THE JOHNS HOPKINS UNIVERSITY STUDIES IN HISTORICAL AND POLITICAL SCIENCE

EIGHTY–SEVENTH SERIES (1969)

1. The Negro in Maryland Politics, 1870–1912
BY MARGARET LAW CALLCOTT

THE NEGRO IN MARYLAND POLITICS, 1870–1912

The Negro in
Maryland Politics
1870-1912

By

MARGARET LAW CALLCOTT

THE JOHNS HOPKINS PRESS

BALTIMORE

Standard Book Number 8018-1023-X
Copyright © 1969 by The Johns Hopkins Press
Baltimore, Maryland 21218
All rights reserved
Manufactured in the United States of America
Library of Congress Catalog Card Number 69-15395

PREFACE

The story of the Negro in post-Reconstruction politics is largely a chronicle of exclusion and denial, of hopes and opportunities raised by enfranchisement and relentlessly put down by varying kinds of disfranchisement. The Fifteenth Amendment, ratified in 1870, seemed to promise free political participation to all citizens regardless of race, but wherever Negroes possessed numerical strength, state after state decimated its electorate in efforts first to curtail and then to eliminate Negro voting power. The story of preliminary disfranchisement, which began in some states as early as the withdrawal of federal troops, and the story of constitutional disfranchisement, which commenced in the 1890s, have been recorded in an extensive body of literature by a very able group of historians.[1] At the same time, however, an important but little noted exception to this general process of Negro exclusion took place in the border state of Maryland.

The promise of the Fifteenth Amendment was kept in Maryland, and Negroes, who comprised roughly one-fifth the population of the state, participated with relative freedom in the electoral process. Suffrage rights were maintained despite widespread white hostility and numerous disfranchisement attempts. Not only were legal rights upheld but, more important, these rights were exercised actively. The rate of Negro voter participation was, from the beginning, about equal to that of whites. Participation was especially high in the southern and eastern counties of the state, where slavery had been concentrated and the number of Negroes was greatest.

1. Preliminary disfranchisement includes the multitude of devices used to curtail Negro voting power prior to the more formal and complete exclusion of constitutional disfranchisement. Devices ranged from outright intimidation of Negro voters to use of the poll tax, complex registration and balloting procedures, and gerrymandering to undercut Negro voting strength. The best single source is C. Vann Woodward, *Origins of the New South, 1877–1913* (Baton Rouge, 1951), and the best state studies are George B. Tindall, *Negroes in South Carolina, 1877–1900* (Columbia, 1952); Vernon L. Wharton, *The Negro in Mississippi, 1865–1890* (Chapel Hill, 1947); Frenise Logan, *The Negro in North Carolina, 1876–1894* (Chapel Hill, 1964); and Charles E. Wyncs, *Race Relations in Virginia, 1870–1902* (Charlottesville, 1961).

As one of the few places where a significant number of Negroes have voted since enfranchisement, Maryland provides a rare opportunity to examine Negro political activity over an extended period of time. Here the Negro was able to build a political tradition, a heritage denied the vast majority of black Americans. This book is a study of that tradition—of Negro response to enfranchisement, of the extent and types of Negro political participation, and of the effects of Negro suffrage on the party system and policies of Maryland.

The central question of this study is how the Negro, who came under the same attack in Maryland as elsewhere, was able to maintain his suffrage rights and achieve his remarkable level of voter participation. Negro success in these endeavors owed little to either white generosity or a notably better climate of race relations. The lesson of the Maryland experience—if it can offer a lesson—lies not in the attainment of a unique racial accord but in the features of a political system that operated to curtail some of the worst excesses of racial discord.

The most outstanding feature of Maryland's political structure was the vigorous two-party system that existed throughout the 1870–1912 period. Maryland's Republican party was transformed into a viable opposition party by Negro enfranchisement, and, unlike the situation in many Southern states, this minority party did not shrivel and die during the long span of Democratic control. There were solid reasons for this persistence, some of them political, some racial, and some deeply rooted in the socioeconomic makeup of the state. The strength of Maryland's two-party system was clearly demonstrated in 1895, when the racially mixed Republican party won control of the state from the normally dominant and practically all-white Democratic party. After a brief period of Republican rule, Maryland Democrats reestablished their sway, primarily by blatant racist appeals, and the stage was set for disfranchisement. The Democratic party launched assault after assault on Negro electoral participation, but these attacks were perceived as attacks on what had become a firmly established party system that served important interests aside from those of race. Large numbers of whites therefore combined with the threatened but nevertheless highly active Negroes to fight off the attacks. The almost mechanistic manner in which the party system reacted to preserve itself was a crucial factor in maintaining Negro suffrage in Maryland.

Although there are heartening elements in the story of the Negro in Maryland politics, there are somber aspects as well. The party system, which contributed so importantly to participatory rights in Maryland, did not work in any substantive way to advance the position of the Negro nor did it protect him from certain harsh setbacks in his status. A wave of segregationist measures, which swept the state along with the disfranchisement movement, went virtually unchecked in the political arena, imposing new humiliations and hardships on the Negro minority. Negro Marylanders, in spite of a remarkable record of responsible voting participation, were unable to advance their legitimate interests significantly or to secure full protection from harassment in a political system that was structured upon free elections and a competitive party system. The limited efficacy of even model political arrangements for dealing successfully with a racist environment is all too apparent in the Maryland experience.

The clearly partisan origins of the disfranchisement movement in Maryland and the accompanying development of rigid segregationist sentiment lend support to the thesis Professor C. Vann Woodward set forth in *The Strange Career of Jim Crow*.[2] Woodward called attention to the growth and intensification of segregation following the political upheavals of the 1890s, developments which ended an era of comparative permissiveness in race relations. Maryland's experience seems to fit readily into this pattern. Although racial segregation was always the rule in Maryland public schools and correctional and eleemosynary institutions, the extension of this policy into public transportation, residential housing, and public accommodations grew out of the purposefully generated racism that marked the return of the Democratic party to power in 1900 and its attempts to solidify its hold on the state.

The high level of Negro voting participation in post–Civil War Maryland is contrary to the findings of most studies of present-day voting behavior, which repeatedly show that Negroes participate at much lower rates than whites. These studies also show that participation is a function of low income, low occupational and educational levels, and of residence in rural rather than urban areas.[3] The high Negro participation which characterized

2. 2nd rev. ed. (New York, 1966).
3. Generalizations about contemporary political participation have been built up from many voting behavior studies over the last three decades. Lester Milbrath's

the Maryland political scene from 1870 to 1900 suggests that there is nothing inevitable about such present-day relationships. Mass Negro participation occurred despite a socioeconomic position that was even more peripheral in the past than it is at present; participation of rural Negroes tended to exceed that of urban Negroes. One key to understanding this contrast between past and present political response can be found in the greatly changed role of the political party in our society. This study covers a period when political party organization and power were at their zenith, both in the state and in the nation. Party organization was professional organization, devoted on a full-time continuous basis to maximizing electoral support. Commanding a vast array of jobs and services and affording access to both power and status, the political party possessed the resources to play a more central role in the electorate then than it does now.

In its theory and methodology, this study owes much to the work of the late V. O. Key, Jr., one of the foremost proponents of a purposefully historical conception of the political system. By example in his own research and by specific admonition, Key warned against non-historical conceptions of the party system and its group components.[4] Writing in 1959, Key called particularly for studies designed to " search out electoral areas in which specific kinds of people are concentrated and to analyse the voting behavior through time of the people of such areas." [5] Of course, the study of political behavior in a historical rather than a contemporary context entails several methodological handicaps. Many of the tools of modern voting-behavior research, which produce enviable precision in analyzing the complex electoral alignments that underlie our political system and the motivations of its group

---

Political Participation: How and Why Do People Get Involved in Politics? (Chicago, 1965) is a good summary of these generalizations and a thorough guide to the studies from which they were developed. Although it focuses primarily on southern Negroes, the most comprehensive treatment of contemporary Negro political participation is that of Donald R. Matthews and James W. Prothro, *Negroes and the New Southern Politics* (New York, 1966).

4. Key's early and even now his most widely known work, *Southern Politics in State and Nation* (New York, 1949), is an exemplary study of political behavior, firmly rooted in historical context. *The Responsible Electorate* (Cambridge, Mass., 1966), Key's last book, reaffirmed the value of the historical approach in illuminating the rational basis of the individual's traditional commitment to his party. Key's warning against a nonhistorical approach is in " Secular Realignment and the Party System," *Journal of Politics*, 21 (May, 1959): 198–210.

5. " Secular Realignment and the Party System," p. 199.

components, are not available to a historical study.[6] The questions that one can ask are severely limited by the types of data that have been preserved, and many of our answers incorporate the imprecision that characterizes much of the available information. Nevertheless, systematic analysis of the great historical storehouse of aggregate and areal data in election and census records yields much of value to the student of political behavior. Important theoretical advantages can also be gained by breaking out of the mold of the immediate past and present, in which so many studies of political behavior have been cast. Historical perspective can provide a valuable corrective to generalizations that have been shaped almost entirely from the materials of present-day political activity.

Many persons have aided me in this study. I particularly wish to thank Professor Donald R. Matthews, under whom this study was begun as a dissertation in political science at the University of North Carolina, and Professor Louis R. Harlan of the University of Maryland, who guided me in the use of the Booker T. Washington Papers. My greatest debt of gratitude is to my husband, George H. Callcott, for his continuous encouragement and aid.

MARGARET LAW CALLCOTT

University Park, Maryland

6. For example, the survey research techniques used so effectively in the landmark studies of Paul F. Lazarsfeld, Bernard Berelson, and Hazel Gaudet, *The People's Choice* (New York, 1944); Bernard Berelson, Paul F. Lazarsfeld, and William McPhee, *Voting* (Chicago, 1954); and Angus Campbell, Gerald Gurin, and Warren Miller, *The Voter Decides* (White Plains, N. Y., 1954).

CONTENTS

TABLES

FIGURES

THE NEGRO IN MARYLAND POLITICS, 1870–1912

CHAPTER 1

NEGRO ENFRANCHISEMENT IN MARYLAND

On an April morning in 1870 Elijah Quigley, a resident of the newly incorporated town of Towsontown, Maryland, walked down the street to the window of the town polling station and presented his ballot to an election official. Clusters of men watched silently but intently as the official took Quigley's ballot and deposited it in the box. For each man there and for thousands of others throughout the state this simple act was a milestone, for Elijah Quigley was a Negro, the first of his race to cast a ballot in Maryland in more than sixty years.[1]

Although Negroes had voted in great numbers in the Southern states since 1867, Maryland Negroes did not receive the franchise until after ratification of the Fifteenth Amendment in 1870. The reconstruction policies of the Congress had forced all of the formerly Confederate states to grant universal manhood suffrage in their state constitutions, but Maryland, a loyal Union state, had been untouched by these policies. Maryland had made no move to extend suffrage to the Negro of its own volition. The Fifteenth Amendment, therefore, was aimed in part at border states, such as Maryland, that had sizable Negro populations and that would not grant them political participation without outside pressure. Negro enfranchisement immediately increased Maryland's potential electorate by approximately 30 per cent,

---

1. *Chestertown Transcript*, April 9, 1870. In other respects this election was insignificant; it was a special local election that chose councilmen for the newly incorporated town. Significant group voting of Negroes did not take place until the fall congressional elections of 1870.

Under the Maryland Constitution of 1776, free Negroes had been allowed to vote if they met certain property requirements. In 1783 a state statute restricted this right to Negroes who were free prior to that year, and in 1810 Negro suffrage was ended completely by a constitutional amendment that limited the franchise to whites. See James M. Wright, *The Free Negro in Maryland, 1634–1860* (New York, 1921), p. 119.

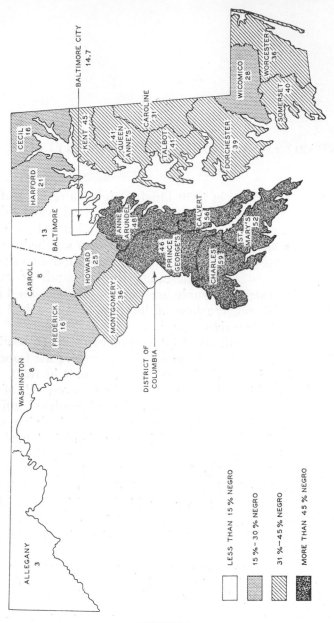

FIGURE 1

PERCENTAGE OF NEGRO POPULATION, MARYLAND COUNTIES AND BALTIMORE
CITY, 1870

adding 39,120 Negroes to the already eligible 130,725 white male citizens of voting age.[2]

Absorption of such a large new element in Maryland's political structure was complicated by the uneven distribution of the Negro population within the state. Maryland's Negro population in 1870 was only 22 percent of the total population, but thirteen of its twenty-two counties far exceeded this overall average. All of the counties with a large Negro population were on the Eastern Shore or in southern Maryland. The population of three counties, all in southern Maryland, was more than 50 percent Negro, and that of ten other counties ranged from 31 percent to 48 percent Negro. Western and central Maryland, on the other hand, had very small Negro populations, both absolutely and proportionately, with the single exception of Baltimore City, where a sizable group of Negroes resided. Almost 40,000 Negroes—one-fifth of the state's Negro population—lived in Baltimore, but they comprised barely 15 percent of that booming urban center's total inhabitants.[3]

Maryland's racial differential (depicted in Figure 1) shaped the reception that was accorded the newly enfranchised Negro by the state's various groups and sections, just as it had shaped the political mold of the state for many years before.[4] The Negro as an issue in politics preceded the Negro as a participant, and Negro enfranchisement in Maryland can be fully understood only against the background of the Civil War decade in that state.

Civil War Politics and Emancipation

The eve of the Civil War found Maryland severely divided over secession. In general, the agricultural and slaveholding regions of the Eastern Shore and southern Maryland tended to be Southern in sympathy, and these regions exerted considerable pressure to propel Maryland into the ranks of the seceding states.

2. U. S. Office of the Census, *Ninth Census of the United States: 1870. Population*, 1: 629.

3. *Ibid.*, p. 163. The 1870 census does not give a racial breakdown of the males of voting age by political subdivisions within the states, but voter-age racial totals for the states are given.

4. The importance of past and present Negro-white population ratios and their relationships to Negro political participation levels are effectively presented in a study by Donald R. Matthews and James W. Prothro, "Social and Economic Factors and Negro Voter Registration in the South," *American Political Science Review*, 57 (March, 1963): 24–44.

Western and northern Maryland, on the other hand, were staunchly Unionist; having the lion's share of the state's industry and peopled by independent farmers, many of German descent, these sections had strong economic and cultural ties with the North and the West. Baltimore City reflected the situation in the state at large: its commercial and industrial interests were sorely divided on secession, some having strong ties with the North, some with the South, and many with both sections.[5] Though feelings ran high in Maryland, it has been remarked that its secession debate was notable for its materialistic tone, the great consideration for most spokesmen being the economic benefits to be derived from a particular course of action, not the justice or injustice of the cause.[6]

From the presidential election in 1860 through the spring of 1861 secession was a real possibility for Maryland.[7] Only two of the four presidential candidates in the 1860 campaign had been given serious consideration by Maryland voters: John C. Breckinridge, the Southern Democratic candidate, and John Bell, the Constitutional Unionist. Breckinridge carried the state by a slim plurality, with 42,282 votes to Bell's 41,760; Lincoln received only 2,294 votes, and Douglas only 5,966 votes. Maryland had apparently cast its lot with the Southern extremists, but the decision was close and it was significant that Bell, a moderate candidate who emphasized union and conciliation, had carried sixteen of Maryland's twenty-one counties, failing mainly in Baltimore City, which Breckinridge won by 2,000 votes.[8] In the months that followed the election Maryland tottered on the brink of secession. Great pressure was exerted on Governor Thomas H. Hicks to call a special session of the legislature, but he held off, knowing that such action might lead to an ordinance of secession.[9]

5. Charles Branch Clark, *Politics in Maryland during the Civil War* (Chestertown, Md., 1952), pp. 14–19.

6. Carl M. Frasure, "Union Sentiment in Maryland, 1859–1861," *Maryland Historical Magazine*, 24 (March, 1929): 217.

7. Charles L. Wagandt, *The Mighty Revolution: Negro Emancipation in Maryland, 1862–1864* (Baltimore, 1964), pp. 17–18.

8. Walter Dean Burnham, *Presidential Ballots, 1836–1892* (Baltimore, 1955), pp. 504–10. Maryland had only twenty-one counties in 1860; today there are twenty-three. Wicomico County was created in 1867 from portions of Somerset and Worcester. Garrett County was formed in 1872 from the western portion of Allegany.

9. Clark, *Politics in Maryland*, p. 25.

Hicks was a Unionist, but the legislature was strongly Democratic and Southern in sympathy.

Secessionist feeling hit its peak in Maryland in April, 1861, with the movement of federal troops through Baltimore on their way south. Incensed by the use of their city as a passageway for Union troops, a mob of Southern sympathizers attacked the Sixth Massachusetts Regiment in a skirmish that left four soldiers and twelve civilians dead and scores of wounded on the streets of Baltimore.[10] The high pitch of popular emotion at this time forced the governor to act, and the legislature was called into session.[11] Just when it seemed that Maryland would succumb to its secessionist advocates, loyal Unionists within the state moved to take control of the situation, and Governor Hicks counseled the legislature to follow a moderate course. Although the session rang with declarations of sympathy for the Southern states, the legislature ended by disclaiming any power to carry the state out of the Union.[12]

Native Unionists also moved to provide formal state political structure for the expression of their views. Pro-Unionists, ignoring old party lines, met in Baltimore in May, 1861, and organized a party that was committed to preserving the Union. Condemning secession on the one hand and abolition on the other, the new Union party appealed to all Marylanders to rally to the defense of the federal government. Maryland Unionists, who ran a full slate of candidates in the special congressional elections of June, 1861, were victorious in all but one of the state's five congressional districts. These elections, which are particularly significant in revealing the real strength of loyalist sentiment in Maryland, were not marred by the federal interference and irregular practices that attended later wartime elections in the border state. The results showed no serious opposition to Unionism in northern and western Maryland, a Union majority of 2,000 on the Eastern Shore, and even a small 150-vote majority in southern Maryland. Only in Baltimore City were the Unionists unsuccessful; the Fourth Congressional District, embracing much of the city, was lost to the opposition. Nationality groups played an important part in the Baltimore vote, with citizens of German extraction generally

10. Wagandt, *Mighty Revolution*, p. 11.
11. Clark, *Politics in Maryland*, p. 25.
12. Wagandt, *Mighty Revolution*, p. 12.

supporting Unionism and citizens of Irish extraction opposing it.[13]

Federal troops were first stationed in Maryland in May, 1861, but it was not until the fall of that year that the military was actively employed to buttress the state's Unionist party. The state's elections of November, 1861, saw many cases of blatant federal interference, beginning with the arrest of the mayor of Baltimore and state legislators who were suspected of Southern sympathy and ending with widespread intimidation of voters. Even the most ardent of Maryland's loyal Unionists, Congressman Henry Winter Davis, who was appalled at the extent of federal interference, complained that the government could not seem to understand that Maryland was a loyal state.[14] The elections, which produced an easy victory for the Unionists, put the state firmly in the hands of a loyal governor and a substantial Unionist majority in the legislature, but the methods that had been employed tarnished the image and diminished the political effectiveness of the new party.[15]

After 1861 it was clear to all realists that secession was a dead issue in Maryland and that the state's destiny lay with the Union. Southern sympathizers still were numerous, and intermittently troublesome, but with the Democratic party virtually driven underground by the arrest of many of its leaders, they could no longer affect the course of the state. The philosophy of those who now controlled Maryland was aptly expressed by the new Unionist governor, Augustus W. Bradford: " The loyal men of Maryland have but one purpose and one hope, but one ambition and one thought, and that is the *Union*, its restoration, its preservation, its perpetuity." [16]

But even as Maryland resolved the dilemma of union or disunion, new controversies arose to agitate the state, and the most serious of these concerned the Negro. In 1860 Maryland's Negro

13. *Ibid.*, pp. 17–19.
14. *Ibid.*, p. 32.
15. It was primarily the conduct of these elections that prompted Charles B. Clark's conclusion that, in the end, it was federal military force that kept Maryland in the Union (*Politics in Maryland*, p. 25). Most historians have emphasized the Southern-leaning tendencies of the state and have implied that, if left to her own devices, Maryland would not have remained loyal. Charles L. Wagandt, in *The Mighty Revolution*, challenges this contention and points out the strength of native Union sentiment; he concludes that Maryland would have remained loyal in any event.
16. Quoted in Clark, *Politics in Maryland*, p. 95.

population was approximately half slave and half free; most of the slaves were held on the Eastern Shore and in southern Maryland and the great majority of free Negroes resided in Baltimore and on the Eastern Shore (see Table 1). Ironically, despite its long and impressive history of voluntary manumission and the fact that at the time of the war Maryland had more free Negroes

TABLE 1

MARYLAND'S SLAVE AND FREE NEGRO POPULATION, 1860

Section of State	Slaves	Free Negroes	Percentage of Negroes Free
Eastern Shore	25,137	28,277	53.2
Southern Maryland	48,905	13,784	21.9
Baltimore City & County	5,400	29,911	84.7
Western Maryland	7,747	11,970	59.7
Total	87,189	83,942	Average 49.0

Source: James M. Wright, The Free Negro in Maryland, 1634–1860 (New York, 1921), pp. 88–89.

than any other state, there was little sentiment among whites for emancipation during the early years of the war. Unionists, who tended to side with non-Unionists in a conservative position on the institution of slavery, resented attempts to associate the Union cause with emancipation. Indeed, many prominent Maryland Unionists were slaveholders, and one of the first resolutions of the 1862 Unionist-dominated legislature was a proposed amendment to the United States Constitution to prohibit federal interference in the domestic institutions of the states. Maryland's reaction to President Lincoln's proposal in 1862 for compensated emancipation of slaves in the loyal states was stony indifference, and congressional abolition of slavery in the District of Columbia in the same year generated outright hostility and fear in Maryland.[17]

Opinion on emancipation began to shift within the state during 1862 and 1863 because of a combination of factors. First, slavery as an institution was greatly weakened in Maryland because of the easy refuge granted by the army and by the neighboring District of Columbia after 1862; runaway slaves were numerous.

17. Wagandt, Mighty Revolution, pp. 36, 46, 59–63.

A federal law of 1863 that allowed Negro conscription intensified the problem; ostensibly enlisting free Negroes only, the Union army struck hard at slavery in Maryland by accepting every Negro it could get.[18] And in many areas the military followed a definite policy of enticing slaves. The resulting instability in the institution of slavery undoubtedly influenced opinion on the desirability of orderly emancipation, particularly among loyalist slaveholders who hoped to gain compensation.

Another potent factor in Maryland's rather surprising about-face on emancipation was the perennial infirmity of political movements, factionalism, which appeared soon after the new Union party had won control of the state. This was a factionalism born of personal animosities and ambition and nourished on an appetite for patronage and power, but its maturity was marked by an increasing differentiation on political issues, particularly on emancipation. Accordingly, a group of men within the Union party seized upon emancipation as the weapon they needed for controlling their party and extending its power over the state. The faction was headed by Henry Winter Davis, a former Know-Nothing congressman, who was joined by men of varying political backgrounds, the most prominent of whom were Archibald Stirling, Henry Stockbridge, John A. J. Creswell, Hugh Lennox Bond, R. Stockett Matthews, Francis Thomas, and Henry H. Goldsborough.[19] With the exception of Davis, who died in 1865, the leaders of this early bolt from the Union party became the nucleus of Maryland's Republican party after the war. The Unconditional Unionists, as this group came to be known, began to work for a state constitutional convention that would free Maryland's slaves, and first gained power in Baltimore, capturing the city's regular Union party apparatus in 1862. The burgeoning Union League movement, which had been formed to promote army enlistments and other patriotic work but which soon became the center of much political activity, was quickly incorporated into the Unconditional Unionist party.[20] By the fall of 1863 the Unconditional Unionists were strong enough to challenge Conservative Unionists to a statewide fight on the issue of emancipation.

18. *Ibid.*, pp. 121, 126.
19. *Ibid.*, chap. 7, "Emergence of Maryland Emancipationists"; also see Bernard C. Steiner, *Life of Henry Winter Davis* (Baltimore, 1916).
20. Wagandt, *Mighty Revolution*, pp. 85, 98.

The 1863 election campaigns were the first major exposition of the pros and cons of emancipation in Maryland and they provide valuable insights into the thought of emancipationist leaders and the arguments that attracted a following to this cause. Emancipation was primarily advocated not on moral grounds but in the hardheaded economic and political terms of class interest. Emancipation spokesmen drew up a three-part brief of the benefits that would flow—not to the Negro but to the lower-class white—from the freeing of the slaves. Economically, emancipation would lessen the competitive disadvantage slave labor presented to the free white workers and small farmers of the state. Politically, emancipation would break the power of the slaveholding oligarchy in the agricultural sections, which had long controlled the state. Finally, but of immediate concern, emancipation would create a large reservoir of Negro manpower for army recruitment, enabling the freed slaves to fulfill Maryland's troop quota as substitutes for poor whites.[21] In the words of the foremost student of Maryland's emancipation movement, " Occasional voices struck at the injustice perpetrated upon the colored race, but it was self-interest that dominated the radical appeal—whether it [was] slave enlistments, economic growth, or more equitable representation." [22]

With help from the federal military, Unconditional Unionists scored a substantial victory at the polls in 1863, winning control of the state legislature and four of the state's five congressional seats. The election was so marred by federal interference, test oaths, and a small turn-out that analysis is hazardous, but it is probable that the emancipationists would have won even in an untrammeled election, though by a much reduced margin.[23] This judgment is supported by the fact that many leading Conservative Unionists shifted their position immediately after the election and moved into the emancipationist camp. Governor Bradford, Union party chairman Thomas Swann, and the members of the Union state central committee—all conservatives or straddlers on the issue before the election—called for an immediate end to slavery in Maryland after the election. It was, in effect, a reunited Union

21. *Ibid.*, pp. 143–50.
22. *Ibid.*, p. 151.
23. *Ibid.*, p. 181; also see William Starr Myers, *The Maryland Constitution of 1864* (Baltimore, 1901), p. 25.

party that called the constitutional convention of 1864 to free Maryland's slaves.[24]

The constitutional convention, composed of sixty-one Union delegates, almost all of them pledged to immediate and uncompensated emancipation, and thirty-five Democrats, who either opposed emancipation or were pledged to seek compensation, met in Annapolis in April, 1864. The most important provision of the new constitution they framed was that slavery would be abolished throughout Maryland on November 1, 1864.[25] Another provision which limited suffrage to white males was retained without debate; neither party at that time envisioned granting political rights to the freed Negro. The basis for representation in the state legislature was changed—a primary aim of the Unconditional Unionist faction, now dominant in the Union party. Although the Constitution of 1851 had made the total black and white population the basis for representation, the new constitution excluded the blacks and established the white population as the sole basis for representation in the House of Delegates. This change shifted power in the legislature from the Eastern Shore and southern Maryland to the northern and western parts of the state, where the Union party was most firmly established. Strict oaths of loyalty to the federal Union for officeholders and voters were written into the new document—and in a most irregular maneuver the framers decreed that the new test-oath would be required of all voters in the referendum on the constitution. In spite of such tactics—indeed, partly because of them—the new constitution was almost defeated at the polls. The final count was 30,174 votes for and 29,799 votes against the document—a margin of only 375 votes in a canvass of 60,000.[26]

Major credit for the near defeat of the Constitution of 1864 was due the newly revived Democratic party, which waged a very effective campaign against its adoption. The revival and reorganization of the Democratic party in Maryland can be traced to the spring of 1864, when it had become clear that the Union party would press for constitutional emancipation. This unequivocal position had alienated many Unionists, who sought refuge in the only organization available—the discredited and almost defunct Democratic party—and this infusion of respectable new

24. Wagandt, *Mighty Revolution*, pp. 190–91.
25. Declaration of Rights, Article 24.
26. Myers, *Maryland Constitution of 1864*, pp. 63, 75, 88.

blood had encouraged the Democrats to mount a statewide campaign for the first time since the start of the war.[27] Raising real issues in 1864, such as the test oaths, and exploiting such fantasies as Negro social equality and school integration, the resurgent Democrats had almost upset the Unionists' plans for emancipation in Maryland.

The Unionists had staked their political future on approval of the test oaths and on reapportionment of the Maryland General Assembly that favored their party; and for a time this strategy was successful. In special elections in 1864, under the new constitution, they succeeded in electing their gubernatorial candidate, Thomas Swann, and in maintaining control of the state legislature.[28] Their margin of control was small, however, and to strengthen their position the Unionists passed a highly partisan registration law in 1865. The Registry Act of 1865 gave the governor power to appoint election registrars in each ward and election district in the state. The registrars, in turn, were empowered to exclude all disloyal persons from the voting lists, and they were given discretionary judgment in determining loyalty and disloyalty. No longer would mere affirmation of the constitutional loyalty oath be sufficient qualification for the right to vote.[29] The Registry Act, of course, produced a clamor of outrage from Democrats and also was unpopular with many Unionists, who feared its use in intraparty struggles.

Unionist policy vis-à-vis the Negro still did not envision political participation by the freedmen. In 1865 the Unionist legislature removed some of the disabilities that had attached to the Negro as a consequence of his slave status, but Negroes were still disqualified as witnesses at law in any case involving whites, and Negroes who had been convicted of a crime could be leased out for private labor as an alternative to prison confinement. The 1865 legislature also ratified the Thirteenth Amendment to the United States Constitution, abolishing slavery throughout the nation, on a strict party-division vote, with Unionists supporting and Democrats opposing ratification.[30]

27. Clark, *Politics in Maryland*, pp. 117, 123–24.

28. The state senate was lost by the Unionists in the election but a Democratic resignation and a Union appointment immediately after the election produced a party tie in the senate, giving Unionist Lieutenant Governor Christopher Cox the deciding vote in cases of strict party divisions.

29. William Starr Myers, *The Self-Reconstruction of Maryland, 1864–1867* (Baltimore, 1909), pp. 18–19.

30. *Ibid.*

Emergence of a New Party System

With the termination of the Civil War and the ensuing national conflict over Reconstruction the political structure of Maryland was shaken by a new upheaval. Less than two years after the war Maryland's Union party, which had controlled the state since 1861, lay shattered and impotent, while the Democratic party, virtually an outlaw party during the war, emerged as the center of political power—a status it was to hold for the next three decades. The basic reason for this shift of power was simply a further manifestation of the difficult problem that had played havoc with Maryland politics for years: the task of defining the role of the Negro in the political life of the state and the nation. The final break-up of Maryland's Union party began as an intraparty conflict over a national issue—the nature of a reconstruction policy for the Southern states.

Most Marylanders, whether Unionists or Democrats, favored immediate restoration of the Southern states to their former standing and power in the Union, the policy of President Andrew Johnson. Governor Thomas Swann and both houses of the Maryland General Assembly publicly endorsed such a policy, and citizens' meetings that were held throughout the state also supported this position.[31] On the other hand, a small but active and influential group of Maryland Unionists opposed this policy and sided with congressional leaders who sought political reconstruction of the Southern states prior to their readmission to the Union.[32] This radical minority was led by many of the same men who earlier had championed the cause of emancipation in Maryland. When it became clear that Congress' version of reconstruction envisioned civil and *political* equality for the Negro, the rift between the two Unionist factions became irreparable. The majority wing of the Maryland Union party repudiated its radical minority and began to act with the Democrats.

In May, 1866, Governor Swann gave his reasons for breaking with the radicals in an open letter (in which he also declined to attend a radical meeting).

31. *Ibid.*, p. 40. The *Baltimore Sun* reported fourteen citizens' meetings throughout the state during February, March, and April of 1866; all but three of these meetings supported President Johnson's reconstruction policy.

32. Richard Paul Fuke, "The Break-up of the Maryland Union Party, 1866" (M.A. thesis, University of Maryland, 1965), pp. 32–33.

I am utterly opposed to universal negro suffrage and the extreme radicalism of certain men in Congress and in our own State, who have been striving to shape the platform of the Union party in the interests of negro suffrage. . . . I look upon negro suffrage and the recognition of the power in Congress to control suffrage within the States as the virtual subordination of the white race to the ultimate control and domination of the negro in the State of Maryland. . . . I consider the issue upon this subject of negro suffrage as well made in the fall elections [congressional and state legislative elections, 1866], and the most important that has ever been brought to the attention of the people of the State of Maryland.[33]

Swann soon paved the way for effective Unionist cooperation with the Democratic party by appointing new election officials throughout the state and instructing them to interpret the loyalty oath and the Registry Act as liberally as possible so as to facilitate the registration of many Democrats who had been excluded from political activity.[34] Voter registration in August and September of 1866 almost doubled the number of legal voters on the books in Maryland.[35]

Radical Unionists, stunned and dismayed by the vehemence of the attack upon them, initially tried to deny the charge that they favored Negro suffrage. Indeed, many in their ranks did not favor Negro suffrage, but their leaders were committed to support the proposed Fourteenth Amendment, which sought to reduce the congressional representation of any state that denied its freedmen the opportunity to vote.[36] Such a policy was vital to congressional radicals in maintaining party control of Congress. In the state elections of 1866 Maryland Radical Unionists attempted to deny any advocacy of Negro suffrage while defending their support of the Fourteenth Amendment.[37] Their position was wholly un-

33. *Baltimore Sun*, May 14, 1866.
34. Myers, *Self-Reconstruction of Maryland*, p. 64; Fuke, "Break-up of the Maryland Union Party," pp. 51–54.
35. Fuke, "Break-up of the Maryland Union Party," p. 56.
36. Maryland's Radical leaders in Congress at this time were Senator John A. J. Creswell and Congressmen John L. Thomas and Francis Thomas.
37. In May, Senator Creswell called a mass meeting in Baltimore to refute the charge that he advocated Negro suffrage, and in June the state convention of the Unconditional Unionists went on record as opposed to any change in the Maryland constitution that would allow Negroes to vote (*Baltimore Sun*, May 19, June 7, 1866).

tenable, and the Conservative Unionist–Democratic coalition won easy control of both houses of the General Assembly and four of Maryland's five congressional seats in the fall election.

In 1867 the conservative wing of the Union party lost its separate identity and, for all practical purposes, was absorbed into the Democratic party. " Conservative," " Conservative-Democratic," and " Democratic " were used interchangeably for several more years to denote the majority party in Maryland, but practical power within the amalgamated party gravitated more and more toward the old-line Democrats. This new center of power was implicit in the spectacle of Conservative Unionists working side by side with Democrats in the 1867 legislature to repeal the Registry Act, which had been passed only two years before for the express purpose of reducing the Democratic vote. It was further revealed in the cooperation of Conservative Unionists and Democrats in framing a new state constitution to nullify the political advantages that had been given the Union party by the Constitution of 1864. Finally, the dominance of the Democrats in the alliance was acknowledged when the gubernatorial nomination of the new party was bestowed upon Oden Bowie, a southern Maryland planter and since 1864 the prime leader in the revival and reorganization of the Democratic party.[38]

The year 1867 also witnessed the formal origin of the Republican party in Maryland. Radical Unionists, who had clung tenaciously to the Union label during the preceding year and had worked hard to minimize their differences with the Conservative Unionists, now frankly declared themselves Republicans and advocates of universal manhood suffrage.[39] Driven into an apparently hopeless political position, they saw one possible route to power and began to build their party accordingly: enfranchisement of the nearly 40,000 Negro freedmen in Maryland of voting age and their incorporation in the Republican party became their goal. In May, 1867, Maryland Republicans began to integrate their party organization; at their state convention white and Negro delegates sat together in the delegations and on the platform. Negro members were appointed also to the party's state central committee,

38. Clark, *Politics in Maryland*, p. 117.

39. At a state convention in Baltimore in February, 1867, Maryland Radicals officially designated their party the Republican Union Party and, for the first time, publicly advocated universal manhood suffrage (*Baltimore Sun*, February 28, 1867).

two from each county and five from Baltimore City.[40] ₁or the first time in history the Negro's voice was heard in the political deliberations of the state.

But even as the Negro was taking his first tentative steps toward political recognition, Maryland Democrats were tightening their hold on the state, determined to exclude both the Negro and his new allies from playing an effective role in the state's politics. Amid Republican clamor that denounced the proceedings as illegal, the Democrats called a constitutional convention in May, 1867, to replace the old Unionist Constitution of 1864 with one that would be more to their liking. The convention, boycotted by the Republicans, was composed solely of Democrats, and the document they framed was designed to perpetuate their control of the state.[41]

The proposed constitution omitted all mention of loyalty oaths for voters and officeholders; henceforth all white male citizens of legal age and residence would be permitted to register, vote, and hold office. Predictably, the new constitution would alter the basis of representation in the General Assembly: total population would again be the basis for representation, rather than the white population alone. Thus the voteless Negro would be used to increase the power of the southern and Eastern Shore counties, where the Democratic party was strong. All state officials—with the exception of the cooperative Governor Swann—and all of the elected officials of the city of Baltimore would be turned out of office by the new constitution and new elections would be ordered.[42] Finally, because of Republican threats to have Maryland included in the states to be reconstructed by Congress, the Democrats granted Maryland Negroes a small concession in their proposed constitution. A half-hearted provision declaring "no person incompetent, as a witness, on account of race or color, unless hereafter so declared by Act of the General Assembly"

40. *Baltimore Sun*, May 15, 1867. The number of Negro delegates to the convention is not given, but four Negro delegates addressed the convention and twelve Negro delegates were elected vice presidents, honorary designations that carried no power.

41. The Republicans' charge of illegality was correct; the convention of 1867 was not called in accordance with the provisions of the Constitution of 1864, either in respect to the timing of the call or representation of the counties in the convention (Myers, *Self-Reconstruction of Maryland*, p. 94).

42. Swann, as his reward for handing the Conservative Union party over to the Democrats, was permitted to serve out his term, which ran to 1869.

removed the last restriction of the old slave code in Maryland.[43] This concession cost the Democrats little, since the Maryland Court of Appeals had already ruled the racial restriction void and had accepted Negroes as competent witnesses in Maryland courts.[44]

Maryland Republicans waged a vigorous campaign to defeat the new constitution at the polls, basing their opposition primarily on the document's failure to enfranchise the Negro. However, the state's lack of sympathy with enfranchisement was vividly demonstrated in the referendum results: the constitution was approved by a two-to-one margin. Republicans failed to carry a single county or Baltimore election district.[45]

An even more decisive repudiation was dealt the Republicans in the statewide elections immediately after the adoption of the Constitution of 1867. In the gubernatorial race the Democratic candidate, Oden Bowie, overwhelmed Republican Hugh Lennox Bond by a three-to-one margin, and the entire membership of both houses of the General Assembly was won by the Democrats.[46] Even though Bowie could not take office until the expiration of Governor Swann's term in 1869, it was clear that the "redemption" of the state by the Democrats was complete in 1867, and the relatively mild "self-reconstruction" of Maryland had ended.[47]

The elections of 1867 were the last important state elections prior to Negro enfranchisement, and the white base of the Repub-

---

43. Constitution of 1867, Article III, Section 53. The slave code provision that authorized the leasing of Negro convicts had been repealed by the legislature in 1867 (Myers, *Self-Reconstruction of Maryland*, p. 87).

44. See *A. H. Somers' Petition for Habeas Corpus*, Montgomery County, Maryland, July 2, 1866. This case is not reported in the *Maryland Reports* but the full text of the decision, delivered by Chief Justice Richard J. Bowie, is reported in the July 7, 1866, edition of *American and Commercial Advertiser* (Baltimore) and the facts of the case are reported in the *Baltimore Sun* of July 9, 1866. The omission of the case from the *Maryland Reports* may be due to the fact that Justice Bowie handed down his decision from his home in Montgomery County and the papers relating to the case may not have been properly transferred to the court's records.

45. The tally was 47,152 votes for the constitution and 23,086 votes against it (Myers, *Self-Reconstruction of Maryland*, p. 128).

46. The final count was Bowie 63,694 votes and Bond 22,050 votes (*Baltimore Sun*, November 13, 1868).

47. William Starr Myers devised the term "self-reconstruction" to describe the period when the Union Constitution of 1864, drawn up and approved by native Marylanders, was in force—that is, from 1864 to 1867.

lican minority party stands out clearly in the returns. In the referendum on the constitution, which Republicans fought vigorously, the total opposition vote was 23,086, 77 percent of which came from Baltimore City and six of the northernmost counties of the state: Allegany, Washington, Frederick, Carroll, Baltimore, and Cecil.[48] The same pattern was repeated in the 1867 gubernatorial poll, in which 85 percent of Republican candidate Bond's support came from Baltimore and the same six counties. These areas shared several common features that help explain why native Republicanism found, if not a controlling position, at least a substantial base from which it could grow in the northern part of the state. Populated mainly by whites, the six counties cited ranked as the six lowest in the state in the percentage of their population that was Negro, ranging from Allegany's 3 percent to a high of only 16 percent in Cecil and Frederick. Baltimore City, a little less than 15 percent Negro, also was well within the lower rank. In Maryland, as in other racially mixed states at that time, Republicanism was strongest in the predominantly white areas of the state, where espousal of the Negro's cause was least likely to cause local repercussions and was more readily tolerated by the population. This area also was the most prosperous and highly industrialized portion of the state; 79 percent of the state's manufacturing establishments were located in these six counties and in Baltimore, representing 92 percent of the state's industrial product value.[49] National Republican

48. Somerset County, on the Eastern Shore, also polled a large vote against the constitution, but this reflected its opposition to the constitution's creation of a new county largely from Somerset territory rather than local Republican sentiment. Without this issue the concentration of opposition in the northern part of the state would have been even more striking, more than 80 percent.

49. U.S. Office of the Census, Ninth Census of the United States: 1870. Population, 1: 36–37, and idem, Statistics of the Wealth and Industry of the United States, 3: 526. Baltimore City and County accounted for the lion's share of the state's industry, but the other five northern counties greatly outstripped the remainder of the state:

	Percentage of State's Mfg. Establishments in 1870	Percentage of State's Industrial Product Value in 1870
Baltimore City & County..........	47	77
Allegany, Washington, Cecil, Carroll & Frederick counties......	32	15
Remainder of state...............	21	8

economic policies had great appeal to many in this industrialized area and gave the local party an economically motivated constituency that would grow as industry grew.

In 1867, however, native Republicanism could not control even the northern part of the state, where most of its strength was centered. After the sweeping repudiation of their program in 1867 it was clear to Republicans that action on the state level was impossible, and all hopes for constructing an effective party organization turned to the passage of a national constitutional amendment that would enfranchise the Negro. For the next two years Maryland Republicans worked as best they could to advance this goal, and the party's commitment to universal manhood suffrage was reaffirmed in its state conventions in 1868 and 1869 without debate or dissent.[50] Though hopelessly outnumbered, Republicans continued to offer candidates in state and congressional elections, and waged fairly vigorous campaigns. In spite of their efforts, they lost their last elective foothold in the state in 1868, when Congressman John L. Thomas, Jr., a Republican, was defeated and a solidly Democratic delegation was returned to Congress.[51]

Federal patronage became the basis for Republican organization after 1868, and with Grant's election to the presidency the fledgling party received a liberal share of appointments. The party's leadership was not changed by the switch from elective to appointive positions. Former United States Senator John A. J. Creswell retained, and even enhanced, his control of the Maryland Republican party when Grant appointed him Postmaster General of the United States. Creswell, along with C. C. Fulton, editor of the *Baltimore American* and chairman of the Republican state central committee, and ex-Congressman John L. Thomas, the new Collector of the Port of Baltimore, composed the Republican elite in Maryland at this time.

The Negro's position within Maryland's Republican party during the years prior to enfranchisement reveals the party's practical—rather than ideological—commitment to Negro suffrage. Negroes had been welcomed to full membership in party councils in 1867, when their aid was sought to defeat the new state constitution. They were summarily dismissed from party

50. *Baltimore Sun*, March 7, 1868, and October 14, 1869.
51. *Ibid.*, November 7, 1868.

membership in 1868, however, after it had become clear that there was no immediate prospect of securing the vote for Negroes in Maryland.[52] From 1868 to 1870 Negroes were excluded from participating in Republican ward meetings, primaries, and conventions, and were relegated to the position of " consulting members " on the state central committee. The exclusion was temporary, however, and did not affect the party's basic goal of securing the franchise for Negroes, which was vital to the party's survival in Maryland. When national ratification of the Fifteenth Amendment was proclaimed in March, 1870, the party's doors were again thrown open to Negroes in their new status as voters.[53]

The Maryland legislature, with a wholly Democratic membership, had unanimously rejected the Fifteenth Amendment, but Democratic reaction to its final ratification and the prospect of Negroes voting in Maryland was, in the first instance, rather mild.[54] The state's Democratic executive committee resolved that Maryland's registration law should be altered to conform with the new constitutional requirement, and within one week the General Assembly complied with the directive.[55] The state's leading newspaper, the *Baltimore Sun*, questioned the constitutionality of the Fifteenth Amendment's ratification but doubted that its effects would be serious enough to call forth a constitutional test.

At the North the colored vote is entirely too insignificant to make the subject of the slightest practical importance. At the South colored men are already entitled to all the privileges of voters, and are eligible to office under the provisions of their own State constitutions. Consequently, the only States where the amendment will work any change in the practical order of things which will be at all felt are the border States— Delaware, Maryland, and Kentucky. In those States, and throughout the country, the rapid growth of the white popu-

52. *Ibid.*, March 7, 1868. The exclusion of Negroes was opposed by a small faction within the party (led by the recent gubernatorial candidate Hugh L. Bond) that wished to continue the party on an integrated basis. Creswell's view, and the view adopted by the party, was that this policy would serve no useful purpose and might hurt the party in the next presidential election.

53. See the last section of this chapter, " The Negro Votes: The Election of 1870."

54. Maryland *House Journal*, 1870, pp. 268-69, and Maryland *Senate Journal*, 1870, p. 291.

55. *Baltimore Sun*, March 30, 1870.

lation from immigration and from natural increase will render the influence of the colored vote year by year proportionately less and less felt.[56]

There are several explanations for such a temperate reaction. The Democratic party had such a firm grip in Maryland at this time that it was easy to underestimate the possibilities of the new situation. The Republican party faced a massive task in organizing the newly enfranchised, and some members of the Democratic party harbored the illusion that the Negro would be politically apathetic or would split his vote between the parties. Moderation, moreover, was a calculated strategy for heading off federal interference in the state's election processes. At the time the Fifteenth Amendment was ratified the Radical-dominated Congress was considering the first of the Federal Enforcement Acts, laws that would give federal officials power to enforce the amendment by, among other things, creation of a federal administrative and police force to oversee the conduct of elections. By seeming to accept and comply with the amendment Maryland Democrats hoped to discourage passage of such acts and to retain undisputed control over the state's elections.[57]

Democratic strategies and illusions were soon shattered. In May, 1870, Congress passed the first Federal Enforcement Act, which was augmented in 1871 by two additional acts, the Federal Election Act and the Ku Klux Klan Act. The intention in all three acts was to protect the Negro in the exercise of his suffrage by bringing state registration and election officials' conduct of federal elections under federal law and by prescribing penalties for discrimination. Civil as well as criminal redress was provided for persons who had been unjustly deprived of their suffrage rights, and all cases to which the acts pertained were to be tried in federal rather than state courts. A vast federal administrative network was provided to enforce the acts: federally appointed registration commissioners and election supervisors were given power to oversee registration and polling processes within the states and federal marshals and deputies were empowered to arrest violators. Federal marshals were empowered to summon federal troops or the state militia to aid them in carrying out their

56. Editorial of March 31, 1870.
57. *Chestertown Transcript*, Editorials of March 5 and April 2, 1870.

duties under the laws.[58] The Enforcement Acts, particularly the first and the second, were to be important factors in Maryland's electoral process.[59]

The Negro Votes: The Election of 1870

The first election in Maryland in which Negroes voted in significant numbers was the congressional election of 1870. Organizational activity among the newly enfranchised began soon after the ratification of the Fifteenth Amendment, and generally this meant the formation of " loyal leagues " or " radical clubs " in communities throughout the state. Meetings usually were held in Negro schoolhouses or churches and instruction in the mechanics of registration and voting was offered.[60] Sometimes, as in Baltimore, the new clubs were referred to as " colored clubs," indicating segregated membership, but in the counties they were seldom so designated.[61]

It is not clear how much of the initiative in this organization of the Negroes came from white Republican politicians and how much from Negroes, because two somewhat contrary observations bear on the question. For example, much of the organization took place prior to the Republican primary elections of August 31, in which Negroes seem to have participated freely.[62] Because state registration of the new voters was not to take place until the latter part of September, there was no great need for white Republicans to push Negro organization prior to the August primaries, particularly because this might have diluted their control of the party. Thus the timing of the organizational activity may indicate independent Negro activity. On the other hand,

58. Walter L. Fleming, *Documentary History of Reconstruction* (Cleveland, 1907), pp. 102–28; also see William Watson Davis, "The Federal Enforcement Acts," in James W. Garner, ed., *Studies in Southern History and Politics* (New York, 1914), pp. 205–28.

59. See pp. 59–61 below for the narrowing scope but continuing use of the Enforcement Acts in Maryland.

60. *Chestertown Transcript*, September 3, 1870; *Port Tobacco Times and Charles County Advertiser*, August 5, 1870.

61. *Baltimore Sun*, August 31, 1870.

62. *Ibid.*, September 1, 2, 1870. At this time, political party primaries were governed entirely by party rules and regulations; thus Negroes were allowed to participate in the internal affairs of the Republican party even before they were officially registered as voters in the state. The August, 1870, Republican primaries chose delegates to district conventions which in turn nominated party candidates for Congress.

contemporary newspapers—generally Democratic papers to be sure—expressed considerable awe at the industry of the Republicans in organizing the new Negro constituency.[63] According to the *Chestertown Transcript*, an Eastern Shore weekly: " The Republicans have exhibited a zeal worthy of a better cause. Night and day they have not relaxed their energies to instruct the negroes in their duty to the Radical party; and they have largely succeeded in inducing them to join clubs pledged to support Radical nominees." [64]

The major organizational task was to register 39,000 eligible new voters, and Republicans got no help from the Democrats in this massive undertaking. Maryland's registration law allowed only three days in the counties and six days in Baltimore for enrolling new registrants for the year. Maryland Republicans petitioned for additional time to process the great number of applicants but received a flat refusal from Democratic Governor Oden Bowie.[65] In spite of the limited time a remarkable job of registration was accomplished; when the lists were totaled it was found that more than 35,000 of the 39,000 eligible Negroes had registered to vote. The success of the registration campaign speaks eloquently of the individual Negro's strong desire for political participation and the Republican party's effectiveness in working with the Negroes of Maryland. (Table 2 shows the number of Negroes who were reported registered in each county and in Baltimore during the autumn registration of 1870.)

Although Negroes participated in the nomination of Republican candidates for Congress in 1870, there is no indication that the Democrats accorded them any part in this important process. Congressional candidates in both parties were nominated by district conventions of delegates who had been elected in primary elections by the party voters on the local level; the entire nominating process was regulated by the party, with no supervision from the state or state law. Reports of the nominating process are scanty, but there are specific accounts of Negroes voting in

63. *Chestertown Transcript*, April 9, May 7, and September 3, 1870; *Port Tobacco Times and Charles County Advertiser*, August 5 and September 2, 1870.
64. Editorial of September 3, 1870.
65. In a letter to Republican State Chairman S. M. Evans (Annapolis, September 14, 1870), Governor Bowie refused to comply with the Republican request, stating that the law provided ample time for registration (*Baltimore Sun*, September 16, 1870).

Republican primaries in all five congressional districts, and in four of the five districts Negroes were elected delegates to the Republican nominating conventions.[66] Reports of the Democratic nomination process make no mention of Negro participation.[67]

TABLE 2

NUMBER OF NEGROES REGISTERED IN MARYLAND IN 1870, BY COUNTY

County	Registrants	County	Registrants
Allegany	200*	Kent	1,562
Anne Arundel	2,521	Montgomery	1,607
Baltimore	1,684	Prince George's	1,500*
Calvert	1,052	Queen Anne's	1,510
Caroline	600*	St. Mary's	1,500*
Carroll	494	Somerset	1,011
Cecil	922	Talbot	1,388
Charles	1,732	Washington	650
Dorchester	1,493	Wicomico	900*
Frederick	1,711	Worcester	1,073
Harford	900*		
Howard	600*	Baltimore City	8,616
		Total	35,236

* County reported an estimated total rather than an exact count.
Source: Baltimore Sun, September 24–November 10, 1870.

The Democrats' complacency or their indifference to the newly enfranchised Negroes was shattered by the success of Republican organizational and registration activity, and cries for countermeasures rose from various parts of the state. There was, however, no consensus on what constituted effective countermeasures; opinion varied widely. On the Eastern Shore the *Chestertown Transcript* called for the organization of "white men's clubs" in all districts of Kent County and proposed that the Democratic party unequivocally present itself as the white man's party.[68] In southern Maryland, where Negroes constituted a majority in several counties, white Democrats were not so sure this was the answer. From Charles County came a plea for guidance and

66. *Baltimore Sun*, September 1, 2, 1870. There is no indication that Negro delegates were present at the First Congressional District Republican convention (on the Eastern Shore), but in each of the other districts Negro delegates addressed the convention, and several were elected officers.

67. *Baltimore Sun*, September 10, 16, 1870.

68. Editorial of May 7, 1870.

for a uniform party policy on the difficult question of Democratic solicitation of Negro votes:

> Does the Democratic party want the colored vote or does it not? If it does want the colored vote it must say so. . . . If there is any class of people who believe that the colored people will vote for any man or party whose position on that subject is the least equivocal, let us assure them that they are woefully mistaken. . . . The Republican party is straining every nerve to get their vote. The Democratic party is standing by with its hands folded. . . .
>   Once joining the Republican party, the negro will stay in it for years. The census is not complete, but from what we can gather from it the negroes are likely to have a small majority in the county. If this vote is all lost to the Democrats, it means a Republican Board of Commissioners of the Tax, Orphans Court, Sheriff and members of the next House of Delegates and the next State Senator, and that these offices will be filled in whole or in part by colored men. . . . If in the face of the existing facts, the Democratic party decides against the reception of the colored vote, we must abide its decision. But we owe it to the people of Charles County . . . faithfully to lay before them what is, in our opinion, the true condition of our political affairs.[69]

The Democratic state central committee declined to hand down a policy on the matter, leaving it to individual candidates to settle within their own districts. The result was an interestingly autonomous campaign in which Democrats in one district avidly courted Negro votes while their cohorts in a neighboring district ran on white supremacy platforms. In the First and Second Congressional Districts, for example, the Democrats ran a " white man's campaign." The First District comprised most of the counties on the Eastern Shore; the Second District embraced Harford County, seven wards in Baltimore City, and parts of Baltimore County. The First District candidate, Samuel Hambleton, left no doubt about his stand when he described the major issue of the day as " one of races—whether the white, Caucasian race, or the negro race, shall rule in this State." [70] Candidate Stevenson

69. *Port Tobacco Times and Charles County Advertiser*, Editorial of September 2, 1870.
    70. *Chestertown Transcript*, October 1, 1870.

Archer, of the Second District, was equally candid; he did not intend to appeal to any man " who did not belong to the white Caucasian race." He wished " either to succeed with the white people or go down with the Democratic party." [71]

Democrats in the Third and Fifth Congressional Districts, on the other hand, courted the Negro vote. The Third District was located wholly within Baltimore City and the Fifth District included all the counties of southern Maryland and parts of Baltimore County. The Colored Democratic Association was formed in Baltimore in August, 1870, and a Baltimore Negro, Jonathan Waters, was elected its president.[72] Waters became the main agent of the Democratic party in soliciting Negro votes, but his activities were strictly confined to the Third and Fifth districts. He traveled throughout the Fifth District, where integrated Democratic rallies were held in several counties, addressing the gatherings on behalf of the Democratic candidate and remaining in a county three or four days for organizational work among the Negroes.[73] Waters and his fellow Democratic campaigners were hard pressed to produce convincing arguments for Negro support of the Democratic ticket, however; their appeals were largely negative, consisting of reassurances that the Democrats would not try to re-enslave Negroes, confessions of error in having opposed enfranchisement, and indirect threats of dire consequences if the Negroes should align themselves solely with the Republicans. The Democrats' most positive claim was that they had framed the provision in the Constitution of 1867 that permitted Negroes to testify in court on an equal basis with whites.

Negro response to Democratic solicitations varied. In the rural areas there seems to have been no difficulty attracting Negro audiences at Democratic rallies; there are reports of successful integrated rallies in Prince George's, Anne Arundel, and Charles counties.[74] In Baltimore, however, Democrats were greatly embarrassed when their big pre-election rally, billed as " a mass meeting of democratic freemen " and preceded by warnings for

71. *Baltimore Sun*, September 16, 1870.
72. *Ibid.*, August 31, 1870.
73. The *Port Tobacco Times and Charles County Advertiser* of October 4, 1870, gives an account of Waters' activity in Charles County; the *Baltimore Sun* of October 10, 1870, reports that Waters had campaigned in Prince George's and Anne Arundel counties.
74. *Baltimore Sun*, October 10, 1870; *Frederick Examiner*, October 19, 1870; *Port Tobacco Times and Charles County Advertiser*, October 21, 1870.

discreet and orderly conduct at this " mixed " meeting, turned out to be an all-white gathering because Negroes failed to appear. Candidate Thomas Swann, of the Third District, attempting to put a good face on what must have been a disappointing situation, termed the demonstration " an outpouring of the white men of Baltimore " such as he had never witnessed before.[75]

In the Fourth Congressional District, composed of the predominantly white counties in northwestern Maryland, neither Republicans nor Democrats seem to have had any particular solicitude for the Negro voter. The Democratic candidate frequently declared that he did not want Negroes to vote for him.[76] And Republicans, after an initial flurry of registration activity, tried to disassociate themselves from the Negro constituency as the campaign progressed. Fearful that white Republicans would stay at home rather than participate in an amalgamated party, they zealously reported every instance of Democratic solicitation of Negro voters in other districts. " How foolish it would be," they pointed out, " for a Republican to stay at home on election day because colored people vote, when Democrats are doing all they can to get a portion of that vote." [77]

As election day approached, federal election supervisors were appointed to oversee the polling and to witness the count of the ballots and the compilation of returns. Hundreds of federal deputy marshals were appointed to assist the supervisors and to arrest anyone who attempted to interfere with an orderly polling of the vote. Federal troops were moved into Maryland, stationed at strategic places throughout the state, and held in readiness for use if needed.[78] The election, on November 8, passed quietly. There was a large vote, but no disorder that could not be handled by the federal supervisors and marshals, and federal troops were not needed or used.[79]

Seventy-nine percent of the state's eligible voters took part in this off-year congressional election. The figures (see Table 3) show that the voting was heaviest in areas with large Negro

75. *Baltimore Sun*, October 31 and November 1, 1870.
76. *Frederick Examiner*, October 12, 1870.
77. *Ibid.*, October 26, 1870.
78. *Baltimore Sun*, November 7, 8, 1870. The election supervisors were appointed by the judge of the United States Circuit Court and the deputy marshals by the United States Marshal under the provisions of the Federal Enforcement Act of 1870.
79. *Baltimore Sun*, November 9, 1870.

TABLE 3

VOTER TURN-OUT IN THE MARYLAND CONGRESSIONAL ELECTION OF 1870,
BY RACIAL COMPOSITION OF COUNTIES

Counties	Number of Eligible Voters *	Total Vote Cast †	Percentage Voting
Group 1 (less than 15% Negro)			
Allegany	7,941	4,833	61
Baltimore	13,449	8,485	63
Carroll	6,751	5,524	82
Washington	7,796	7,040	90
Total	35,937	25,882	Average 74
Group 2 (15%–30% Negro)			
Cecil	6,288	4,912	78
Frederick	10,454	9,403	90
Harford	5,155	4,674	91
Howard	3,145	2,639	84
Wicomico	3,473	2,877	83
Total	28,515	24,505	Average 85.2
Group 3 (31%–45% Negro)			
Caroline	2,735	2,333	85
Dorchester	4,409	3,778	86
Kent	4,143	3,563	86
Montgomery	4,863	4,227	87
Queen Anne's	3,723	3,653	98
Somerset	4,124	3,363	81
Talbot	3,770	3,260	86
Worcester	3,542	3,091	87
Total	31,309	27,268	Average 87
Group 4 (more than 45% Negro)			
Anne Arundel	5,859	5,024	86
Calvert	1,838	1,942	105 ‡
Charles	3,366	3,138	93
Prince George's	5,018	4,441	89
St. Mary's	3,241	3,090	95
Total	19,322	17,635	Average 92.6
Baltimore City §	54,762	39,245	71.6

* U.S. Office of the Census, *Ninth Census of the United States: 1870. Population,* 1: 629.
† *Baltimore Sun,* November 11, 1871.
‡ In Calvert County 104 more persons voted than were eligible, according to the census data. In averaging Group 4 turn-out this figure was reduced to 100 percent.
§ Baltimore, whose population was less than 15% Negro, could be included in Group 1.

populations, indicating that many of the newly enfranchised Negroes participated and that Negro participation stimulated white voting in these areas. Counties with a small Negro population tended to have a lower turn-out than counties with a large Negro population.

There is every indication that most Negro voters supported the Republican ticket. In the Fifth District, where Democrats made their best efforts to capture some of the Negro vote, four counties —Anne Arundel, Calvert, Charles, and Prince George's—went Republican. In Charles County, where Negroes had been repeatedly wooed by Democrats at integrated rallies, barbecues, and even breakfast meetings prior to the election, the local newspaper reported that only about one hundred of the county's 1,732 registered Negroes voted Democratic while more than 1,500 Negroes supported the Republican party.[80] Here, as elsewhere in the state, it was relatively easy for contemporary observers to estimate Negro support for the Republican ticket; Republican workers gathered Negro voters at meetings early in the morning before the polls opened and then escorted them to the polls in groups.[81]

In spite of the high turn-out and seemingly strong support from the new Negro voters, Republicans failed to carry a single congressional district in 1870 (see Table 4); theirs was still a minority party, except in four counties in southern Maryland. But if Negro enfranchisement failed to make the Republican party a majority party in Maryland, it improved the party's competitive position immensely. In 1867, before enfranchisement, Republicans had polled only one vote to very three votes for the Democrats, and only one vote for every two Democratic votes in 1868. In 1870, with the addition of blacks to the electorate, Republicans polled four votes for every five votes received by the Democrats.[82]

The 1870 returns show that the Republicans fared best in western Maryland (the Fourth District) and southern Maryland (the Fifth District). The predominantly white counties in western Maryland formed the traditional base of the state's Republican party and were the source of its strongest support before enfranchisement. Republicans fully expected to carry the Fourth District

80. *Port Tobacco Times and Charles County Advertiser*, November 11, 1870.
81. *Baltimore Sun*, November 9, 1870; *Chestertown Transcript*, November 12, 1870.
82. *Baltimore Sun*, November 13, 1868, and November 11, 1871.

TABLE 4

Party Vote in the Maryland Congressional Election of 1870,
by District and County

District and County	Democratic	Republican
First District		
Caroline County	1,291	1,042
Cecil County	2,770	2,142
Dorchester County	2,034	1,744
Kent County	1,874	1,689
Queen Anne's County	2,031	1,622
Somerset County	1,816	1,547
Talbot County	1,760	1,500
Wicomico County	1,944	933
Worcester County	1,982	1,109
Total	17,502	13,328
Second District		
Baltimore City, Wards 1–7	8,904	4,878
Baltimore County, Districts 5–7, 9–12	2,794	1,484
Harford County	3,000	1,674
Total	14,698	8,036
Third District		
Baltimore City, Wards 8–20	15,065	10,398
Fourth District		
Allegany County	2,843	1,980
Carroll County	2,966	2,558
Frederick County	4,739	4,664
Washington County	3,756	3,284
Total	14,304	12,486
Fifth District		
Anne Arundel County	2,318	2,706
Baltimore County, Districts 1–4, 8, 13	2,640	1,567
Calvert County	937	1,005
Charles County	1,545	1,593
Howard County	1,483	1,156
Montgomery County	2,436	1,791
Prince George's County	2,220	2,221
St. Mary's County	1,671	1,419
Total	15,250	13,458

Source: Baltimore Sun, November 11, 1871.

in 1870, because their margin of loss in 1868 had been less than 600 votes and because 3,000 Negroes had meanwhile been added to the voting lists.[83] Their failure to carry this district indicates substantial defection of white Republicans because of the Negro issue, and the relatively low turn-out of this district, 81.3 percent, indicates that much of this defection took the form of nonparticipation. But time and effective organization could remedy this situation, and the western part of the state would remain a strong base for Republicanism in Maryland. In southern Maryland the Republicans found a new base of power as a result of enfranchisement, where the party's membership was almost wholly Negro. In a few counties the Negro vote would be sufficient, but in most places Republicans had to attract some white support to gain control. Winning white support would prove extremely difficult in areas where the white population looked with fear and contempt upon the large number of Negroes in their midst, but it would not always prove impossible. Southern Maryland had become, and would remain, an intensely competitive area in Maryland politics.

On the state level, the Republican party had demonstrated that it possessed a following and organizational ability capable of presenting a genuine challenge to the dominant Democratic party. If it could retain and build upon these two elements it stood a real chance of gaining power. In the meantime the position of the Republican party furnished a check of sorts on the majority party. The Democratic party would have to maintain a high degree of party unity and work and campaign hard to maintain its control of the state. Thus the base for a two-party system in Maryland had been constructed by enfranchisement of the Negro and his incorporation into the state's Republican party.

83. *Frederick Examiner*, September 28, 1870.

CHAPTER 2

THE DEMOCRATIC PARTY AND THE NEGRO, 1870–1895

The Nature of Democratic Power

Although Negro enfranchisement established a solid base for the Republican party in Maryland, the Democratic party retained its dominant position in the state for the next twenty-five years. From 1870 until the election of a Republican governor in 1895, all major state offices and the control of both houses of the legislature remained in Democratic hands. Maryland regularly voted Democratic in presidential elections, and of the seventy-seven congressional representatives elected during this period sixty-seven were Democrats.[1]

To all outward appearances Maryland was solidly and safely a Democratic state. Underlying this long period of Democratic dominance, however, was a genuinely competitive party system that was capable of providing a check on the policies and personnel of the majority party. The Democratic margin of control was never large enough to permit the luxury of relaxed, easy campaigning or sustained indulgence in the intraparty factionalism that the composition of the party invited. Democratic candidates rarely assumed office by default; the Republican party consistently ran opposition candidates in state and in federal elections.[2] Campaigns varied in their intensity but elections were seldom foregone conclusions, and both parties worked vigorously to maximize their vote.

1. In 1872 Maryland's presidential vote went to Horace Greeley who ran as a Liberal Republican but was endorsed by the Democratic party.
2. Partial exceptions occurred in 1875 and in 1878. In 1875 the Republican party did not nominate candidates for governor, attorney general, or comptroller; it endorsed the nominees of the Citizens' Reform party, a Baltimore City–based group of independents and renegade Democrats. The Republicans ran their own legislative candidates in most of the counties, however. In 1878 Republicans failed to offer congressional candidates in the Second and Third districts. See the *Baltimore Sun*, October 30, 1875, and November 6, 1878.

The competitive nature of the party system in Maryland can be seen in the relatively narrow margins of control the Democratic party maintained in major elections throughout the period (Table 5). Although Democrats were elected in each of the six guber-

TABLE 5

MARYLAND DEMOCRATIC PARTY'S SHARE OF THE TWO-PARTY VOTE
IN GUBERNATORIAL AND PRESIDENTIAL ELECTIONS, 1871–1892
(Percentages)

Gubernatorial Elections

1871	55.6
1875	54.0
1879	56.9
1883	53.4
1887	53.3
1891	58.0

Presidential Elections

1872	50.3 *
1876	56.0
1880	54.4
1884	53.0
1888	51.4
1892	55.1

* The vote for Liberal Republican Horace Greeley, who was also endorsed by the Democratic party, is used for the 1872 election and accounts for the abnormally low margin in this year.

natorial elections from 1871 through 1891, their margin of victory was never one to inspire complacency within the party. The story was much the same in presidential elections. Democratic candidates carried the state in each election but, on the average, their margin was even lower than that of gubernatorial candidates.

Democratic control was most tenuous in the rural areas. Twice during the era—once in a gubernatorial and once in a presidential election—Democrats failed to carry the vote in the counties and were saved from defeat only by their margin in Baltimore City.[3] The regularity of a highly competitive Republican position in the rural areas of the state was also important. In each gubernatorial and presidential election from 1871 through 1892 the Democrats' percentage of the two-party vote in the counties fell below

3. The losses occurred in the presidential election of 1872 and the gubernatorial election of 1875. Both were unusual elections, however: in 1872 the Democratic forces ran under a Liberal Republican banner and in 1875 the Republicans ran under a Citizens' Reform banner.

their share of the vote in the state as a whole, while their margin in Baltimore City just as regularly surpassed their state performance (see Figure 2). Thus Baltimore City, polling approximately

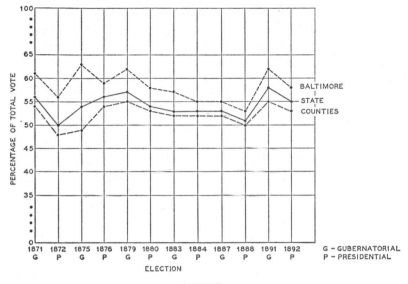

FIGURE 2

DEMOCRATIC PARTY'S SHARE OF THE TWO–PARTY VOTE IN BALTIMORE CITY,
THE STATE, AND THE COUNTIES, 1871–1892

one-third of the vote of the state during this period, was the stronghold of Democratic power. Baltimore was important not only for the numerical strength it furnished the party but also for the reliability of its support. The city went Democratic in every gubernatorial, presidential, and congressional election between 1870 and 1895 and, with only one exception, sent a wholly Democratic delegation to each session of the state legislature during this time.[4]

The Democrats' success in Baltimore owed much to the organizational talents of Isaac Freeman Rasin and the effective political structure he built and commanded for more than forty years. Rasin, the "boss" of the city's regular Democratic organization

4. Republicans carried the third legislative district of Baltimore in 1889, electing six Republicans to the House of Delegates; the remainder of the Baltimore delegation, twelve delegates, was Democratic (*Sun Almanac* [Baltimore], 1890, p. 58).

from the mid-1860s until shortly before his death in 1907, was a prototype of the successful urban machine politician. Born in Kent County in 1833 into an old landed family of French ancestry and educated at Washington College in Chestertown, he had come to Baltimore as a young man and had received his early training in the violent politics of the Maryland Know-Nothing movement of the 1850s.[5] Soon he switched to the Democratic party, and became a member of its city executive committee in 1864. From that time on, observers claimed, he exercised an influence " so complete and dominant over party affairs here [in Baltimore] as to amount almost to dictatorship." [6] Operating always in the background, he never held important public office, nor did he seek it. For eighteen years, from 1867 to 1885, he was clerk of the Court of Common Pleas of Baltimore; in 1886 he was appointed naval officer of the Port of Baltimore by President Cleveland, and served as such until 1890; and from 1892 to 1895 he was insurance commissioner for the state of Maryland. All of these positions gave Rasin sufficient time for the consuming task of maintaining a political machine, as well as conferring access to a considerable amount of patronage.

Rasin was known as the man who " made places " for more people than any other politician in Maryland.[7] A revealing account of the inner workings of Rasin's machine is found in the reminiscences of John J. Mahon, Rasin's long-time lieutenant and later his successor, whose rise in the organization illustrates Rasin's use of patronage to maintain his machine.[8] Mahon, the son of Irish immigrant parents, a nineteenth-century high school drop-out and self-confessed young tough, first met Rasin in 1870.

By that time I was 19 years old; I was pretty well running the old Ninth ward. I had been in a lot of fights and had a crowd of fellows who followed me around and were not

5. John R. Lambert, "Reconstruction to World War I," *The Old Line State: A History of Maryland*, ed. Morris L. Radoff, 3 vols. (Baltimore, 1956), 1:108. Primarily a tactician rather than an ideologue, Rasin seems to have carried none of the nativism of Know-Nothingism into his Democratic organization; his machine worked well with the foreign-born of Baltimore, but the political rowdyism associated with the Know-Nothing movement was also an ever-present element.

6. *Baltimore Sun*, March 13, 1904.

7. *Ibid.*

8. "Sonny Mahon's Own Story: The Autobiography of a Baltimore Boss" appeared as a series of articles in the *Baltimore Sun*, October 1, 8, 15, and 22, 1922.

afraid of anything. In a ward fight we could pretty well clean up anything that came against us.

Politics in those days wasn't any kid-glove business. It was rough, and we were as rough as you make them. It was not long before the leaders uptown began to take notice that they could not carry the Ninth ward in the primaries without us, and I began to get known around a little.[9]

Recognizing his promise, Rasin summoned young Mahon to his office.

I went around to the office of the Clerk of the Court of Common Pleas, which was the job Old Man Rasin held onto for 18 years. It was from this office that he ran the organization. . . .

That first conversation was a funny one. We talked about things in the Ninth ward and about the fall campaign. The Old Man cussed out a lot of people and I listened. The upshot of that conversation was that I became Rasin leader in the ward and got a job in the State tobacco warehouse at $2 a day.[10]

A few years later Rasin raised Mahon to the position of mayor's messenger, and then city council doorkeeper, jobs that paid about $900 a year. Mahon then decided he was ready to go into the city council, and broached the idea to Rasin.

I talked with the Old Man about it, and he wanted me to go there and be his representative. Of course, there wasn't any trouble about it. I could have nominated and elected anybody I wanted in that ward, and everybody knew it. So I was a candidate and got more than the usual majority.

I served, all told, 14 years in the Council. . . . I worked for Old Man Rasin while I was in the City Council and represented him in a lot of fights there and in Annapolis.[11]

After fourteen years the attractions of elective office palled for Mahon and Rasin found a place for him in his own office in the Court of Common Pleas. Then, in 1884, Grover Cleveland's election to the presidency opened a whole new world of patronage to

9. *Baltimore Sun*, October 1, 1922.
10. *Ibid.*, October 8, 1922.
11. *Ibid.*, October 15, 1922.

Maryland Democrats. Rasin had Mahon appointed special agent for the Treasury Department in Baltimore, a post Mahon valued highly.

> The salary of that was $8 a day and I thought I had all the money in the United States. . . . It was the first time in a good many years that the Democrats had had a chance at the Federal patronage. Rasin was supreme boss in the city and Gorman was in the Senate in the height of his power. As Jim Lewis [another Rasin lieutenant and ward leader] used to say, those were the days when "knighthood was in flower." [12]

Rasin is little remembered today, even in Maryland, but in his own day his political career was considered unparalleled. The *Baltimore Sun* claimed " there has never been a man in the political history of either party who has succeeded in maintaining his supremacy as boss of the party organization for so long and continuous a period as has Mr. Rasin." [13]

Democratic strength owed much to Baltimore City, but there also were other areas the party could count on for regular support. Although the vote in these areas usually was close, time after time certain counties fell into the Democratic column. An index of party regularity, based on the percentage of Democratic victories in all gubernatorial, House of Delegates, presidential, and off-year congressional elections between 1870 and 1895, reveals that ten counties constituted the rural backbone of Democratic strength (Table 6, Group 1).[14] Five additional counties (Group 2) show distinct Democratic leanings but lack the reliability of the previous ten. The eight remaining counties (Group 3) supported the Republican more often than the Democratic party and mark areas of Democratic weakness. Geographically, Democratic strength radiated from Baltimore, embraced the middle counties and most of the Eastern Shore, and was checked when it reached the out-

---

12. *Ibid.*
13. March 13, 1904. After Rasin died, in 1907, John Mahon took over his organization (*Baltimore Sun*, October 22, 1922).
14. Off-year congressional elections are used rather than all congressional elections to provide a more varied comparison. A county's rating in congressional elections that were held in presidential election years usually was the same as its presidential election rating.

TABLE 6

INDEX OF DEMOCRATIC PARTY REGULARITY, MARYLAND COUNTIES
AND BALTIMORE CITY, 1870–1895
(Percentage of Times Unit Voted Democratic)

Counties	Gubernatorial Elections (6)	House of Delegates Elections (*)	Presidential Elections (6)	Off-Year Congressional Elections (7)	All-Election Average (†)
Group 1					
Wicomico	100	100	100	100	100.0
Montgomery	100	97	100	100	98.1
Queen Anne's	100	97	100	100	98.0
Howard	100	100	83	100	97.6
Carroll	83	100	83	84	95.5
Harford	100	98	83	84	95.1
Worcester	100	90	100	100	94.0
Kent	100	96	83	84	93.0
Cecil	67	100	83	84	92.7
Baltimore	83	92	100	100	92.3
Group 2					
Anne Arundel	83	79	67	57	75.8
Dorchester	83	83	17	57	72.7
Prince George's	83	67	83	71	70.9
Talbot	83	68	50	71	68.0
Caroline	67	58	67	57	60.4
Group 3					
Somerset	50	56	17	43	49.0
Washington	50	46	33	43	44.7
Charles	50	45	17	14	37.5
Calvert	67	38	17	14	34.8
St. Mary's	50	42	0	14	32.5
Frederick	17	25	17	43	25.3
Allegany	17	22	17	14	20.6
Garrett	0	27	0	28	19.5
Baltimore City	100	97	100	100	97.4

* Number of elections varies from 22 to 216, according to the number of delegates representing each unit.
† Number of elections varies from 41 to 235 because of variations in the number of delegates elected from each unit.

posts of Republican strength in southern and western Maryland. Racially, it was at the extremes of demographic composition—that is, in the " blackest " and the " whitest " counties of the state—that the Democratic party was most often unsuccessful. Of the eight counties in which the Democratic party was weakest (Group 3), three counties—Charles, Calvert, and St. Mary's—had the state's highest percentages of Negro population for the period and three counties—Garrett, Allegany, and Washington—had the lowest percentages.[15]

Credit for construction of the Democratic rural machine must go to Arthur Pue Gorman, four times a United States senator from Maryland and the most prominent political figure the state produced in the post–Civil War era. A native of Howard County, Gorman began his political career in the House of Delegates in 1868. In 1870 Gorman met Rasin, whose influence in Baltimore already was paramount, and the following year he was elected Speaker of the House, probably with Rasin's support.[16] Gorman won control of the state party machinery in 1874, and for the next thirty years he and Rasin worked together, two master politicians who held a tight grasp on the reins of party power. Rasin remained in the background while Gorman rose rapidly to state and national prominence.

In 1881 Gorman began the first of his four terms in the United States Senate, serving continuously to 1899, and from 1903 until his death in 1906. His political reputation was enhanced by his successful management of Grover Cleveland's presidential campaign in 1884 and by his role as chairman of the Senate Democratic caucus. Because of his success he was often mentioned as a possible Democratic presidential choice, in 1892 and 1904,[17] but his involvement in national politics never caused him to neglect the state. Because United States senators were elected by state legislatures, Gorman maintained a firm hold on the state's party machinery by continual involvement with its personnel and policies

15. The pattern is not exact, however; two strongly Democratic counties, Carroll and Baltimore, had very small Negro populations, smaller than in Frederick County, which usually voted Republican. Somerset County also is inexplicable in these terms; it fell in the middle range in Negro-white population but more often than not voted Republican.

16. Lambert, " Reconstruction to World War I," in *The Old Line State*, 1:109; also see Lambert's biography, *Arthur Pue Gorman* (Baton Rouge, 1953).

17. Lambert, " Reconstruction to World War I," in *The Old Line State*, 1:112–13.

and by his continuing alliance with Rasin's organization in Baltimore. The Gorman-Rasin alliance seems to have been one of equals despite the disparity in their political positions. Each was supreme in his own sphere and each was vital to the overall success of the Democratic party. Rasin always referred to Gorman as " the state crowd " and to himself as " the city people." [18]

Despite the power and success of the Gorman-Rasin organization, intraparty opposition to its leadership was continuous. The Maryland Democratic party embraced a peculiarly diverse grouping of interests, which had to be held together to create an electoral majority, and these interests could not always be meshed. Agrarian interests in the counties competed for favor and attention with commercial interests and with the growing labor movement in Baltimore City. Reconciliation of such conflicting interests was a difficult feat and it was a measure of Gorman's and Rasin's tactical ability that they usually succeeded. One group within the party, however, continually defied their leadership and finally was able to defeat the two men by turning to the opposition party. Beginning in 1873 and continuing for as long as the Gorman-Rasin organization existed, a countermovement within the Democratic party opposed the machine's leadership. Known variously as the Citizens' Reform party, the Old Line Democrats, and the Independent Democrats, the movement was based in Baltimore City, where it was most active; it had no permanent organization, but a continuity of personnel and outlook identify it as a continuing movement.[19]

Led in the 1870s by such men as Severn Teackle Wallis, a prominent Baltimore attorney, and J. Morrison Harris, an attorney and former congressman, the reform movement drew its support primarily from Baltimore businessmen and merchants.[20] In the 1880s it received the support of the Baltimore and Ohio Railroad in the person of John K. Cowen, the road's general counsel and future president, and the intermittent backing of the Edwin F. Abell family, owners of the state's most influential newspaper,

18. *Baltimore Sun*, March 13, 1904.
19. Disaffected Democrats called themselves Reformers in the 1870s and their organization was the Citizens' Reform party. In 1881 they agreed to call themselves Old Line Democrats, but after 1882 they were most often referred to simply as Independent Democrats.
20. *Baltimore Sun*, September 29, 1875. The *Baltimore Sun* frequently referred to the dissident Democrats as a businessmen's group.

the *Baltimore Sun*.[21] The program of the independent Democrats
was one which is usually associated with urban progressivism:
opposition to "machine politics" and "corrupt elections" and
support of electoral reform, regulation of primaries and lobbying,
and civil service.[22] All these reforms, though irreproachably
respectable, were also measures designed to undercut the regular
organization's mode of operation by restricting its supply of
patronage and by making its control of nominations more difficult.
Furthermore, underlying the political progressivism of the independents was an economic conservatism dedicated to the maintenance of corporate economic privileges, which frequently col-
lided with the policies of the regular wing of the Democratic
party. Indeed, the level of political activity and the volume of
protest against "ring rule" generated by the independents in
Maryland bore a close relationship to the intensity of the regular
Democrats' efforts to effect tax reform during the era.[23]

In short, the nature of Democratic power in Maryland was that
of a party closely challenged by its opposition, relying heavily
on the organizational talents of two men, and threatened from
within its ranks by those who denounced its methods of achieving
power. Factionalism, its chief danger, required a constant bal-
ancing of interests by its leadership. Where this failed, the
leadership resorted to the heavy-handed and sharp practices of
machine politics, supplemented by ideological appeals to tradi-
tionalism and maintenance of white solidarity in the face of an
enemy who consorted with the Negro.

The Substance of Democratic Politics

For several years after the restoration of Democratic rule in
1867 and 1868 it was hardly necessary for the Democratic party
even to offer a program to its constituents. It was enough that
the party bore the Democratic-Conservative label and that it
opposed the Republican or "Radical" party. Indeed, the plat-

21. Lambert, "Reconstruction to World War I," in *The Old Line State*, 1: 110.
22. Severn Teackle Wallis, a prominent Baltimore lawyer and reform leader,
gave a detailed exposition of the independents' grievances and aims early in their
movement's history in an address before a Citizens' Reform mass meeting in
Baltimore in 1875; see the *Baltimore Sun*, September 29, 1875.
23. See the next section of this chapter, "The Substance of Democratic Politics,"
for a more detailed treatment of the policy clashes of regular and independent
Democrats.

form adopted by the Democratic state convention in 1871 was devoted almost exclusively to national issues.[24] Maryland Republicans complained bitterly about the irrelevancy of a Democratic state campaign waged solely on such issues as " the plight of the Southern states " under Reconstruction. For a time, however, such emotional issues satisfied the mass of Marylanders, and the party held resolutely to this safe ground as long as it could.

Worsening economic conditions in the country, culminating in the depression of 1873, and the growing strength of the farmers' movement gradually forced the Democratic party to respond to internal pressures for economic and political action. Maryland farmers, the backbone of the rural wing of the party, were particularly aggrieved by the favored position of corporations in the state, many of which were exempt from state taxation.[25] Here as elsewhere, railroads bore the brunt of the attack as the farmers, smarting from the conviction that farmland was bearing a disproportionate share of the tax burden, forced the party to action. In 1872 the General Assembly imposed the first state tax on railroads operating in Maryland: half of 1 percent on annual gross receipts.[26] Small though the imposition was, it was a gesture toward the party's rural constituency, and was resented by business interests in the Democratic party. In the following year, 1873, the first open challenge to the regular Democratic organization was launched, in Baltimore City, when the Citizens' Reform party was formed. This independent party ran candidates against the regular Democratic slate in the Baltimore municipal election and in the state legislative election in Baltimore districts in 1873, but both efforts were unsuccessful.[27]

As regular Democrats worked in the legislature in 1874 to enact a bill providing for a general reassessment of property in the state, the independent movement blossomed into full-fledged revolt.[28] In the gubernatorial campaign of 1875 the Citizens'

24. *Baltimore Sun*, July 20, 1871.
25. *Baltimore Sun*, Editorial of September 17, 1873.
26. *Laws of Maryland*, 1872, chap. 234, p. 370. The Baltimore and Ohio Railroad was exempt from this law because it paid the state one-fifth of the passenger receipts of its Washington branch line. In 1878 the B & O asked to be relieved of this payment and the state consented, provided the railroad agree to comply with the gross receipts tax law (*Laws of Maryland*, 1878, chap. 155, pp. 241–50).
27. *Baltimore Sun*, October 23 and November 5, 1873.
28. *Laws of Maryland*, 1874, chap. 514, p. 853.

Reform party entered candidates for governor, attorney general, and comptroller against the regular Democratic ticket. Republicans, scenting an opportunity for gain in the factionalization of the dominant party, endorsed the Reform candidates for state office, confining their own nominations to local levels.[29]

The campaign of 1875, an exceptionally bitter campaign, was fought over three issues. The paramount issue, but not the one that generated most discussion, was the economic issue. Independents and their Republican allies denounced regular Democrats for extravagance in government, a rise in taxes, and state indebtedness. Admitting that taxes had risen, Democrats countered by pointing out that taxes were lower and more justly proportioned between landed and corporate wealth than they had been under the Unionists.[30] Independents, galled by their inability to control the Democratic organization, lashed out at the party as a corrupt and ring-ruled machine, charging fraud in its nominating and electoral processes. Independents, prior to their defection, had worked within the Democratic party to secure the nomination of a candidate who was acceptable to them, William T. Hamilton of Hagerstown, but he was defeated in a brilliant convention coup engineered by Arthur Gorman.[31] Democrats sought to counter the charge of bossism by raising another salient issue and pointed to the independent group's cooperation with " the black Republican party," asking " whether the large majority of the white voters of this State shall be overruled by a minority of the white voters in this State aided by the 29,232 colored voters? . . . Can any pretext of reform be made a reason for bringing [this] about? " [32]

The election of 1875, purely a state contest which was not federally supervised, was marked by fraud and violence, particularly in Baltimore City, where Negroes and whites alike were terrorized as they attempted to vote. Shooting incidents between the races were reported in five of the city's wards, and continuous efforts of the police were required to prevent widespread rioting in the southern part of the city. Arrests for the day totaled 209, about equally divided between whites and Negroes. Fraudulent election practices accompanied the violence. Repeat voting was

29. *Baltimore Sun*, September 23, 1875.
30. *Ibid.*, September 9, 16, 17, 1875.
31. Lambert, " Reconstruction to World War I," in *The Old Line State*, 1:108–9.
32. *Baltimore Sun*, Editorial of November 1, 1875. The *Baltimore Sun* supported the regular Democrats in this election.

common, as were " shingle " ballots—extra ballots enclosed and deposited within a legitimate ballot. The greatest fraud, however, consisted of Democratic ballots with a picture of Republican President Grant above the regular Democratic slate, a device designed to confuse the Negro voter.[33] Responsibility for most of the disreputable aspects of this election seems to rest with the Rasin machine, but since the Democratic party owed its victory on this occasion to its margin in Baltimore, the reputation of the whole party was tarnished. Even the *Baltimore Sun*, which had supported the regular Democrats, complained about their excesses in this election and began to support some of the reforms advocated by the independent movement.[34]

The campaign of 1875 was the only statewide third-party challenge to the Democratic party during the period. After its failure, dissident Democrats confined their party activity to Baltimore City, and in state races supported the Republican party whenever they felt threatened by the policies of the regular Democratic organization. Within Baltimore City, however, independent Democrats continued to act as an opposition party during the 1880s and early 1890s. They regularly nominated candidates to oppose the Rasin organization, and the Republican party, weak and divided in the city, either endorsed the independents' candidates or cooperated with them in drawing up fusion tickets. Although the independents never got control of the city during this time, they regularly placed a sizable minority on the city council and usually gave the organization a close race for mayor and for statehouse delegates.[35]

Regular Democrats, far from being elated by their victory in 1875, were shaken by the bitterness that had been engendered in the contest and were fearful of the ultimate consequences of continued independent-Republican cooperation. Maintenance of party dominance seemed to call for concessions to the dissidents, and the regulars, with their modest tax reforms safely on the books, began to cast around for means to woo the independents back into the party fold. The opportunity came in 1879, and the concession

33. *Ibid.*, November 3, 4, 1875. Ballots were designed and printed by the parties at this time, not by the state.
34. Editorial of November 5, 1875.
35. *Sun Almanac*, 1883, p. 33; 1884, p. 41; 1885, p. 45; 1886, p. 47; 1887, p. 58; 1888, p. 47; 1889, p. 65; 1890, p. 53; 1891, p. 50; 1892, p. 51; 1893, p. 72; 1894, p. 118; and 1895, p. 67.

was dramatic: the Democratic party bestowed its nomination for governor on William T. Hamilton, the independents' choice for this office prior to their defection in 1875. Hamilton's nomination was not only sanctioned but was arranged by the same man who had deprived him of it earlier, Arthur Gorman, now chairman of the Democratic state central committee and in firm control of the party's state organization.[36] The Democratic platform also was designed to please the independents, featuring calls for economy in government, lower taxes, and a new statewide registration of voters.[37] The maneuver was successful, and Hamilton was elected by the largest majority the Democratic party had received since Negro enfranchisement. The 1879 election was as quiet and orderly as the previous one had been rowdy, and it was notable that appeals to racism were almost completely absent from this campaign.[38]

Most Democrats pointed with pride to Hamilton's term as a reform administration, but its accomplishments were few.[39] The promised voter registration act was passed, providing not the periodic re-registration independents had hoped for but continuing the old cumulative system of annual revision of the lists by the registrars after the prescribed new registration had taken place. The new registration form included a space for noting the " color " of the registrant, something the previous procedure had not required, but there was no effort to make the registration of Negroes more difficult. An act that regulated primary elections also was passed, prescribing penalties for attempted bribery, intimidation, and repeat voting, but again independents were disappointed by the failure of the legislature to make the law mandatory. Each political party could decide whether it wanted to operate under the provisions of this law.[40]

36. Lambert, " Reconstruction to World War I," in *The Old Line State*, 1:111.

37. *Baltimore Sun*, August 8, 1879.

38. *Ibid.*, November 6, 1879.

39. John Mahon gave an interesting explanation for the failure of Hamilton's reform program. He recalled that both Gorman and Rasin were afraid of Hamilton and reluctantly agreed to his nomination only because of his strength with the independents; they knew that when he was in office he would not work with the organization, either on patronage or legislation. According to Mahon, their strategy " was to tie him up the best they could with a Gorman-Rasin State Senate and a Gorman-Rasin Board of Public Works, and then sit as tight as they could until his four years was over." *Baltimore Sun*, October 22, 1922.

40. *Laws of Maryland*, 1882, chap. 22, p. 28, and chap. 290, p. 439. The decision was left to the state executive committee of each party.

The remaining element in the Democrats' unlikely coalition of interests, and the next to clamor for attention in party councils, was labor. With the industrial growth of Baltimore City and the inability of the Rasin machine to work out a local accommodation with Baltimore independents, labor became increasingly important to the Democratic party in the 1880s. The Democratic state organization had been able to mollify the independents, at least temporarily, but there was to be no peace between the Democratic city organization and the independents. Rasin was regularly opposed by independent-Republican fusionists in all elections in the city, and his machine—a " people's " machine grounded on small favors and petty patronage for the workingman and immigrant groups—became interested in the demands of the growing labor movement in the city.

The primary interest of labor at this time was protection of its right to organize, and this demand was espoused by the Democratic party in 1883. Indeed, the Democratic and the Republican platforms in that year promised to protect the right of labor to organize by state statute, and in the ensuing gubernatorial campaign each party tried to outbid the other for labor's support.[41] The Democrats were successful in their bid, and in 1884 the first labor legislation of consequence was enacted in Maryland.[42] Statutes exempted labor unions from the state's conspiracy law and established procedures for the incorporation of unions.[43] A ten-hour maximum workday was set for coal miners, and an embryonic safety code that regulated working conditions in manufacturing establishments was enacted.[44] Like other group interests in the party, however, labor did not receive all that it asked: two important labor bills, one prohibiting child labor under ten years of age and the other setting an eight-hour maximum day for women and children employed in factories, died in the 1884 legislature.[45]

During the late 1880s the rift between the business element and the agrarian-labor wing of the Democratic party again began to

41. *Baltimore Sun*, September 20, 28, 1883.
42. A ten-hour maximum day for children under sixteen had been established in 1874, but this law was modified in 1876 to apply only to children working in manufacturing establishments, leaving those engaged in agriculture completely unprotected (*Laws of Maryland*, 1874, chap. 3, p. 5, and 1876, chap. 125, p. 193).
43. *Ibid.*, 1884, chap. 266, p. 366, and chap. 267, p. 367.
44. *Ibid.*, chap. 427, p. 573, and chap. 265, p. 365.
45. *Baltimore Sun*, March 31, 1884

widen, and again the basic cause was economic. The Democratic party found itself caught in a peculiar sort of tax bind: it bore responsibility for governing a fast-growing state, for maintaining, and in some instances expanding, the services of the state, but at the same time it was committed to various elements in its ranks not to raise the state tax rate.[46] Still, the problem need not have become acute—except for the fact that the state's total assessable tax base, instead of increasing as it should have in a growing industrial state, was diminishing. The state comptroller reported that the total assessable property base for 1885 was $5,000,000 less than the base in 1877, the year after the last assessment was made.[47] Governor Henry Lloyd who pointed out the situation in his annual address to the General Assembly in 1886, signaled the readiness of the Democratic party to attack the problem:

> Ten years have passed since our last general assessment, and notwithstanding new and large enterprises involving the outlay of large sums of money, which have sprung into existence, the improvement and development of many of our resources, and the appreciation of values incident to our increase of population and general growth of wealth, we find our taxable basis today less than it was a decade ago.[48]

The situation was aggravated by the excessive decrease in Baltimore City; the total state decrease from 1877 to 1885 was $5,000,000, but the decrease in Baltimore during this time was $11,000,000.[49] The flight of wealth from visible property to investment and personal property was accomplished more easily and artfully by the city dwellers than by their country cousins.[50] Estimating that at least $200,000,000 in mortgage capital alone was completely untaxed in Maryland, Governor Lloyd recommended " a new and immediate assessment under a law

46. The state tax rate had remained constant since 1878 (*Sun Almanac*, 1888, p. 85).
47. " Report of the Comptroller of the Treasury of the State of Maryland," *House and Senate Documents*, 1886, pp. xiv–xv.
48. *House and Senate Documents*, 1886, p. 9.
49. " Report of the Comptroller," *House and Senate Documents*, 1886, pp. xiv–xv.
50. There also was more reason for city dwellers to hide their assets from the tax collectors: the state tax rate was a minor consideration; city tax rates were infinitely higher. The state rate had remained constant, 18.75 cents per $100 assessed value, since 1878; Baltimore City's rate averaged $1.58 per $100 from 1876 to 1887; and county rates averaged about 75 cents per $100, varying somewhat from county to county (*Sun Almanac*, 1888, p. 85.).

broad enough in its letter and spirit to enable the assessors to reach all manner of property, that the burdens of taxation may be more equally distributed and substantial equality and uniformity of taxation may prevail throughout the State." [51] In addition to such assessment the Democratic party sought basic alterations in the state constitution that would permit more effective taxation and regulation of business. The Constitution of 1867 specified that every twenty years a referendum on constitutional revision should be held, and the Democrats took this opportunity to press for a constitutional convention.[52]

These new threats to business heightened the independents' political activity and pushed them closer to the Republican party, on the state as well as the local level. The closer relationship was symbolized in the political metamorphosis of John K. Cowen, spokesman for the Baltimore and Ohio Railroad and one of the state's most powerful business leaders. Originally a Democrat, Cowen had long been identified with the independent faction of the party; in 1887 he left the Democratic party completely and, as the featured speaker at the Republican state convention, lashed out viciously at Gorman and the program of the Democratic party. Republicans, playing for the independents' support, opposed constitutional revision at this time and incorporated many of the independents' electoral reforms in their platform. They made no mention of reassessment.[53]

The gubernatorial election of 1887, which pitted Democrat Elihu E. Jackson against Republican Walter B. Brooks, demonstrated anew the importance of the independent faction to the Democratic party. Its defection was so great that the Democrats' margin of victory was cut to its lowest point since the party had reestablished its control of the state in 1868, falling even below its 1875 margin.[54] Independents and Republicans also dealt the Democratic party a substantial policy rebuff in this election by defeating the proposal for constitutional revision, leaving the regulars little hope of achieving more control over business interests by this method.[55]

---

51. "Message of Governor Henry Lloyd," *House and Senate Documents*, 1886, p. 9.

52. *Baltimore Sun*, July 28, 1887. For the motivation behind the party managers' desire for a constitutional revision, see Lambert, *Arthur Pue Gorman*, pp. 134–40.

53. *Baltimore Sun*, August 25, 1887.

54. See p. 34 above.

55. The call for a constitutional convention was defeated 105,735 to 72,464 (*Sun Almanac*, 1888, p. 49).

The story of the Democratic party from 1887 to 1895 is that of a party increasingly at war with itself, confused in its policy aims, and generally on the decline. The agrarian-labor wing of the party continued to press for reassessment and tax reform, and some minor reforms were effected, particularly during Governor Jackson's administration. In 1890 laws were enacted that taxed all corporations chartered in Maryland at the rate of one-eighth of 1 percent of their capital stock value, that instituted a 1 percent tax on the gross receipts of foreign corporations doing business in the state, and that raised the tax on railroads from one-half of 1 percent to 1 percent.[56] But each time the party seemed on the verge of achieving a major reform, the effort failed. In 1890, after a bitter campaign in which Gorman and the regulars characterized the independents as " selfish men, identified with corporate greed," a Democratic legislature finally succeeded in passing a general reassessment bill—only to see it given a pocket veto by their Democratic governor.[57] Why Governor Jackson, who only a few months before had strongly backed reassessment, let the long-desired measure die in this manner is not altogether clear, but confusion and disorder within the party hierarchy undoubtedly played a part.[58] Confusion resulted from the attempt of party leaders to do too many things at once. At the same time the reassessment bill was passed, Democratic party leaders voted a proposed constitutional amendment through the legislature which would have permitted the state to levy an income tax.[59] Fearing that reassessment prior to the referendum on the proposed amendment would prejudice the amendment's chances at the polls, party leaders evidently decided at the last minute to scuttle reassessment and bank everything on the amendment. Their strategy proved to be extremely faulty; the amendment was rejected at the polls, leaving the regulars with neither reassessment nor authority to levy an income tax.[60]

Failure of this amendment, despite its progressive intent, proved to be a blessing in disguise for the state, and certainly for the

56. *Laws of Maryland*, 1890, chap. 536, pp. 611 ff.; chap. 608, pp. 780 ff.; chap. 559, pp. 671 ff.; and chap. 245, pp. 268 ff.

57. *Baltimore Sun*, October 14, 1889, and April 4, 16, 1890.

58. "Message of Elihu E. Jackson, Governor of Maryland, to the General Assembly of Maryland," *House and Senate Documents*, 1890, pp. 6–7.

59. *Laws of Maryland*, 1890, chap. 242, pp. 264–65.

60. *Sun Almanac*, 1892, p. 53. The vote was 38,118 against and 32,211 for the amendment.

state's Negro citizens. The proposed amendment would have removed the provision of Article 15 of the 1867 Constitution's Declaration of Rights, which prohibited the levy of a poll tax in Maryland.[61] Prohibition of a poll tax was at this time construed as prohibition of any capitation or head tax, and repeal of this prohibition was considered a necessary prelude to the state's authority to enact an income tax. At the same time, however, repeal of this provision would have opened the door to enactment of a poll tax in the narrower meaning of the term, a tax on the right of franchise. There is no indication that Democratic leaders were planning a franchise tax at this time, although Republicans laid this charge against them.[62] In any event, the amendment's failure meant that a specific prohibition against a poll tax remained part of the Maryland Constitution, barring the way to this method of disfranchisement in later years.

In 1892 Democrats again found their party embroiled in a fruitless economic policy imbroglio. A second reassessment bill was guided successfully through the legislature, with the party's apparent blessing, only to receive another Democratic governor's pocket veto.[63] Governor Frank Brown, in spite of his party's long-standing commitment, yielded to open pressure from the Baltimore business community to kill the measure.

Party demoralization reached its nadir after a spectacular scandal that broke in 1890, when it was discovered that State Treasurer Stevenson Archer had embezzled more than $100,000 in state funds. The Democratic party had always taken great pride in its fiscal integrity and its reign, to this point, had been remarkably scandal-free. Archer, serving his third term as treasurer when the scandal broke in March, 1890, was removed from office in April by Governor Jackson and charged with " malfeasance in office and misappropriation of the funds of the State." [64] The affair was doubly damaging to the party because

61. *Laws of Maryland*, 1890, chap. 242, pp. 264–65. Questions about the legal force of sections of the Declaration of Rights, a sort of preamble to the Maryland Constitution of 1867, have been raised in recent years, primarily because of wording. Section 15, for example, states that " the levying of taxes by the poll is grievous and oppressive and ought to be prohibited." Recent opinion holds that such a statement is merely a declaration of principle and is not enforceable in the courts unless supplemented by legislation. In the 1880s and 1890s, however, this statement was considered a constitutional prohibition.

62. *Baltimore Sun*, August 28, 1891.

63. *Ibid.*, April 9, 1892.

64. *Ibid.*, March 30 and April 16, 1890.

Archer also was state chairman of the Democratic party, and rumor had it that the misappropriated funds had found their way into the party's coffers. The rumor was denied repeatedly, by Archer and by every other party official of importance, but neither the legislative committee that investigated the case nor the ensuing criminal prosecution of Archer produced evidence of where the money had gone.[65] In one of the shortest trials in the state's history, Archer pleaded guilty to the embezzlement of $132,000 and was sentenced to five years in the penitentiary.[66] The plea of guilty, which precluded any real investigation or presentation of the case in court, kept publicity at a minimum.

The quality of legislation produced by the Democratic party during these declining years was generally undistinguished. In the area of political reform the high point was a new election law in 1890, requiring use of the "Australian" or secret ballot in general elections and providing that ballots be furnished by the state and be uniform in size and appearance.[67] Originally the law applied only to half the state, but in 1892, after its successful application in the preceding gubernatorial election, it was extended to the rest of the state.[68] Despite strong demand for a general law regulating primary elections, none was forthcoming; instead, beginning in 1892, a series of local laws that regulated primaries was enacted, which did little more than extend the penalties for election fraud in general elections to primary elections.[69] Registration reform was accorded the same inadequate treatment that had been applied to election reform. Baltimore City was at last granted biennial re-registration of voters, but the rest of the state had to operate under the old cumulative

65. Archer's written confession specified that "no part of the State's money or securities was ever used by me in gambling, stock speculation or for political purposes, nor have I at this time one dollar of it left" (*Baltimore Sun*, July 8, 1890). The legislative investigating committee also made a special point of denying that Archer had used any of the money for party purposes, but it could not show how the money had been spent (*Baltimore Sun*, June 13, 1890).

66. *Baltimore Sun*, July 8, 1890.

67. *Laws of Maryland*, 1890, chap. 538, p. 614.

68. *Ibid.*, 1892, chap. 300, p. 420. Maryland still has a unique system whereby the General Assembly may pass a "general law" but exempt from its provisions those counties that do not care to operate under it.

69. In 1892 systems of primary regulation were enacted for Baltimore City and for Baltimore, Queen Anne's, and Montgomery counties; in 1894 Cecil County was added to the list (*Laws of Maryland*, 1892, chaps. 238, 261, 508, and 548; 1894, chap. 355).

system whereby only an initial registration was required.[70] The party's record in social legislation was even worse; the best the Democrats could produce was a child labor law that prohibited the employment of children under twelve years of age in factories in Baltimore City and Allegany, Garrett, Anne Arundel, Charles, Talbot, Dorchester, and Montgomery counties. Under a legislative procedure peculiar to Maryland, sixteen of the state's counties elected not to come under the operation of this " general law " and hence were specifically exempted, leaving child labor unregulated in most of the state.[71]

Policy and leadership failures of this kind did nothing to mend the breaches in the party. Indeed, the failures were a symptom of the widening gulf between the various elements in the majority party and proof of their growing ability to frustrate each other's aims. The independent-business wing of the party was frustrated at not being able to put through the political reforms it felt would make the party more responsive to popular opinion. The farmer-labor group was frustrated at not being able to get the economic and social reforms it felt were demanded by the development of industrial capitalism. And the party's leaders must have been frustrated by the increasingly vociferous charges of bossism that were hurled at them despite their almost total inability to deliver on any of the policy aims they set out to achieve. The Democratic party was headed for major trouble, which in 1895 overwhelmed it.

The Negro under Democratic Rule

A *Baltimore Sun* editorial of November 18, 1884, effectively portrays the basic attitude of Maryland's Democratic party toward the Negro during its postwar period of dominance: " The best thing that can be done for the colored people is to let them alone. If they are treated kindly, the fears that beset them will soon be dissipated and they will be put in the best condition for working out their own deliverance, politically and otherwise."

After the initial shock of seeing the Negro become a citizen and voter and after the uneasiness over the effect this would have on practical control of the state, white Democrats soon accepted

70. *Ibid.*, 1892, chap. 368, p. 513.
71. *Ibid.*, 1894, chap. 317, p. 443. The practice of local exemption from state law was a procedure which developed by mutual consent in the Maryland state legislature; it was not a procedure which had any sanction or basis in the Maryland Constitution of 1867.

the new situation. This is not to say that race prejudice moderated or faded away as the whites became accustomed to Negro political activity; their belief in the inherent inferiority of the Negro was still a basic tenet, so ingrained in most whites that it rarely occurred to anyone even to discuss it. But racism was not virulent during this time, as it was to become later. There was little disposition in the Democratic party to harass the Negro, either ideologically by attempting to exploit the reservoir of race prejudice in the general population or practically by devising schemes and policies to restrict his newly gained political and civil rights. There was also, however, little disposition on the part of the ruling whites to do anything to help the Negro. During the 1870s and 1880s Negroes looked in vain to the Democratic party for even a promise of aid in improving their lot. Viewed neither as threat nor responsibility, Negroes for the most part were ignored by Maryland Democrats.

Democrats' acceptance of Negroes as political participants is indicated by the infrequency with which the race issue was raised in political campaigns. In only three of the twenty-three state and federal elections between 1871 and 1894 was racism a major feature of a Democratic campaign or a deliberate part of campaign strategy, sanctioned and adopted by the party hierarchy.[72] The first exception occurred in the gubernatorial campaign of 1875, when the Democratic party felt particularly threatened by a combination of independent bolters and Republicans. In an atmosphere of extreme economic tension, both within and outside the party, Democrats utilized racist arguments to enforce party solidarity and to relegate basic economic conflict to a secondary status.[73] Racism as a campaign weapon produced mixed results for the party: Democrats got their electoral victory amid such violence that their standing, particularly in Baltimore City, was seriously impaired.

In 1883 Democrats again beat the racist drums, but their efforts seem much less deliberate. Because the Danville, Virginia, race riot had broken out shortly before Maryland's gubernatorial election and had received considerable attention in the Maryland press, Maryland Democrats were unable to resist the opportunity

72. Racism as a campaign weapon of individual candidates or party workers undoubtedly played a part in all elections; our analysis deals only with instances in which the party as a whole openly embarked upon a racist course.
73. See p. 44 above.

to capitalize on this unfortunate outgrowth of a Virginia campaign to unseat William Mahone and his racially mixed Readjuster party. Citing the Virginia riot as a logical outcome of fusion rule, Democrats warned that support of "black Republicanism" would produce the same bloody results in Maryland. Their racist effort, however, was a last-minute affair, and, at its height, Democratic gubernatorial candidate Robert McLane made a public appeal to "decent and educated colored people" to support the Democratic ticket.[74]

Deliberate exploitation of racial prejudice was most obvious in the 1889 off-year legislative election during Governor Elihu Jackson's administration, as Gorman regulars struggled to increase their control in the legislature in order to put through the tax reforms that had been promised two years earlier in the party platform. Gorman had been rebuffed in 1887 by the defeat of the constitutional convention call, and the organization's program had got nowhere in the first session of the Jackson legislature. Regulars blamed this stalemate on the independents and their cooperation with Republicans, and in the 1889 campaign they hit back by making free use of class and race as issues. For the first time all the "big guns" of the Democratic party directed their fire at the racially mixed Independent Democratic-Republican coalition. Gorman commanded the attack and set the tone:

> From one end of this land to another the question between the white and black races is uppermost in the minds of the people. It was not started by the democratic party. We do not make war on the colored people. They are here among us, and we have tried to advance them as far as we could. We will educate them, treat them kindly, but we have determined that this government was made by white men and shall be ruled by white men as long as the republic lasts.[75]

Gorman was vague about the possible consequences of fusion rule, saying only that "behind the scenes" the fusionists "have told the negroes that they shall have what they want," but other party leaders were more imaginative. L. Victor Baughman, the Democratic candidate for state comptroller and head of the ticket in this off-year election, warned that fusion rule would see colored

74. *Baltimore Sun*, November 3, 1883.
75. *Ibid.*, October 22, 1889.

policemen and firemen installed in Baltimore and that mixed schools were a real possibility.[76] The Democratic platform which also raised the mixed schools issue, pledged to resist any such attempt, even though there was no evidence the opposition had even remotely considered supporting school integration.[77] A convention of Maryland Negroes, meeting in Baltimore earlier in the year, had asked that Negroes be permitted to attend the all-white Maryland Agricultural College inasmuch as there was no comparable state institution for Negroes. They had, however, received no support from any political party or faction, and had been condemned by prominent Negro leaders in the Maryland Republican party.[78] Racism did not pay off well for the Democrats in 1889, as Republicans placed a larger delegation in the legislature than ever before and won control of part of the Baltimore City delegation for the first time since redemption.[79] On the other hand, Democrats retained control of both houses, and the Gorman program made progress in the next session of the legislature.[80] Thus the usefulness of racism as a Democratic campaign tactic remained an open question.

For most of the elections that were held during the 1870–94 period, however, the Maryland Democratic party did not choose to campaign on racism; it either ignored the Negro altogether or made half-hearted efforts to solicit Negro votes. Immediately after enfranchisement the party formed the Colored Democratic Association, headed by a Baltimore Negro, Jonathan Waters, to solicit Negro support.[81] In 1872, however, Waters was cornered on the streets of Baltimore by a group of white and colored Republicans and shot by " an unknown assailant." [82] His wound was not fatal, but there are no further reports of Waters' political activity. Negro Democratic leadership seems to have passed to another Baltimore Negro, Walter Sorrell, who fared better than Waters and was rewarded for his political activity by appointment to a clerical position in the House of Delegates in 1880, the first

76. *Ibid.*, October 14, 23, 1889.
77. *Ibid.*, September 27, 1889.
78. *Ibid.*, February 14, 26, 1889.
79. *Ibid.*, November 7, 1889. The composition of the legislature that was elected in 1889 was: senate, 18 Democrats, 8 Republicans; house, 59 Democrats, 32 Republicans.
80. See p. 50 above.
81. See p. 27 above.
82. *Baltimore Sun*, November 9, 1872.

Negro to hold a position under the state government in Maryland.[83] On the whole, however, Democratic political activity among Negroes was sporadic, generally confined to the Baltimore area, and consisted mainly of organizing colored Democratic clubs on the ward level. The formation of Negro Democratic ward clubs in Baltimore is reported for 1870, 1872, 1876, 1879, and 1893.[84]

Open solicitation of Negro support through Democratic party platforms or by party candidates was even less frequent than the more covert solicitation of Negro agents and of Negro clubs, but there were occasional instances of the former. To allay the fears of Negroes who had been told that a Democratic victory in 1876 would mean a return to slavery, the platform of the Maryland Democrats acknowledged that "the Constitution of the United States secures perfect equality to all citizens, of whatever race or color, before the law," and it pledged to "guarantee to every citizen all his rights of person and property without regard to race or color."[85] Such pledges were exceptional, however; Democratic platforms usually made no mention of the Negro. Democratic candidates were equally remiss or embarrassingly awkward in their appeals for Negro support, as when gubernatorial candidate Robert McLane appealed to the "decent and educated colored people."[86] One of the few other Democrats who openly courted Negro support was Ferdinand C. Latrobe, a many-term mayor of Baltimore —who based his appeal on his longtime membership in the American Colonization Society, an organization whose aim was the resettlement of black Americans in Africa.[87] Latrobe, however, developed greater sophistication and became a Democratic champion of Negro demands for employment of Negro teachers in Baltimore's Negro schools.[88]

The absence of political racism in the 1870–94 period also was shown by a lack of concern when a Negro candidate ran for public office. Maryland Negroes did not run for office in anything like the number who stood for election in some of the Southern

83. *Ibid.*, April 5, 1880.
84. *Ibid.*, August 31, 1870; July 18, 1872; September 16, 1876; September 6, 1879; and October 25, 1893.
85. *Ibid.*, September 14, 1876.
86. See p. 55 above.
87. *Baltimore Sun*, October 23, 1883.
88. *Ibid.*, October 22, 1887.

states, and usually they ran as independent candidates unendorsed by any political party. These Negro candidacies caused very little comment. The first Negro who ran for public office in Maryland was James H. Montgomery of Cumberland, who stood for Congress in the Sixth District in 1874. Republicans were more exercised over Montgomery's candidacy than the Democrats because the Sixth was a district the former stood a fair chance of carrying, and the Negro candidate threatened to undercut their Negro backing. Republicans claimed that Montgomery's candidacy was a Democratic trick, but many Negroes were dissatisfied with the regular Republican candidate, Lloyd Lowndes, who opposed the civil rights bill that was pending in Congress, and Montgomery's candidacy may have been a genuine expression of Negro unrest. Negro support failed to materialize, however, and Montgomery received only twenty-five votes; the bulk of the Negro vote went to Republican Lowndes.[89]

Other Negro candidates had a similar experience. Negro independent candidates ran for the city council in Baltimore in 1880, 1882, 1885, and 1886, but none received more than a handful of votes. In 1886 a second Negro, S. Q. Sanks of Baltimore, stood for Congress in the Fourth District, but, like his predecessor, he garnered only about twenty-five votes.[90]

Not until 1890 was a Negro candidate successful in his bid for elective office in Maryland. Harry Scythe Cummings, a young attorney, was elected to the Baltimore city council as the representative of the city's eleventh ward. Cummings, a graduate of Lincoln University and the University of Maryland Law School, had been active in Republican politics for many years, and he became the first Maryland Negro to secure party endorsement of his candidacy. Running from a heavily but not predominantly Negro ward, Cummings beat his white opponent by 105 votes.[91] Neither Cummings' candidacy nor his victory seems to have aroused concern among the white community; city newspapers reported his election in a matter-of-fact manner and commented favorably upon his educational and professional background.[92]

89. *Cumberland Daily News*, October 29 and November 7, 1874.

90. *Baltimore Sun*, October 26, 1880; October 26, 1882; October 29, 1885; and October 28 and November 3, 1886.

91. *Ibid.*, November 5, 1890. Voter registration in Baltimore's eleventh ward in 1890 was 2,073 whites and 1,949 Negroes (*Sun Almanac*, 1891, p. 43).

92. *Baltimore Sun*, November 5, 1890; *Baltimore American*, November 5, 1890.

Maryland Negroes seem to have been reasonably secure in the exercise of their voting rights under Democratic rule, largely because of the Federal Enforcement Acts and their use in Maryland from 1870 through 1892.[93] Although the scope of the laws was gradually eroded during this period, primarily by adverse court decisions, some potent controls for protecting Negro suffrage remained in force.[94] The federal administrative machinery for overseeing state officials' conduct of registration and election procedures in federal elections remained intact, along with federal penalties for a state's discrimination against citizens because of race, color, or previous condition of servitude. Federal supervisors or United States marshals and deputies were present in Maryland at each federal election from 1870 through 1892.[95] In practical political terms this meant that every two years Maryland Democrats, who controlled the state's election machinery, were subjected to federal supervision by officials who were charged with seeing that Negroes got a fair chance to vote—and who usually had a partisan interest in a high Negro vote.

The amount of supervision exercised by these federal officials, as well as their number, varied from election to election. Election supervisors, appointed by the judge of the federal circuit court,

93. The Federal Enforcement Acts were passed in 1870 and 1871 (see p. 22 above). Congress repealed most of the provisions of the Enforcement Acts (those that had not previously been invalidated by judicial decisions) in 1894. The 1892 federal elections were the last in which the acts were in force (William Watson Davis, " The Federal Enforcement Acts," James W. Garner, ed., *Studies in Southern History and Politics* [New York, 1914], p. 228).

94. Decisions of the Supreme Court in 1876 struck down provisions in the first Enforcement Act that had permitted federal supervision of state elections, as distinguished from federal elections (U.S. *v.* Reese, 92 U.S. 214; U.S. *v.* Cruikshank, 92 U.S. 542). These rulings had little effect in Maryland, where no federal supervision of state elections (held in off years and separate from federal elections) was exercised even before the decisions. Accounts of state elections in Maryland in 1871, 1873, and 1875 comment upon the absence of federal supervisors and marshals (*Baltimore Sun*, November 8, 1871; November 5, 1873; and November 3, 1875). In 1880 Congress denied the use of federal troops to supervisory personnel responsible for enforcing the acts, and in 1883 the Supreme Court invalidated the Ku Klux Klan (the third Enforcement) Act on the grounds that the Fifteenth Amendment conferred protection against state, not private, discrimination (*Public Laws*, 46th Cong., 2d sess., p. 81, and U.S. *v.* Harris, 109 U.S. 3).

95. Specific mention of either federal election supervisors or marshals is made in the election accounts of the *Baltimore Sun* of November 8, 9, 1870; November 5, 6, 1872; November 6, 7, 1876; November 4, 1878; November 2, 1880; November 8, 1882; October 28 and November 3, 4, 1884; November 3, 1886; November 7, 1888; October 29, 1890; and November 9, 1892.

were authorized only to report irregularities in the polling process, but deputy marshals, sworn in by the United States marshals for the districts, had power to arrest offenders. In Maryland's 1870 congressional election, the first in which Negroes had the opportunity to participate, federal supervisors and deputy marshals were reported to have been present at every polling place in Baltimore City from the opening of the polls until the final ballot count.[96] Again in 1872, supervisors and deputies were present at the polls. A force of 322 deputies was used in the city, thirty-five of whom were Negroes.[97] By 1878 the total number of deputies had grown to 600, and 1,200 deputies were used to police the Baltimore polls in 1882.[98] Appointment of such a large force was an excellent source of election-day patronage, since remuneration for supervisors and for deputies was $5.00 a day.[99] As late as 1890 the use of federal officials to police Maryland polls was still widespread; on the request of local voters, federal supervisors were appointed to oversee the polls in each ward of Baltimore and in each precinct in ten counties.[100] And as late as 1892 Negroes still were used as deputy marshals, although the reports indicate that they were used only to arrest Negro offenders.[101]

The increasing inability to secure convictions under the Enforcement Acts, which eventually nullified their effectiveness in the lower South, could not be counted on in Maryland by potential violators.[102] The state's substantial Republican population performed jury duty, along with its other citizens, and the chances of drawing a jury that would disregard gross violations of Negro voting rights were not high in the border state. The combination of a strong indigenous Republican party and federal supervision of the election process proved to be an effective check on discrimination against Negro voters in Maryland.

Although the Enforcement Acts were used only in federal

96. *Baltimore Sun*, November 8, 1870.
97. *Ibid.*, November 5, 1872.
98. *Ibid.*, November 4, 1878, and November 8, 1882.
99. *Ibid.*, November 5, 1872, and November 3, 4, 1884.
100. *Ibid.*, October 29, 1890.
101. *Ibid.*, November 9, 1892.
102. William Watson Davis reports that from 1871 to 1897 federal courts handled 7,372 cases under the Enforcement Acts in the entire United States; there were 1,423 convictions, 903 acquittals, and 5,046 dismissals. The overwhelming majority of cases arose in the South, and only 162 cases originated in Maryland during the period 1871–97 ("The Federal Enforcement Acts," in James W. Garner, ed., *Studies in Southern History and Politics* [New York, 1914], p. 224).

elections in Maryland, the state's Democrats seem not to have taken advantage of the lack of such supervision in purely state elections to repress the Negro vote. Voter participation in Maryland from 1870 through 1895 was remarkably high, and a comparison between seven state-supervised and six federally supervised elections during the period shows no pattern of discrimination (Table 7). The average turn-out for presidential elections was slightly higher than for gubernatorial elections, but the small difference could easily be accounted for by the normal greater interest in national elections.

Maryland Negroes, although generally accepted in their limited role of citizen-voter under Democratic rule, usually failed in their attempts to persuade Democratic lawmakers to grant the policy reforms the black community desired. Even minor requests that would have made no real change in the status of Negro-white relations met with indifference or hostility from Democratic-controlled legislatures. In 1878, for instance, Negro leaders made the first of many efforts to secure repeal of certain discriminatory clauses in the Maryland constitution and statutes. The Constitution of 1867, for example, still contained provisions that limited suffrage to white male citizens, even though the Fifteenth Amendment had technically and actually nullified such provisions,[103] and Negro lobbyists appeared before a committee of the state senate with petitions urging that these repugnant and archaic clauses be stricken.[104] Even so minor a request, however, was refused by the legislature; Democratic leaders complained of the expense of amending the constitution to bring it into line with federal law and practice.[105] Negroes never succeeded in having the constitution formally amended to remove the obnoxious restriction; in later printings of the document, however, the restriction was omitted, and a footnote cited its incompatibility with the Fifteenth Amendment.

More substantive demands from the Negro community met the same sort of Democratic indifference. State legislation limited jury service in state courts and the practice of law before state courts to white persons. In these instances the law operated to exclude Negroes, but efforts to get the state legislature to remedy

103. The restrictive clause appeared in Article 7 of the Declaration of Rights and Article 1, Section 1 of the Constitution.
104. *Baltimore Sun*, February 14, 1878.
105. *Senate Journal*, 1878, pp. 924, 938.

TABLE 7

COMPARISON OF VOTER TURN-OUT IN MARYLAND'S STATE AND FEDERALLY SUPERVISED ELECTIONS, 1871–1895

Gubernatorial Elections (State Supervised)				Presidential Elections (Federally Supervised)			
Year	Eligible Voters*	Total Vote†	Turn-out (%)	Year	Eligible Voters*	Total Vote†	Turn-out (%)
1871	174,530	132,728	76.1	1872	179,215	133,948	74.7
1875	193,270	157,991	81.8	1876	197,955	163,846	82.6
1879	212,010	159,472	75.2	1880	216,694	172,227	79.5
1883	228,130	173,401	76.0	1884	231,942	186,019	80.2
1887	243,378	190,076	78.1	1888	247,190	210,921	85.3
1891	260,113	192,037	73.8	1892	265,409	213,275	80.4
1895	281,297	240,105	85.4				
		Average	78.1			Average	80.5

* The number of eligible voters is figured by using U.S. Census reports of the number of male citizens of age in Maryland in 1870, 1880, 1890, and 1900 and interpolating for intervening years.
† Voting totals are taken from the *Baltimore Sun* for 1871 through 1881 and from the *Sun Almanac* for 1882 through 1895.

the situation failed. Bills to remove racial restrictions from state jury service and the practice of law failed to pass the legislature in 1878, and in 1884 a bill to allow Negro lawyers to practice in state courts passed the senate but failed in the house.[106] Then, in 1880, the United States Supreme Court ruled that states could not exclude Negroes from jury service, and in March of that year the names of twelve Negroes were added to the jury lists in Baltimore City.[107] Negro lawyers were admitted to state practice in 1885, when a Maryland court ruled that the state legislation restricting practice to whites was a denial of equal protection of the law under the Fourteenth Amendment.[108]

Improvement of Negro education, a major concern of the black community, received active backing from the Republican party— and there was good reason for concern. In 1870 Governor Oden Bowie, calling attention to the fact that Maryland had made no provision for Negro public education, had advanced the Democratic party's solution for this problem.

> In connection with the subject of the system of education throughout the State, the fact occurs to my mind that a portion of our population consists of colored freedmen, for whose education no legislative provision has yet been made. If at a period, immediate or remote, they are to become citizens, possessed of the elective franchise, would not sound policy, then, dictate such education of the colored population as would prepare them intelligently to exercise the elective franchise, and as citizens to judge for themselves of the proper workings of our political system, and not be misled by the crafts and clamors of designing and unscrupulous politicians? . . . It is not proposed to add to the burdens of taxation for the purpose of educating the colored population, nor to suggest that colored children be admitted into the schools with whites; but that the taxes which are paid by the colored tax-payers for school purposes be set apart for

106. *Baltimore Sun*, March 23, 1878, and March 12, 1884.

107. Strauder *v.* West Virginia, 100 U.S. 306 (1879), and *Baltimore Sun*, March 23, 1880. Negroes had served as jurors in federal courts in Maryland prior to this time; the decision concerned state courts.

108. *Baltimore Sun*, March 20, 1885. The decision, by the Supreme Bench of Baltimore, admitted Charles S. Wilson, a Negro, to the bar of Maryland. Decisions of the Supreme Bench were not officially reported until 1888, and newspaper accounts must be relied on for cases prior to that date.

the education of the colored children, and that educational facilities be extended to this class of our population, and such encouragement given as will show that we have due consideration for their welfare and prosperity.[109]

The legislature responded by having the state school taxes paid by the colored population set aside for the maintenance of Negro public schools.[110] One year later, however, even the Democrats had to admit that this system of financing Negro education would not work—after the state board of school commissioners reported that the state fund for Negro education in 1871 totaled $4,611.40, an amount they admitted was "practically worthless." [111]

The Republican party, which took up the cause of Negro education in 1871, accused the Democrats of "criminal neglect" in failing to provide an adequate educational system, and an adequate public education for all children became a major plank in the Republican platform.[112] The Democrats responded to this challenge in 1872 by passing a major amendment to the state's basic school law, requiring each county to establish a free public school for colored youth in each election district. The school terms were to be the same length for both races, provided the average daily attendance did not fall below fifteen pupils, but school attendance was not compulsory for either white or Negro children. The state pledged annual support for the Negro schools from the general school fund, and appropriated $50,000 for the colored and $525,000 for the white schools.[113] By 1873, it was reported, Negro schools were available in all Maryland counties, and in 1874 the state specified that Negro schools must offer instruction in the same branches of learning as the white schools.[114]

This basic mode of operation continued without substantial change throughout the period of Democratic dominance. Although state support for Negro schools increased somewhat between 1872

109. "Message of Governor Oden Bowie to the General Assembly of Maryland," *House and Senate Documents*, 1870, pp. 14–15.

110. *Laws of Maryland*, 1870, chap. 311, pp. 555–56.

111. "Report of the Board of State School Commissioners," *House and Senate Documents*, 1872, pp. 11–12. This figure excludes the Baltimore City school system, which had a fully organized system of Negro schools and appropriated $30,000 for their support during 1871.

112. *Baltimore Sun*, September 13, 1871.

113. *Laws of Maryland*, 1872, chap. 377, p. 629.

114. "Annual Report of the State Board of Education," *House Documents*, 1874, pp. 12–13; *Laws of Maryland*, 1874, chap. 463, p. 686.

and 1895 and appropriations for white schools declined, the per capita expenditure for Negro children never reached parity with that for whites. In 1874 the state appropriated $460,000 for its white schools, or $2.31 for each white child of school age; the Negro schools received $100,000, or $1.65 per school-age child. By 1890 the appropriation for white schools had declined to $400,000, or $1.69 per school-age child; state support for Negro schools ranged from $100,000 to $125,000 annually, depending on revenues—producing a median expenditure of $1.46 per child.[115]

The disparity in the support of white and Negro education under Democratic rule was increased by a wide variance in local support of the two systems. Some counties refused to grant any local support to their Negro schools, leaving them to subsist entirely on their state appropriation and private donations. In practice this meant that Negro schools had to cease operations when their meager resources were used up, in spite of the state law that specified equal terms for white and Negro schools; Democratic administrations did not try to compel counties to furnish local support for their Negro schools. As late as 1895 seven Maryland counties furnished no local tax support to their Negro schools, and only a few years earlier the list had totaled eleven—almost half of the state's counties.[116] To make matters even worse, all the noncontributing counties had large Negro populations.[117]

In education as in other areas, Negro needs were generally neglected or ignored during the era of Democratic dominance. The challenge of aiding this minority group to assume its rightful place in the political and social framework of the state was largely unmet, and the black community was left to cope as best it could with the immeasurable problems arising from centuries of socioeconomic deprivation.

115. *Laws of Maryland*, 1874, chap. 332, pp. 478 ff., and 1890, chap. 500, pp. 550 ff.

116. "Twenty-fifth Annual Report of the State Board of Education," *House and Senate Documents*, 1892, p. 23; "Twenty-ninth Annual Report of the State Board of Education," *House and Senate Documents*, 1896, p. xxiii.

117. "Twenty-ninth Annual Report of the State Board of Education," *House and Senate Documents*, 1896, p. xxiii. In 1895 the noncontributing counties were Anne Arundel, Charles, Prince George's, Queen Anne's, St. Mary's, Somerset, and Worcester; in 1891 these same counties, plus Calvert, Caroline, Montgomery, and Wicomico counties, were noncontributors.

CHAPTER 3

THE REPUBLICAN PARTY AND THE NEGRO, 1870–1895

Maryland Republicanism

Enfranchisement of the Negro heralded a new era for the Republican party of Maryland, changing a seemingly hopeless minority party into an organization with real power in two widely separated areas of the state—a party with reasonable expectations of achieving power on an even broader basis. The Negroes' first electoral participation, in 1870, had indicated that Republicans could count on a base of power in southern Maryland, and during the next twenty-five years Charles, Calvert, and St. Mary's counties, with their predominantly Negro populations, became Republican strongholds. The predominantly white counties of the mountain region, momentarily frightened away from their Republican allegiance by Negro enfranchisement, soon found their way back into the fold and constituted a second area of Republican strength. In these two sections Republicans elected local officials, state legislators, and congressmen who furnished the party the positions and power necessary to maintain a going political concern.

The eight counties that formed the backbone of Maryland Republicanism during the 1870–95 period and their degree of party regularity are shown in Figure 3; the bulk of Republican officials was elected from these counties.[1] On the local level this meant Republican county commissioners, sheriffs, county treasurers, surveyors, and registers of wills, and control of the host of appointive positions and service jobs in local government.[2] On the state level the party always maintained representation in the

1. See Table 6 for a breakdown of party regularity in the various kinds of state and federal elections during the period. Low scores in Table 6, an index of Democratic party regularity, indicate high Republican performance.
2. The number of elective officials varied from county to county, but county commissioners and sheriffs were elected in all counties.

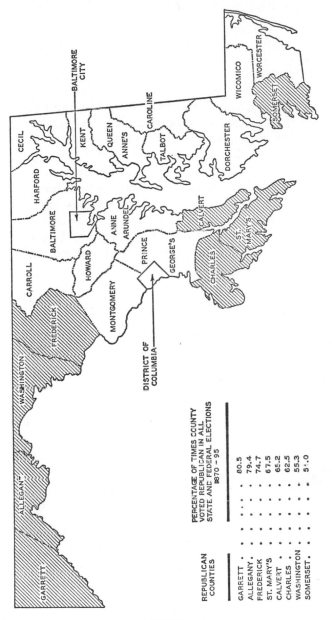

FIGURE 3

AREAS OF REPUBLICAN STRENGTH IN MARYLAND, 1870–1895

General Assembly, but the size of its delegation varied widely during the period. In the state senate, Republican representation ranged from a low of 8 percent of the membership in 1872 to a high of 46 percent in 1884. Representation in the senate at this time was based on a geographic formula: one senator from each county and three senators from Baltimore City; and senate terms were staggered so that only one-half of the membership came up for election at one time. In the House of Delegates, Republican representation fluctuated from a low of 6 percent in 1891 to a high of 35 percent in 1889. House representation was based on a crude population formula: the counties with least population were entitled to two delegates, and the number increased to six delegates, in a rough correlation with a county's population. Baltimore City was allowed eighteen delegates. In a typical year Republicans composed about one-fourth the membership of each house. The party composition of the Maryland General Assembly between 1872 and 1894 is shown in Table 8.

TABLE 8

PARTY COMPOSITION OF THE MARYLAND GENERAL ASSEMBLY,
1872–1894 *

| | House of Delegates | | | | Senate | | | |
Year	Dem.	Rep.	Others	Total	Dem.	Rep.	Others	Total
1872....	70	12	0	82	24	2	0	26
1874....	59	20	5	84	22	3	1	26
1876....	61	17	6	84	20	4	2	26
1878....	65	12	7	84	18	5	3	26
1880....	63	21	0	84	19	7	0	26
1882....	60	31	0	91	16	10	0	26
1884....	63	28	0	91	14	12	0	26
1886....	80	10	1	91	22	4	0	26
1888....	71	20	0	91	22	4	0	26
1890....	59	32	0	91	18	8	0	26
1892....	81	6	3	90	22	4	0	26
1894....	68	23	0	91	21	5	0	26

* The legislative session of 1870 is omitted because Maryland Negroes had not received the franchise prior to its election.

Maryland Republicans usually sent at least one representative to Congress during this period, usually from the mountain district of western Maryland. Occasionally they elected two congressmen, and at their peak in 1894 they managed to split the state's six-man delegation with the Democrats, sending three Republicans to Congress. The party composition of the Maryland congressional delegation from 1870 through 1894 is shown in Table 9.

Like most minority parties in a two-party system that is based on single-member district representation, the Republican party in Maryland was underrepresented in the councils of government in proportion to its strength in the electorate. Republicans' typical representation in the state legislature was only about 25 percent

TABLE 9

PARTY COMPOSITION OF THE MARYLAND CONGRESSIONAL DELEGATION, 1870–1894

Election Year	Democrats	Republicans	Total
1870	5	0	5
1872	4	2	6
1874	6	0	6
1876	6	0	6
1878	5	1	6
1880	5	1	6
1882	4	2	6
1884	5	1	6
1886	5	1	6
1888	4	2	6
1890	6	0	6
1892	6	0	6
1894	3	3	6

of that body's membership, but Republicans on the average won almost 45 percent of the vote in the state's gubernatorial contests. Although Republicans usually captured only one sixth of the state's congressional delegation, their average share of the vote cast in presidential elections in Maryland during this period was almost 47 percent.[3]

This disproportion between electoral strength and representation reflected the presence of large Republican minorities in almost every Democratic stronghold in the state. Republican acquisition of power was a sectional phenomenon, limited to western and southern Maryland, but Republicanism among the electorate was statewide. Negro enfranchisement freed the party

3. See Table 5 for the narrow margin of Democratic control of the state in gubernatorial and presidential elections.

from the confines of sectionalism and provided it a constituency of varying size but steady loyalty in virtually every county of Maryland. Even counties that time after time ended up in the Democrats' column contained Republican minorities sizable enough to compel vigorous campaigning and exact a degree of " responsibility " from the majority party. The strength of Republican minorities in traditionally Democratic counties is shown in Table 10, with the counties listed in order of their Democratic reliability

TABLE 10

REPUBLICAN STRENGTH IN TRADITIONALLY DEMOCRATIC COUNTIES,
1887 AND 1891

County	Democratic Reliability Rating *	Republican Percentage of Two-Party Vote †	
		1887	1891
Wicomico	100.0	34	37
Montgomery	98.1	44	44
Queen Anne's	98.0	36	41
Howard	97.6	45	41
Carroll	95.5	48	46
Harford	95.1	46	39
Worcester	94.0	37	33
Kent	93.0	48	45
Cecil	92.7	47	43
Baltimore	92.3	43	35
Anne Arundel	75.8	44	41
Dorchester	72.7	47	46
Prince George's	70.9	49	46
Talbot	68.0	49	46
Caroline	60.4	48	41

* Rating represents the percentage of times county voted Democratic in all gubernatorial, House of Delegates, presidential, and off-year congressional elections from 1870 to 1895 (also see Table 6).
† From election data in the Sun Almanac, 1888, p. 49, and 1892, p. 53.

for the 1870–95 period, followed by the Republican share of the two-party vote in the gubernatorial election of 1887, the closest state election of the period, and the gubernatorial election of 1891, the Republicans' worst defeat during the period. The presence of these " submerged " minorities meant that the Republican party was underrepresented in normal years, but it also meant that the party stood a fair chance of someday achieving statewide control. In every section of the state Republicans were reasonably competitive with their Democratic rivals; indeed, with the single exception of Wicomico, every county in Maryland voted Republican in some state or federal election between 1870 and 1895 (see Table 6).

The Republicans were weakest, both in organization and in electoral strength, in Baltimore City. Contemporary accounts portray the city's Republican organization as continually involved in factional disputes and chronically at odds with the state party leadership. Basic party organization was overhauled four times between 1870 and 1895 in efforts to work out a satisfactory method of handling the city organization's perpetual difficulties and restoring harmony between the state and city portions of the party.[4] Most of the difficulty seems to have stemmed from federal patronage disputes. Baltimore received valuable federal plums in the positions of postmaster, collector of the port, marshal, and district internal revenue collector, and competition for these remunerative offices, with control of the subordinate positions they entailed, was intense. The battle for these posts kept the city's Republicans at each other's throats, made continuity of party leadership impossible, and rendered the city organization a liability to the party rather than an asset.

In 1891 Theodore Roosevelt, then United States Civil Service Commissioner, came to Baltimore to investigate alleged civil service violations in the conduct of the city's Republican primaries. His investigation confirmed the existence of widespread violations, and his report to President Benjamin Harrison was an apt description of contemporary Baltimore Republican politics. Concerning the party primaries of the spring of 1891, Roosevelt reported:

As far as I could find out from the witnesses there seemed to be no question of principle at stake at all, but one of offices merely. This was recognized as much by one faction as by the other. . . . Several of the newspapers commented on and one or two of the witnesses complained bitterly of the alleged fact that most of the officeholding or officeseeking ward workers on both sides showed more activity and zeal in this contest, waged within the party, than they had ever shown

4. Party organization was revised in state conventions at Frederick in 1876 and at Baltimore in 1879, 1891, and 1893 (*Baltimore Sun*, September 13, 1879; April 10, 1891; and September 7, 1893).

in the contest for party supremacy at the polls, and my observation leads me to believe that such was the case. Seemingly, many of them regarded victory in the primaries as of more importance than victory at the polls because the former gave them control of the party machinery and would, therefore, in their own language, entitle them to " recognition " in the distribution of patronage. . . .

As a whole, the contest was marked by great fraud and no little violence. Many of the witnesses of each faction testified that the leaders of the opposition in their ward had voted repeaters, democrats and men living outside the ward in great numbers, and I am inclined to believe that in this respect there is much reason to regard the testimony of each side as correct in its outline of the conduct of the other. . . .

Most of the witnesses spoke of the cheating in a matter-of-fact way, as being too common and too universal in primaries generally to be worthy of notice, and a great many of them did not seem to bear any special malice against their opponents for having cheated them successfully—if anything, rather admiring them for their shrewdness—and frankly testifying that it was only lack of opportunity that had hindered them from doing as much themselves.[5]

The petty factionalism of the local Republican organization was one reason for the formation of a third party in Baltimore. The business and middle-class interests, from which the independents came, dissatisfied though they were with the Democratic party, were unwilling to associate themselves directly with the local Republican organization. Part of the independents' rebellion against the Democrats had come about because of disgust with machine politics, and certainly the Baltimore Republicans provided no agreeable alternative. Independents might nevertheless have been wooed into the party if a share in its leadership had been offered them or if their program of party reforms had been adopted. Local Republican potentates, however, were too busy fighting among themselves to entertain any notion of relinquishing power or its perquisites in an effort to build electoral strength. As a result, independents and Republicans had to settle for separate organizations, which made shifting electoral alliances and deals

5. Quoted in the *Baltimore Sun*, August 17, 1891.

with each other, but neither was able to build the strength necessary to wrest control from the common opponent.

Leadership of Maryland's Republican party during the 1870–95 era did not fit into the simple pattern that the Gorman-Rasin organization made possible for the Democratic party. Republican leadership was shifting and decentralized, more a matter of influence and prestige than of the naked power that characterized Democratic leadership. Although the Republican party had its "big" men, none attained the power or prestige of Gorman nor the durability of Rasin. The man who probably carried most weight in Republican councils for the greater part of the period was John A. J. Creswell. Born in 1828 into a prominent slaveholding family of Cecil County, Creswell had originally been a Whig, and with the coming of the Civil War was caught up in political activity in behalf of Union interests in the state. He rose rapidly in Unionist ranks, from the House of Delegates in 1861 to acting adjutant general in charge of Maryland's quota of Union troops in 1862, to Congress in 1863, and to the United States Senate in 1865.[6] In spite of his slaveholder origins, Creswell aligned himself with the radicals in the widening split within the Union party and became one of the founders of Maryland's Republican party, guiding it in the direction of universal manhood suffrage.[7] The high point of his political career was reached in 1869, when President Grant appointed him United States Postmaster General, a position he held for the next five years. Throughout the time he held office he was undisputed leader of the Maryland Republican party. After his resignation as Postmaster General in 1874, Creswell retired to his home in Elkton to practice law, and in the late 1870s he momentarily lost control of the party to his old ally, C. C. Fulton, editor of the *Baltimore American*. The rift involved patronage disputes and ill feeling brought about by Creswell's failure to support Fulton for the party's gubernatorial nomination in 1875. Within two years, however, Creswell was back in charge, and his influence again became paramount in party matters for the next ten years.[8] Until his death in 1891, Creswell's position as the grand old man of the party was quite secure.

Another Republican leader whose influence and prominence

6. B. F. Johnson, ed., *Men of Mark in Maryland*, 4 vols. (Baltimore, 1910), 3:398–412.

7. See pp. 10 and 15–16 above.

8. *Baltimore Sun*, September 21, 1877, and September 13, 1879.

spanned the period was James Albert Gary, one of the state's leading industrialists. Gary, born in Connecticut in 1833, was a child when his family moved to Maryland, where his father established a cotton manufacturing business and joined the Whig party. Control of the flourishing family enterprises passed in 1870 to young Gary, who added banking and insurance to the original cotton textile interests. Gary gravitated toward the Republican party, and in 1872 accepted its nomination for Congress. He soon became a leader within the party, usually working with the Creswell wing, and in 1879 he was nominated for governor on the Republican ticket. In 1883 he procured the party's gubernatorial nomination for his son-in-law, Hart B. Holton. Gary's political interests extended beyond state politics into the national arena; he played a prominent part in every national Republican convention from 1872 to 1896 and was an effective campaigner for Republican presidential nominees. In 1897 he was appointed United States Postmaster General by President McKinley, a position he held until 1898, when illness forced him to resign.[9] By the mid-1890s Gary had succeeded not only to Creswell's official position but also to his place of prominence in Maryland's Republican party.

Even with their prominence and longevity, however, Creswell and Gary did not monopolize power within the Republican party. Maryland's Republican leadership embraced such diverse and sometimes colorful figures as the Henry Stockbridges, father and son, both of whom were respected Baltimore lawyers and jurists; Lloyd Lowndes, an attorney-businessman from western Maryland and eventually the party's first successful gubernatorial candidate; George L. Wellington, a professional politician from western Maryland whose mastery of organization finally gave Republicans control of the state and himself a seat in the United States Senate; Sydney Mudd, white overlord of the party's predominantly Negro wing in southern Maryland; and Charles Jerome Bonaparte, the eccentric and aristocratic reformer who headed the progressive movement in Maryland. Beyond these men power extended in even wider circles. Devolution of power did not, however, extend so far as to include Negroes in the leadership ranks. Power within the Maryland Republican party remained a monopoly of the white man, even though Negroes composed more than 50 percent of the party's membership for most of the period.

9. Johnson, ed., *Men of Mark in Maryland*, 2:135–37.

The Negro in the Party

Although the addition of the Negro to its constituency gave Maryland's Republican party a new lease on life, the party never accorded the Negro more than a menial place within its organization. The Negro was expected to form the loyal rank and file, to vote often and always a straight ticket, to be content with token representation in party councils, to accept party programs handed down by white leaders, and never to doubt that the Republican party was his chief benefactor and only protector. In large measure he fulfilled these expectations. For while the Negro was grossly underrepresented and undervalued in proportion to his electoral strength, he was at least accorded a place and recognition of sorts in the Republican hierarchy, which was more than he was offered elsewhere.

Throughout the 1870–95 period, a small measure of Negro representation in Republican party councils was the rule rather than the exception—a token or symbolic offering to the Negro group. State conventions of several hundred delegates usually had about half a dozen Negro delegates.[10] Occasionally a Negro was included in Maryland's delegation to a Republican national convention but usually these prestigious positions were reserved for whites, and Negroes were sent only as alternates. In 1880 and 1888 Maryland's delegation to the Republican national convention included one Negro member; in 1892 two Negroes went as delegates. Negro alternates attended the conventions of 1884, 1888, and 1892. In 1884 a Negro was placed on the party's slate of presidential electors by the state convention, a move that was considered quite a concession by the party's white leaders and a signal honor by its Negro followers.[11]

Negro representation on the party's governing committees was always small and even more irregular in occurrence than it was in party conventions.[12] The state central committee was the governing body of the party in the intervals between state conventions. During the 1870s this committee was composed of

10. It is difficult to ascertain the exact number of Negro delegates to the various Republican state conventions because there was no consistent policy of reporting the race of delegates. Delegates usually were listed by name, and sometimes Negroes were indicated by a *c* or *col.* after their names.

11. *Baltimore Sun*, May 7, 1880; April 25, 1884; May 18, 1888; and May 5, 1892.

12. Again, it is difficult to ascertain the number of Negro members because of inconsistent reporting of race.

one member from each county and one from Baltimore City; in 1880 its membership was enlarged to give each county and Baltimore the same number of members as their representatives in the General Assembly.[13] This enlargement, however, made the central committee so unwieldy that power was delegated to an executive committee of twenty-seven, composed of one member from each county and four from Baltimore City. Thus from 1870 to 1880 practical power resided in the central committee, and from 1880 to 1895 in the executive committee. During the 1870s at least two or three Negroes served on the central committee, and in 1879 three are known to have served. With enlargement of the central committee in 1880 Negro representation, instead of increasing or at least holding its own, actually decreased; where three Negroes had served the year before in a committee of twenty-four, only one Negro served in the new 110-member body.[14] This worsening state of affairs seems to have persisted throughout the 1880s. Negroes may have been excluded from membership in the central committee at various intervals during this decade, and it is almost certain that they were entirely excluded from membership on the powerful executive committee. Not until 1893 does the designation " colored " again appear in the lists of Republican central or executive committee members.[15]

Negroes also were slighted in the distribution of party patronage. Denied real influence in party councils, they had little to say about the jobs at the party's disposal, and very few positions went to Negroes. At a protest meeting in 1880, Dr. H. J. Brown, a frequent spokesman for Negro unrest and an organizer of the Colored Equal Rights League, reported that the only place the Negro got a fair share of recognition in federal patronage in Maryland was the United States Marshal's office, where three of the seven employes were Negro. A few Negroes had minor positions in the customs house and the post office, but not one was employed in the internal revenue or subtreasury offices. In the counties, Brown said, many of which were Republican solely because of the Negro vote, there was not a colored postmaster, federal clerk, lighthouse keeper, or the like in any position of federal authority. Brown concluded that the condition of the

13. *Sun Almanac*, 1879, p. 47, and 1880, p. 44.
14. *Baltimore Sun*, September 8, 1875; November 13, 1879; and January 15, 1880.
15. *Sun Almanac*, 1882–92, and 1893, p. 47.

Negro vis-à-vis federal employment was worse in Maryland than in any Southern state.[16] At a colored Republican convention in 1881, discrimination in federal employment was further detailed. Delegates charged that Maryland Republicans had 1,311 federal positions at their disposal and that exactly twenty-four of them had gone to Negroes. Most of these twenty-four Negroes were employed in janitorial positions, and none of them held a job that paid as much as $1,500 a year.[17]

Republican timidity in backing Negro candidates for office was another evidence of the Negro's lowly position in the Maryland party. Elsewhere in the South at this time Negro Republicans were running for and securing offices as high as the United States Congress, as well as positions of genuine state importance. In Maryland from 1870 to 1895, only one Negro candidate received Republican party backing, and this was for a purely local office. In 1890 Harry Scythe Cummings ran for the Baltimore city council with Republican endorsement. Cummings was successful and became the first elected Negro officeholder in Maryland.[18]

If Republican leadership was slow to share the rewards of office with Negroes, it was more generous with promises. Party platform pledges provide an inexpensive and sometimes effective method of courting support, particularly if the opposition party refuses to make such appeals. Platform planks also provide clues to a minority group's position within a party and the level of aspiration the parent organization is willing to support. In this regard, then, Maryland Negroes clearly were offered more by the Republican party than by the Democrats. Republican platforms usually contained a plank, aimed at black constituents, either promising to remedy a Negro grievance or pledging support for a threatened right. Such pledges, though numerous, were narrow in scope and aspiration.

16. *Baltimore Sun*, January 15, 1880. A circular issued by Brown's protest group (which became the Colored Equal Rights League) later gave a more detailed breakdown of Negro federal employes in Maryland, showing seventeen Negroes among the 200 employes in the customs house and three Negroes among the 160 employes of the post office. The Colored Equal Rights League was formally organized in Baltimore on February 10, 1880, and the Reverend John Handy was elected its president. The league determined to work not only for a fairer share of patronage for Negroes but also for colored teachers in the colored schools, admission of Negroes to the state bar, and selection of Negroes on juries in the state courts (*Baltimore Sun*, January 30 and February 11, 1880).

17. *Baltimore Sun*, March 25, 1881.

18. *Ibid.*, November 5, 1890.

Most Republican platform promises addressed themselves to the problem of securing better Negro education in Maryland. Pledges of improved educational facilities for Negroes appear in the Republican platforms of 1871, 1877, 1879, 1881, 1883, 1887, and 1889, but they varied greatly in strength of language and commitment.[19] Weak planks in 1877 and 1879 merely called for " increased educational facilities for the masses " and " improvement " in the state's educational system for Negroes.[20] In 1871, however, Republicans accused Democrats of " criminal neglect " in failing to provide public education for Negro children, and in 1887, after declaring that Negroes were " entitled to the same provision for the education of their children as is enjoyed by the children of whites," they pronounced Democratic discriminations against the colored schools " a disgrace to the State." [21]

Negroes occasionally received Republican support in other areas. In 1881 a weak civil rights plank was adopted, and in the late 1880s increasing concern was shown for the Negro's right to vote and for the mounting attack on this right in the Southern states.[22] In the platforms of 1888 and 1889 Maryland Republicans took an unequivocal stand in favor of " unqualified franchise and equality of all men before the law," and denounced the Democratic party for " its systematic and persistent attempts to deprive the colored citizens of the right of franchise." [23] Beyond this, however, Maryland Republicans did not go: no other important policy statements pertain to the Negro during the period.

Even in the pattern of political rhetoric and promises there were significant lapses, times when the party conspicuously avoided platform appeals to Negro voters. In the elections of 1873 and 1875, when Republicans concentrated on cooperating with white independents, Republican platforms were totally devoid of appeals to the Negro.[24] Some Negro leaders professed to see the same sort of situation developing in 1887 and claimed that white Republicans were eager to sacrifice their Negro allies in exchange for a union with renegade Democrats. The Maryland Progressive

---

19. *Ibid.*, September 13, 1871; September 21, 1877; September 13, 1879; October 6, 1881; September 26, 1883; August 25, 1887; and October 2, 1889.
20. *Ibid.*, September 21, 1877, and September 13, 1879.
21. *Ibid.*, September 13, 1871, and August 25, 1887.
22. *Ibid.*, October 6, 1881.
23. *Ibid.*, May 8, 1888, and October 2, 1889.
24. *Ibid.*, September 13, 1873, and September 23, 1875.

Assembly, a Negro protest group, took a paid advertisement in the *Baltimore Sun* to press the charge.

> Our eyes have been opened, and what we now behold is that our white Republican leaders have and do now propose to consider us as so many thousand machines, to be operated to their own advantage at their will. At the last Republican State convention, held in this city, the interests of the colored members of the party were entirely ignored, in order that the white Republicans might gain the favor and association of a few Democrats, who call themselves " reformers and independents." Read the platform then adopted, and you will at a glance be convinced that our interests were not thought of.[25]

This charge was not entirely accurate inasmuch as the 1887 platform contained one of the strongest Negro education planks the Republican party ever adopted, but the Negro group was correct in recognizing the threat posed to their position by the Republican party's courtship of the independents.

Negroes, acutely aware of their subordinate position in Maryland's Republican party, protested frequently about their treatment. As early as 1872 and 1873 efforts were made to form an independent organization, under Negro leadership, in order to pressure Republican leaders into granting Negroes more recognition and control in party affairs.[26] Such efforts were sporadic and largely unavailing. There was not much continuity in the organizations spawned by these attempts or the personnel behind them; even the names of the dissident Negro groups changed with great frequency. The Colored State conventions of the 1870s were succeeded in the 1880s by the Colored Advisory Committee, the Colored Equal Rights League, the United Brotherhood of Liberty, and finally by the Maryland Progressive Assembly.[27] The Colored Equal Rights League and the United Brotherhood of

25. *Ibid.*, October 20, 1887.
26. *Ibid.*, June 20 and July 18, 1872, and August 29, 1873.
27. The Colored Advisory Committee was active as a protest group in 1879 and 1883, the Colored Equal Rights League in 1880, the United Brotherhood of Liberty in 1885 and 1886, and the Maryland Progressive Assembly in 1887 (*Baltimore Sun*, October 11 and November 13, 1879; February 11 and March 12, 1880; August 16, 29, 1883; and October 14, 20, 1887). For the United Brotherhood of Liberty, also see A. Briscoe Koger, *Dr. Harvey Johnson, Minister and Pioneer Civic Leader* (Baltimore, 1957), pp. 11–12, and August Meier, *Negro Thought in America, 1800–1915* (Ann Arbor, 1963), p. 70.

Liberty displayed some continuity in the leadership of the Reverend Harvey Johnson, pastor of the Baltimore Union Baptist Church and a co-organizer of both groups, and achieved a measure of success in their endeavors. Although ineffective on the political front, each group scored a significant legal gain for Maryland Negroes: the Equal Rights League was instrumental in getting Negroes on juries in the state courts in 1880, and the Brotherhood of Liberty was active in the successful effort to have Negroes admitted to the state bar in 1885.[28]

Most of these protesting groups originated in Baltimore, where a sizable Negro middle class resided, and usually they attempted to extend the movement to the Negro communities in the rest of the state. The groups, however, were short-lived and seem to have had little impact on the Republican establishment. Perhaps their real importance lies in the opportunity they provided for articulation of the bitterness and disillusionment a large number of knowledgeable Negroes felt toward the Republican party. Few could deny the charge of a protest spokesman that his fellow Negroes had allowed themselves to be used " as the pack mules, sumpters, and dromedaries of the Republican party, without advancing their interest in the state, or any practical acknowledgement of their efforts beyond electing or keeping white Republicans in office." [29] Few can fail to sympathize with the Negro leaders who were refused an audience with Republican gubernatorial candidate Walter Brooks in 1887. Brooks had pleaded prior commitments, but the Negroes reported:

> We have since learned Mr. Brooks' engagements were to attend the horse races then in progress at Pimlico, and we naturally conclude that he has more interest in the success of a horse race than in the elevation of the negro race in Maryland. We have not been permitted to interview him, and would not now if we could.[30]

An expression of disillusionment usually was the extent of the Negro response in such matters. Their own organizations were politically ineffective and they had no real alternatives; the Democratic party did not desire their support, and it offered them

28. See pp. 61 and 63 above.
29. *Baltimore Sun*, November 13, 1879.
30. *Ibid.*, October 20, 1887.

nothing. Nonparticipation or withdrawal from political activity, a possible course, found little favor among Negroes. The newly enfranchised Negro was proud of his hard-won right to vote, anxious to assert himself through it, and aware of its tentative nature. He accepted his inferior position in the Maryland Republican party partly from emotional loyalty to the party of emancipation and partly from lack of any place else to go. He continued to provide the major part of Republican electoral support, and in the long run this enforced policy paid off. His steady support through the years produced a party that was strong enough, and dependent enough upon him, that it could serve as his champion when the critical issue of his basic right to participate politically was questioned.

CHAPTER 4

REPUBLICANS IN POWER, 1896–1900

The reality of Maryland's two-party system was vividly demonstrated in the mid-1890s when the long-dominant Democratic party, harassed by internal strife and increasingly unable to govern effectively, was turned out of power in the state election of 1895. For the first time since its inception responsibility for the government of Maryland fell to the Republican party; and the shift in power was complete. In the 1895 election Republicans won the three top state posts—governor, attorney general, and comptroller—and an overwhelming majority in the lower house of the General Assembly. The following year Maryland went Republican in the presidential election and sent a solidly Republican delegation to Congress. In 1897 the party completed its electoral coup by winning control of the upper house of the General Assembly. For the first time, Republicans spoke for Maryland in national, state, and local councils. Their reign was short, but their ascension to power and their orderly discharge of its responsibilities had far-reaching effects on the future policy and political structure of the state.

The Election of 1895

A complex intermixture of state and national politics, rooted in and intensified by the serious economic problems of the era, brought about the downfall of Maryland's Democratic party in 1895. The Democratic organization had found itself totally unable to handle the problem of property reassessment and adjustment of the disparity between taxation of real property and investment capital.[1] Policy that was acceptable to one wing of the party was repeatedly sabotaged by another. The agrarian wing of the party became increasingly disgruntled, convinced that it was bearing an inordinate share of the burden of state and local

1. See pp. 47–51 above.

taxation and yet unable to do anything about it. On the other hand, the business wing of the party, subjected to regular assaults on the existing tax structure, was kept in a continual state of alarm and found the resulting uncertainty inimical to its interests. The seriousness of the situation was intensified by the depression of 1893, which fell heavily on all segments of the economy. National politics played an important part in the defeat of the Maryland Democratic party primarily because of the prominent dual position held by United States Senator Arthur Gorman in state and national Democratic councils.

Gorman, boss of Maryland's Democratic organization, also was in a position of national power as head of the Democratic caucus in the United States Senate, and thus was responsible for maintaining party harmony and a working majority in the Senate. It was in this role, or in his interpretation of it, that he ran afoul of the policy aims of the Cleveland administration and alienated important factions in his home-state organization. In 1893 the two top-priority items of the newly elected Cleveland administration were repeal of the Sherman Silver Purchase Act and substantial reduction of the McKinley Tariff. Faced with a Senate narrowly controlled by Democrats, who were themselves divided on both of these issues, Gorman assumed the role of compromiser and tried to reach accord within the party by diluting the administration's policy. For his efforts to compromise on repeal of the Silver Purchase Act, Gorman won the lasting enmity of President Cleveland and the sound-money faction in Maryland, which supported the President. His part in the tariff controversy was equally unrewarding. The Wilson-Gorman Tariff, which replaced the McKinley Tariff, earned Gorman the charge of " party perfidy " from the President and the hostility of the tariff-reform forces of the Democratic party who felt that the law fell lamentably short of redeeming their party's pledge for tariff reduction.[2]

Thus in the Maryland campaign of 1895 Gorman's national prestige was at low ebb, and because the Gorman-Rasin organization and the state Democratic party had become virtually synonymous over the years, the enmity felt toward the former was vented upon the latter. Gorman, whose Senate term ran until 1897, was not a candidate in 1895, but " Gormanism " became the main issue of the campaign and his enemies resolved

2. John R. Lambert, *Arthur Pue Gorman* (Baton Rouge, 1953), pp. 183–238.

that he must be defeated even at the cost of turning the state over to the Republicans. The *Baltimore Sun*, a strong supporter of Cleveland's administration, led the revolt against Gorman and its own party and marked out the lines along which the swelling ranks of independents would wage the campaign. " GORMANISM WINS; THE DICTATOR'S WISHES CARRIED OUT BY THE CONVENTION " was the *Baltimore Sun*'s headline after dark horse John E. Hurst, a backroom selection of Gorman and Rasin, received the Democratic gubernatorial nomination over a host of more prominent candidates.[3] " Bossism " became the battlecry and the sole issue raised by the independents, who rationalized their desertion of the party with the argument that " the bosses must be destroyed in order that the party may live." [4] Because the state's leading newspaper was in the camp of the opposition, regular Democrats had difficulty getting their messages to the people. Senator Gorman, who waged one of the most active campaigns of his career, conceded that the onslaughts of the *Sun* seriously hurt his party. The Democrats were thrown on the defensive by repeated charges of " bossism," " Gormanism," and " ring rule," and even some of their adherents began to echo these accusations.[5]

With Democratic in-fighting so intense, Republicans had only to nominate an unobjectionable candidate, close ranks behind him, and stay clear of trouble until election day to have a reasonably good chance of winning their long-awaited victory. This they did, after a brief flurry of intraparty competition for what promised to be a highly rewarding nomination. The Republican favorite was Lloyd Lowndes, a prominent attorney and businessman from Cumberland, whose only political experience was one term in Congress, from 1872 to 1874. Lowndes, however, was challenged for the Republican nomination by William T. Malster, who represented the Baltimore wing of the party in alliance with the predominantly Negro southern Maryland machine of Congressman Sydney Mudd.[6] The *Baltimore Afro-American*, Maryland's oldest continuously published Negro newspaper, which endorsed Malster even before the convention, noted that Negro delegates at the convention generally supported Malster.[7] Negroes objected to

3. *Baltimore Sun*, August 1, 1895.
4. *Ibid.*, Editorial of August 20, 1895.
5. Lambert, *Arthur Pue Gorman*, p. 249.
6. *Baltimore Sun*, August 16, 1895.
7. August 3, 17, 1895.

Lowndes because of his opposition to the Civil Rights Act of 1875, a position, incidentally, which did him no harm in Independent Democratic circles.[8] But the division within the Republican ranks was not deep, and as the Malster-Mudd faction came to see that Lowndes would carry the day, they closed ranks behind him and made his nomination unanimous.[9] Lowndes' convention manager, Congressman George L. Wellington, who was made chairman of the Republican state central committee, proved to be an able political organizer in the ensuing state campaign. The Lowndes-Wellington organization conducted a vigorous but dignified campaign, and, following the lead of the Republican platform, confined its campaign efforts to a few carefully selected state issues.

The Republican platform of 1895 promised Marylanders a property reassessment that would include real and personal property, but the promise was general and no attempt was made to specify the form that reassessment would take. Republicans also promised revision of the election laws to require periodic reregistration of voters, provision of free textbooks to public school students by the state, a constitutional amendment setting a limit on municipal indebtedness, and a local-option merit system for selection of municipal and county employes. There was no plank in the Republican platform appealing to the party's Negro constituents, and the campaign that followed did nothing to remedy this omission. All in all it was a bland, uncontroversial program.[10]

The Democratic platform, in contrast, reflected the chaos within the party. Even more general in terminology than the Republican document and promising much less, the Democrats' program was riddled with internal contradictions that even deliberate vagueness could not mask. Beginning with an endorsement of the Cleveland administration, Maryland Democrats went on to laud passage of the Wilson-Gorman Tariff, which Cleveland himself had disavowed. On the state level, Democrats reaffirmed their party's pledge for reassessment and, in the next breath, heartily endorsed the administration of outgoing Governor Frank Brown, who had vetoed a hard-fought Democratic reassessment bill only three years earlier. The only unequivocal stand in the Democratic platform was in favor of "sound money."[11] Clearly, the Demo-

8. *Baltimore Sun*, August 4, 1895.
9. *Ibid.*, August 16, 1895.
10. *Ibid.*
11. *Ibid.*, August 1, 1895.

crats did not have a program that could inspire enthusiasm or even confidence in their followers, and during the campaign the platform was largely ignored by party spokesmen. Instead, Democratic campaigners launched a two-prong attack on their opponents, appealing to race and class hatreds.

Racism was the major weapon in the Democratic arsenal. Democrats asserted that if the Republicans were victorious Marylanders could expect passage of a state civil rights law giving Negroes full access to inns, restaurants, theaters, barber shops, and public conveyances. It was further asserted that the Republican nominee, Lowndes, had promised an equal division of offices among the races and that Negro policemen, firemen, judges, and clerks of elections would displace whites if Lowndes were elected. Racially mixed public schools were said to be inevitable under Republican rule. The Democrats' final campaign rally in Baltimore featured a huge night-time parade in which torch-lit transparencies decried mixed schools, a float depicted a mixed school presided over by a colored school teacher who flogged white children, and at the end of the parade a small boy carried a banner that asked: "Papa, would you vote to put a negro alongside your little boy in school?" [12]

The class issue, when it was raised, was presented in equally vivid terms. The *Port Tobacco Times and Charles County Advertiser*, a small weekly newspaper in economically depressed southern Maryland, emerged as one of the strongest supporters of Gorman and the regular Democratic organization in the 1895 campaign. Although it spoke from a county predominantly Negro in population, the paper barely mentioned the race issue, concentrating its fire on the alliance between Republicans and "the silk-stocking gentry of Baltimore, known as the Cleveland Democracy." [13] The paper described the Republican nominee for governor as

a full-fledged representative of the McKinley protective tariff class which has burdened this country with an iniquitous measure greatly to its detriment. He is a wealthy corporation attorney and president of a number of the richest corporations in the State. In addition to this, he is a director in monopolistic concerns, and consequently a tax-dodger. . . .

12. *Ibid.*, October 28, 29, and November 3, 1895.
13. November 8, 1895.

Aside from Mr. Lowndes' well-established record against reassessment, he could not with any kind of good faith favor an honest reassessment after the alliances that he has deliberately made in this campaign. That is what the Baltimore tax-dodgers know and that is the reason they will desert their party to support him.[14]

Reliance on race and class prejudices was the last resort for a party reeling under the charges of bossism and without a substantial issue of its own. The *Chestertown Transcript*, an Eastern Shore weekly, revealed the low state of Democratic morale in its very pleas for continued support of the party.

Conceding that corruptions exist and that party managers have shown themselves unworthy of the high trust placed in them; accepting all these things as true, what is to be gained by turning the entire organization over to the enemy and letting all go down in general wreckage? . . . Would ring rule be less galling under a Republican than under a Democratic administration? [15]

This kind of lukewarm support boded ill for Democrats' chances at the polls, and when the votes were in, it was clear that their defeat was no accident but a thorough repudiation of the party by the people.

Republican Lowndes not only beat Democrat Hurst by more than 18,000 votes but carried virtually every area of the state. The totals were: [16]

Lloyd Lowndes (Republican)   124,936
John E. Hurst (Democrat)   106,169
Joshua Levering (Prohibition party)   7,719
Henry F. Andrews (" People's " and
  Socialist-Labor parties)   1,381

Sectionalism played no part in the outcome, as Baltimore and nineteen of the state's twenty-three counties went Republican.[17]

14. Editorials of September 6 and October 18, 1895.
15. Editorial of October 31, 1895.
16. *Maryland Manual*, 1896, p. 198. Andrews headed two tickets in the election; he received 989 votes as the " People's party " candidate and 392 votes as the Socialist-Labor candidate.
17. Only Montgomery, Queen Anne's, Wicomico, and Worcester counties gave a majority to Democrat Hurst.

Lowndes ran stronger in Baltimore than in the rest of the state, but his margin in the rural areas left no doubt that he was preferred throughout the state.[18] Nor was this merely a personal victory for Lowndes; Republican success extended down the ticket. Seventy Republicans and twenty-one Democrats were elected to the House of Delegates, and nine Republicans and six Democrats to the state senate.[19] Control of the senate remained with the Democrats because of their large number of hold-over senators, but the party division was close: a total of fourteen Democrats and twelve Republicans.

The most unusual aspect of the 1895 election—aside from the Republican victory itself—was the high rate of voter participation. Voter registration figures for the years immediately preceding and following the election suggest that the 1895 campaign mobilized almost every registered voter in the state: [20]

	Maryland	*Baltimore*
Registered voters in October, 1894..	252,194	97,340
Vote cast in 1895 election.........	240,205	100,978
Registered voters in October, 1896..	265,417	112,424

Participation was high not only relative to the number of registered voters but also in terms of the number of citizens who were eligible to vote.[21] In Baltimore City and the state as a whole, new highs for voter turn-out in gubernatorial elections were established: 84.8 percent and 85.4 percent respectively. Republican success owed a good deal to this increased voter participation. The Democratic vote total in 1895 was down only several thousand from that in recent successful campaigns, but the Republican vote was up by several tens of thousands.[22] It was activation of usually

---

18. *Maryland Manual*, 1896, p. 198. The city-county vote breakdown for Lowndes and Hurst was:

	Baltimore	*Counties*
Lowndes (R)..............	54,920	70,016
Hurst (D)................	43,320	62,849
Republican margin..........	11,600	7,167

19. *Maryland Manual*, 1896, p. 7.
20. *Sun Almanac*, 1895, p. 57, and 1897, p. 65.
21. See Appendix B.
22. The most recent comparable elections were the 1891 gubernatorial and the 1892 presidential elections (*Sun Almanac*, 1892, p. 53, and 1893, p. 68):

1891	Democrats:	108,539	Republicans:	78,388
1892	Democrats:	113,866	Republicans:	92,736
1895	Democrats:	106,169	Republicans:	124,936

nonparticipant voters that made the difference and gave Republicans their victory.

The coincidence of a Republican victory and an unusually high level of voter participation in a normally Democratic state is a curious phenomenon, but understandable in the circumstances of the times. High voter participation was a feature of this whole troubled decade in Maryland, not merely of the 1895 campaign.[23] The severity of the economic and social dislocations of the 1890s contributed to political interest, and discontent normally worked against the party in power. Moreover, a viable second party was waiting in the wings, and thus, unlike the situation in other states, it was not necessary to take over the ruling party or secede from it and form a new party in order to give substance to protest. The electorate could easily shift from the dominant party to the consistently close-running second party. Maryland's Republican party had demonstrated its vitality in twenty-five years of close and persistent challenge to Democratic rule. It possessed respectable national ties and a record of responsibility in governing its pockets of strength in the state. Finally, it lacked a heritage that the Republican party in the South had to live with—the heritage of hate handed down from Reconstruction days. All these factors combined to make the Republican party an acceptable vehicle for protest and change in Maryland in 1895.

The protest embodied in the Maryland conflict, however, was quite different from that which animated the national political scene during the same era. Populism, then reaching its zenith as a national political force, played little part in the political changeover in Maryland and as a separate party movement found practically no support in the state. In 1892 and 1894 Populist congressional candidates had run in several Maryland districts—with a singular lack of success, usually winning even less support than the perennial Prohibitionist candidates.[24] In 1895 the Popu-

23. Comparison by decade shows the following average voter turn-out in all presidential, gubernatorial, and congressional elections held within the time period (see Appendix B for more detailed information):

	Maryland	Baltimore	Number of Elections
1870s	75.0%	70.2%	10
1880s	77.5	70.9	10
1890s	79.5	78.2	10
1900–12	66.1	65.5	14

24. In 1892 Populist congressional candidates were offered in the Second, Fourth, and Fifth districts and received 103, 138, and 790 votes respectively (*Sun*

list gubernatorial candidate met the same fate: Henry Andrews, endorsed for governor by both the " People's " and the Socialist-Labor parties of Maryland, ran a very poor fourth, behind the Republican, the Democratic, and the Prohibitionist candidates.[25] Whatever Populist sentiment existed in Maryland probably was entrenched within the Democratic party, and there is no reason to think that the Republican victory in Maryland in 1895 owed anything to Populist support. Instead, the upset seems to have been a product of economic conservatism joined with political progressivism; both were expressions of the Baltimore commercial class, who spurned the economic reforms of the time but were vigorous proponents of political change. The election's essentially conservative nature was reaffirmed in 1896 when Maryland voters overwhelmingly rejected William Jennings Bryan, the first Democratic presidential candidate to fail in the state since the Civil War.

The alliances that were formed in the 1895 election remained in effect for the presidential campaign. The Baltimore independents, led by the *Baltimore Sun* and John K. Cowen of the Baltimore and Ohio Railroad, formed the Honest Money League to do battle for Republican William McKinley, while Gorman and Rasin carried the banner for Bryan.[26] The vote configurations of the two elections, which are remarkably similar, also lend credence to an interpretation of both elections as essentially a conservative manifestation. Lowndes and McKinley carried identical areas; McKinley ran somewhat better than Lowndes throughout the state but this was due largely to a higher turn-out, not to further inroads on the Democratic vote. The hard core of Democratic strength was steadfast in both elections.[27]

Almanac, 1893, p. 69). In 1894 Populist congressional candidates were offered in the First, Fifth, and Sixth districts and received 394, 355, and 307 votes; in each instance they ran behind Prohibitionist candidates in the same districts (*Sun Almanac*, 1895, pp. 63–64).

25. Andrews' total vote was 1,381 and the Prohibitionist candidate's total was 7,719 (*Sun Almanac*, 1896, p. 64).

26. Lambert, *Arthur Pue Gorman*, pp. 252–56.

27. The similarity of vote configurations for the two elections is most dramatically shown in the county-by-county returns (see the *Sun Almanac*, 1896, p. 64, and 1897, p. 104) but is also apparent in the following summary:

	1895 Election		1896 Election	
	Rep.	Dem.	Rep.	Dem.
Baltimore	54,920	43,320	61,965	40,859
Rest of state	70,016	62,849	75,013	63,887
Total	124,936	106,169	136,978	104,746

The Republicans' mandate in Maryland, then, was a mandate for change only in a very superficial sense. The voters expected a change in parties, personnel, and some of the political ground rules, but they neither looked for nor desired fundamental alterations in economic or social arrangements. Still, it is a measure of the interdependence of things political, social, and economic that what had been viewed as mere surface political change soon began to show signs of deeper ramifications. A political fact of life, ignored during the 1895 campaign by Democratic bolter and Republican alike, was that Maryland Negroes constituted an important and legitimate interest group within the Republican party. This fact soon became an issue that had to be dealt with.

Republican Rule and the Negro

The Republican administration of Governor Lloyd Lowndes gave Marylanders approximately what it had promised. To white Marylanders it had promised limited reform in a number of policy areas, which it delivered. To Negro Marylanders it had carefully promised nothing; this promise, too, was largely fulfilled.

Reassessment was the first and most important policy undertaking of the new Republican administration in 1896; in his inaugural address Governor Lowndes asked the General Assembly to make a new assessment of property, both real and personal, its first order of business. The legislature responded by passing Maryland's first reassessment act in twenty years—a moderate measure, probably the only kind that could have been enacted in view of the long history of discord in this matter.[28] The state tax base was boosted by slightly more than $67,000,000 but, with no change in the tax rate, increased the state's revenue for the following year by only $120,000.[29] The 1896 law did plug one of the loopholes by which investment capital had escaped taxation by levying a tax on mortgages held on property within the state. This category of property had been specifically exempted in earlier laws, a policy which had drawn increasing criticism over the years. The rate imposed by the new law was moderate, 8 percent on the gross annual mortgage interest, but the reform was established.[30]

28. *Senate Journal*, 1896, p. 72.
29. "Message of Lloyd Lowndes, Governor of Maryland, to the General Assembly at Its Regular Session, January, 1898," *House and Senate Documents*, 1898, p. 6.
30. *Laws of Maryland*, 1896, chap. 120, pp. 151 ff.

The election law of 1896 was the reform that Republicans took most pride in, and although it fell short of expectations, it was a high point in election regulation in Maryland. The law provided a stringent tightening of secret ballot procedures, so that, after its passage, voting secrecy was not merely permitted but required. Voting booths, closed and curtained, replaced the open voting shelves of earlier practice; and the privacy of the booth was enforced by forbidding entry to everyone except the individual voter, unless aid from an authorized election official was needed. Ballots had to be folded to hide their markings before they could be deposited in the prescribed plate-glass ballot boxes. Provisions for uniform ballots, printed and distributed by the state, and for easy straight-ticket voting were retained. In addition, a workable and self-enforcing provision to ensure bipartisan selection of the supervisors, judges, and clerks of election was included in the law—a goal long desired by Republicans and reform-minded Democrats.[31] Efforts to strengthen the law by the addition of a corrupt practices act and a mandatory primary law failed, but Republicans were justly proud of having produced the fairest election law Maryland had seen for quite a while.

Republicans also scored a significant advance in public education. In 1896 the legislature passed a free textbook program for the indigent pupils of all grades in the public schools and it initiated a general program of free textbooks, beginning in the primary grades, for all pupils regardless of need. An initial $150,000 was appropriated to inaugurate the program.[32] The Republican administration tried to encourage industrial education in the public schools with its offer to underwrite the salaries of manual training instructors in localities that were willing to furnish the facilities for this training, and the offer applied equally to white and to colored schools.[33] In the first two years of Republican rule the basic state appropriation for public education remained the same as that appropriated by the preceding administration—$400,000 annually for white schools and $125,000 for colored schools.[34] In 1899 and in 1900, however, these amounts were increased by $25,000 for each system, and Republicans, when they left office, were correct in claiming that they had

31. *Ibid.*, chap. 202, pp. 327–31.
32. *Ibid.*, chap. 135, pp. 215–17.
33. *Ibid.*, 1898, chap. 273, pp. 814 ff.
34. *Ibid.*, 1896, chap. 369, pp. 664 ff., and chap. 347, pp. 634 ff.

made greater appropriations for public education than any previous administration.[35]

Negro Marylanders, although they shared in the general reforms and policy advances enacted by the Republican administration, received little in the way of special legislation or policy to equalize their position with that of the white community. Negroes probably fared best in education; the free textbook program was of more benefit to them than to the average white—a result attributable less to Republican generosity than to the Negro's low economic status. The increases in state support for white and Negro schools, while equal in amount, were proportionately greater for the Negro schools. The most important gain for Negro Marylanders was a new legal provision, an inconspicuous part of the state education appropriation acts for 1899 and 1900, that compelled the counties to maintain equal-length school terms for Negroes and whites or forfeit all state school support.[36] This was a genuine effort to force counties that made little or no contribution to Negro schools to provide local support. Some counties channeled all their local school revenue to white education, remitting only the inadequate state funds to Negro schools and closing them down when this aid was exhausted.

In Baltimore, Negroes made slight progress under Republican rule toward their long-standing goal of putting additional Negro teachers in the city's Negro schools. In the counties, whites taught in white schools and Negroes taught in Negro schools, under sharply differing salary scales. Baltimore had only one salary scale, but whites had a near monopoly on positions in its Negro schools; of the approximately 235 positions in Baltimore's Negro schools, white teachers held slightly more than 200.[37] There was no mixing of faculties in the city's Negro schools; they were either all-white or all-Negro. Negro leaders had long deplored the city's policy of permitting white teachers to staff Negro schools, which denied members of their race the opportunity to fill these relatively lucrative jobs. Lashing out at the city's " mixed schools " system, they demanded that the new administration help Negroes achieve their goal of truly separate schools.[38]

Governor Lowndes, in one of his rare public pledges to his

35. *Ibid.*, 1898, chap. 406, pp. 1011 ff., and chap. 409, pp. 1018 ff.
36. *Ibid.*, chap. 406, p. 1011, and chap. 409, p. 1019.
37. *Baltimore Sun*, March 24, 1896.
38. *Baltimore Afro-American*, Editorial of October 19, 1895.

Negro constituency, responded by promising to foster " the present system of separate free schools for their [Negro] children with teachers of their own race, if they so desire them." [39] For Baltimore Republicans, however, this went too far. When a Negro city councilman, Marcus Cargill, introduced an ordinance directing that all future vacancies in Negro schools be filled by Negro teachers, he was sabotaged by his own party. Cargill's ordinance was amended by the Republican-controlled council in such a way that its author was compelled to oppose its final passage, declaring that under the amended ordinance " it would take fifty years to get a full corps of colored teachers in our public schools." [40] The crippling amendment, supported by all of the Republican councilmen except Cargill, directed that vacancies in Negro schools be temporarily filled by white teachers until there were enough vacancies that a whole faculty could be turned over to Negroes. This provision, designed to prevent racial mingling of faculties, tremendously delayed the actual opening of positions to qualified Negro applicants. A three-year residence requirement for Negro teachers also was added by the amendment, although this was not required of white teachers.[41] The only real gain to the Negro community was the assurance that Negroes were entitled to these teaching positions. Many more hard battles were required actually to place Negroes in these jobs.

Some immediate job benefits, in the form of municipal and state patronage positions, accrued to the Negro community as a result of Republican rule. The jobs were primarily manual labor positions, but in many instances they represented the first time particular areas of employment were opened to Negro labor. The city of Baltimore had never hired a Negro in any capacity before 1896. Early in 1896 the new Republican mayor announced the appointment of the first Negroes to city jobs, assuring his white constituents that Negroes would not be placed in positions where they would come in contact with white employes.[42] Over the next few years this policy came to mean the employment of Negroes in custodial, janitorial, sanitation, and messenger positions by the city; most of them were employed by the city sanita-

39. " Message of Governor Lloyd Lowndes at His Inauguration to the Senate and the House of Delegates," *Senate Journal*, 1896, p. 74.
40. *Baltimore Sun*, March 24, 1896.
41. *Ibid.*
42. *Ibid.*, January 31, 1896.

tion department and put to work in segregated gangs cleaning the streets. By 1898 there were three such gangs, of twenty-five to thirty laborers each, presided over by a Negro superintendent.[43]

Negro superintendents of sanitation districts held posts of prestige and power, and could hire and fire the laborers beneath them. One of the superintendents, Dr. George Wellington Bryant, the first Negro hired by the city in 1896, became the center of the major scandal of the Republican administration. Bryant was dismissed from his job in 1897 and accused of defrauding both the city and the men working under him by charging fees for enrolling job applicants and withholding part of the wages of his employes. The charge of defrauding his employes had to be dropped for lack of anyone willing to testify against him, but Bryant was convicted of fraud against the city and sentenced to six months in prison. Bryant was pardoned by Governor Lowndes before the expiration of his sentence, and Democrats made much of the incident in the 1899 gubernatorial campaign, charging Lowndes with encouraging Negro lawlessness and consorting with a Negro " jail-bird." [44]

Despite the Bryant incident, Republicans continued to appoint Negroes to various low-level patronage jobs in both the city and the state during their term in office. The *Baltimore Ledger*, a Negro weekly, reckoning the benefits of four years of Republican rule, estimated that some $200,000 in annual wages had been paid to the Negro community by the city as a result of Republican hiring practices.[45] Republicans also provided a similar amount of patronage on the state level. Again, these jobs were primarily laboring jobs, but a few clerical positions were given to Negroes. The state's liquor license board employed a Negro clerk, as did the judiciary committee of the House of Delegates.[46] More typically, however, Negroes found state employment in road repair work, in state tobacco warehouses and state fisheries, and in custodial work at Annapolis.

Laboring-class Negro Republicans could count some tangible rewards from having their party in power, but middle- and upper-class Negroes were slighted by Republican patronage policies.

43. *Baltimore Ledger*, April 2, 1898.
44. *Baltimore Sun*, March 28, 1897; April 19, 1898; and October 24, 1899.
45. November 4, 1899.
46. *Ibid.* Baltimore City also employed a Negro clerk in the office of the Register of Wills.

Negro leaders repeatedly sought appointments to the governing boards of state and city institutions that dealt primarily with Negro clientele or inmates, such as the Cheltenham Reformatory for Colored Boys, but their requests were ignored. The Republican administration made no important appointment of this sort during its entire term, either at the state or city level.[47] Nor did state Republican leaders exert themselves to obtain federal appointments for Negroes; the *Baltimore Ledger* charged that Maryland's Republican senators and representatives had not recommended a single Negro appointment to President McKinley.[48] Reverend S. Timothy Tice of Annapolis summed up the dissatisfaction of Negro leaders with Republican patronage policy: " Six republican Congressmen, two republican Senators and a republican Governor, all placed in power by Negro voters, and yet, not a single recognition shown. The only places doled out have been a few second or third-rate clerkships, and spittoon-cleaning jobs." [49]

The Republican hierarchy persisted in ignoring growing Negro demands even as the party approached the 1897 midterm state elections. During the spring, numerous Negro protest meetings were held in Baltimore; demands for better jobs for Negro Republicans, a larger voice in party councils, colored candidates for the state legislature, and representation in the police and fire departments were made with increasing urgency. Negro leaders threatened to run an independent ticket of Negro candidates in the midterm elections unless some of their requests were met by party leaders. Republican leaders, such as Governor Lowndes, United States Senator and state party chairman George L. Wellington, and city chairman William Stone, were unimpressed with the Negro uprising and refused to heed the mounting dissatisfaction. They favored continuing the organization's previously successful policy of orienting the party toward positions and candidates acceptable to the independent Democrats.[50]

Other Republican leaders, however, saw important opportunities in the rising Negro militance; white insurgent Republicans, especially William Malster of Baltimore and Sydney Mudd of Charles County, saw a chance to advance their own political interests and even to assume control of the party organization.

47. *Ibid.*, July 30, 1898.
48. August 13, 1898.
49. *Baltimore Ledger*, Letter to the Editor, August 13, 1898.
50. *Baltimore Sun*, March 12, April 4, May 13, and August 27, 1897.

This Malster-Mudd faction was the same group that had challenged Lowndes and Wellington at the Republican convention in 1895. Although Mudd was a congressman, the faction was out of favor with the party hierarchy and had bitter feelings about its lack of patronage. The struggle between the two white groups for control of the party was fought out in the Republican mayoralty primary in Baltimore. The party hierarchy presented a carefully selected and eminently respectable businessman, Theodore Marburg, who could appeal to the independent Democratic vote. Republican insurgents backed Malster as their candidate and, behind the scenes, promised Negro Republicans that they would have representation on the party's legislative ticket if Malster were successful.[51] On these terms Negro support went overwhelmingly to Malster, who won the city primary and soon, in conjunction with Congressman Mudd, succeeded in capturing control of the entire state party organization.[52] Malster's victories probably represented the high point of Negro political achievement in Maryland since enfranchisement. By rebuffing the regular Republican hierarchy, the Negro minority had again demonstrated its cohesiveness and electoral potency, but it still had to collect its share of the victor's rewards.

In the betrayal that followed, the cynicism of white Republicans was matched only by the angry helplessness of black Republicans. On September 8 reports that the Malster organization would run a colored candidate from each of Baltimore's three legislative districts were leaked to the press. This action lulled and placated Negro leaders at the very time the Malster forces were choosing delegates to the district nominating conventions. On September 9 the delegates were safely elected, on schedule, and on September 13 Negro leaders were informed that Negro representation on the ticket was, after all, impossible.[53] Malster's men cited pressure from county Republicans and independents as the cause for their breach of faith, but Negroes knew they had been used. "You intended to deceive us," said Harry Cummings, Negro Republican candidate for the city council, who promised retaliation for the treatment accorded his people. "When I go back to my people I shall tell them that we were beaten by your perfidy, and

51. *Ibid.*, April 9 and September 14, 1897. The secret promise to Negro leaders was acknowledged by George R. Gaither, one of Malster's campaign managers, after Malster's primary victory.

52. *Baltimore Sun*, August 27 and September 10, 1897.

53. *Ibid.*, September 8, 10, 14, 1897.

you may know what the consequences will be—your ticket will be cut from top to bottom. I do not intend that I shall rest under a suspicion of unfair dealing with my people." [54]

Negro leaders could not make good on such threats, however. An attempt to get a colored independent ticket on the ballot failed when the board of election supervisors ruled that more than half of the collected signatures were invalid.[55] With nowhere else to go but to the hated Democratic party, election day found most of the Negro leaders back in the Republican fold, and Malster carried the city by a comfortable plurality.[56]

This episode implanted the seeds of dissolution within the Republican regime—but the Negro was not, as abstract justice might have decreed, the sower of destruction. The party's factionalism, revealed and heightened by these events, became the debilitating force which would sweep the Republicans out of office after only four years of rule. The Malster-Mudd coalition proved incapable of either holding the Republican party together or retaining independent Democratic support. In 1897 Republican rule began to degenerate into a long intraparty fight as Malsterites, firmly entrenched in Baltimore, tried to maintain control of the state and the party.

The legislative session of 1898 also was notable primarily for sustained political wrangling. The Republican majority was unable even to agree on a Speaker for the House of Delegates, and the Democratic minority made this crucial decision for them. There were long and bitter disputes over selection of the Republican who should succeed United States Senator Arthur Gorman.[57] The party made no progress in fulfilling the limited reform program of the previous Republican legislature, and the only legislation of consequence produced by the 1898 session was purely political: Baltimore received a new city charter and increased powers for its new Republican mayor. Republicans had a field day mapping new wards and legislative districts for Baltimore and rearranging the congressional districts of the state—while Democrats howled complaints of trickery and gerrymandering.[58]

54. *Ibid.*, September 14, 1897.
55. *Ibid.*, October 22, 1897.
56. *Ibid.*, November 3, 1897.
57. *Ibid.*, January 8, 26, 1898. Louis E. McComas, a former congressman from western Maryland, was finally elected to the Senate position.
58. *Laws of Maryland*, 1898, chap. 123, pp. 241 ff.; chap. 10, pp. 69 ff.; and chap. 338, pp. 997 ff.

Even Negro Republicans were parties to the petty factionalism and disorganization: two Negro lobbying groups, with essentially the same aims, converged on Annapolis and dissipated the little strength they possessed by attacking each other. The Colored Citizens' League and the Colored People's Conference, led by rival Negro newspaper editors, both sought the establishment of a state-supported industrial and normal school for Negroes. Wasting most of their energy on attempts to discredit each other, neither organization made any headway with the largely indifferent legislature.[59]

By the end of 1898 it was clear that disorganization and poor management had cost the Republican party the support of the independent Democratic movement, which had helped it to power. The *Baltimore Sun*, the most vocal and influential organ of the independents, having deserted the floundering Republicans, was energetically previewing the tactics the Democrats would use to reestablish their political sway. There was an upsurge in its reportage of Negro " rowdyism " in the city and favorable comment on the values of suffrage restriction, beginning in the autumn of 1898 and continuing through the critical election year of 1899.[60]

In the spring of 1899 the Democrats reclaimed Baltimore from Republican rule, using the slogan " This Is a White Man's City," and racism also was the dominant issue in the fall gubernatorial campaign.[61] The Democratic platform stressed the " menace to the peace and good order of the State " that the Negro supposedly presented under Republican rule and urged that the only remedy was to return to power the party that " represents the vast majority of the intelligent manhood of the State." [62] Governor Lowndes was severely criticized for his pardon of George Wellington Bryant, the Negro official who had been convicted of fraud against the city of Baltimore. Incidents such as this, the Democrats claimed, had increased Negro lawlessness by holding out the promise of political influence to secure immunity from punishment. The whole Democratic campaign was designed to create fear that there would be a total breakdown of law and order if

59. *Baltimore Sun*, February 18–26, 1898.
60. See especially the issues during November, 1898, and April and October, 1899.
61. *Baltimore Sun*, April 23, 1899.
62. *Ibid.*, August 3, 1899.

the Republicans were returned to office, and, with the state's leading newspaper cooperating in this endeavor, the strategy was effective.

The Republicans were crippled by the chaos within their organization. Although the Malster-Mudd coalition had lost Baltimore to the Democrats in the spring, it had full control of the party's machinery in the city, and it seemed determined to control the state organization as well. To this end, and with Governor Lowndes' acquiescence, the faction deposed the able and powerful chairman of the Republican state central committee, George L. Wellington, and replaced him with one of its own men. But Wellington, a United States senator and the architect of the successful 1895 campaign, did not take his deposal quietly. He had long counseled the Republican party to base its strategy on accommodation with the independent Democrats, but it had spurned first his advice and now his person. Wellington retaliated by publicly resigning not only from the central committee but from the Republican party itself. Predicting certain defeat for the Republicans in the coming election, Wellington issued an open letter in which he declared his " immeasurable and unutterable contempt " for Governor Lowndes.[63] In November, 1899, the Democrats easily regained control of the entire state.[64]

Republican rule in Maryland had been brief but instructive. On balance, the Republican party had given the state a creditable administration and had proved itself a reputable alternative to the dominant Democratic party. Independents had learned the practicality of bolting the dominant party and combining with the minority party, and had enhanced their power accordingly. Regular Democrats also had been impressed with this lesson; they would direct their future course toward repeated attempts to so cripple the minority party that such a combination would never again be successful. Republicans had learned something about both the strengths and the weaknesses of their racially mixed party, and that they could achieve power with the Negro in their ranks. The problem of the Negro's role in the party and in the larger society, however, was more difficult and loomed larger than ever before.

63. *Ibid.*, September 22, 23, 1899.
64. *Ibid.*, November 8, 1899. The Democratic ticket, headed by John Walter Smith, was elected by a majority of about 15,000 votes. Democratic majorities were returned to both houses of the legislature.

CHAPTER 5

THE DISFRANCHISEMENT MOVEMENT, 1900–1912

The return of the Democratic party to power in 1900 marked the beginning of a decade-long struggle to restrict Negro suffrage in Maryland. The Democratic old guard, shaken by the disaster of 1895, determined to secure future hegemony over the state and the party through Negro disfranchisement. Not only would disfranchisement break the back of the Republican party, establishing relatively certain one-party rule of the state, but it also would simplify intraparty control by eliminating any practical avenue of appeal from organizational decisions by party dissidents and independents.

Aware of their slim margin of legislative control, the Democrats launched their disfranchisement campaign cautiously, seeking to accomplish their purpose by indirection. The Democrats' first move was enactment of a series of complicated ballot regulations. These regulations, designed to make voting more difficult, were accompanied by a steady stream of racist invective that fed upon itself and grew more virulent with each campaign. Soon the Democratic organization was caught up in its self-generated atmosphere of racial hate, and what had begun as a practical measure for strengthening the party organization became an ideological struggle that sapped party resources and organizational strength. When reduction of the Negro vote by legislatively prescribed ballot devices seemed insufficient, wholesale disfranchisement by state constitutional proscription became the goal. Consumed by this goal, the Democratic party three times went before the electorate with constitutional amendments to deny the Negro his vote.

In the end, the movement to disfranchise the Negro in Maryland failed. The Negro retained his constitutional right to vote, and the two-party system, which operated so effectively to preserve that right, lived on. In the light of contemporary events in other states, this was a notable victory both for the Negro and for Maryland—but a victory that can be measured only in such comparative terms. No one gained from this long and bitter struggle. The disfranchisement issue consumed the political energy of the people of the state for at least a decade; it polluted the political atmosphere of the entire community by the hatred it generated; and it exacted a heavy toll from the Negro in the Jim Crow laws that were spawned and fastened upon him at that time.

Tampering with the Ballot

Rumors of impending election law changes began to circulate in Annapolis almost as soon as the newly elected Democratic legislature assembled there in January, 1900.[1] Although the Democrats had regained power through an intensely racist campaign, they could not pretend they had a mandate for an election law change; they had not raised the issue in either their platform or their campaign. The Democratic platform of 1899 had pointed to the Republicans' reliance on the Negro vote, but Democrats had not even suggested that this was a situation they planned to change. Indeed, they had pledged " to do equal and exact justice to all, without regard to race, and to guarantee to the colored people of the State the fullest protection in all their rights." [2] With victory and state power safely in hand, however, these noble sentiments were set aside and did not rise to trouble the party again for many years. The issue for the Democratic party after 1900 was how, not whether, to restrict Negro suffrage.

The Democratic leadership had to move slowly; the election law of 1896, with its easy straight-ticket-voting and familiar partisan emblem provisions, had widespread support. Although it had been passed by the Republicans, the law had been drawn up and endorsed by the Reform League of Baltimore, a respected civic group that numbered many independents, Democrats, and Republicans among its members. A major change in the law required careful preparation and strict party discipline to effect, and it was a major change the Democrats wanted—one that would eliminate both the party emblems and the opportunity for straight-ticket voting. Democrats sought a ballot on which candidates were grouped by office rather than by party, and party affiliations

1. *Baltimore Sun*, January 27, 1900.
2. *Ibid.*, August 3, 1899.

were written out rather than designated by the familiar emblems. In short, they wanted to make the ballot more difficult for the illiterate voter to mark correctly.[3]

It soon became evident that it would be unwise to attempt such a piece of major legislation in the 1900 legislative session. Party control of the senate was too slight and difficulties in maintaining party discipline began to appear.[4] Despite a strong demand from southern Maryland for immediate action, party leaders decided not to gamble on the matter and settled for a legislative study of how such a change, if enacted, would affect the state's electorate. A canvass of each county's voter registration books was made to discover the number of illiterate white and Negro registrants. According to this survey, 26,616 illiterate Negroes and 18,307 illiterate whites were registered to vote in Maryland. Negro illiterates, however, accounted for 47 percent of all Negro registrants, while white illiterates made up only 8 percent of all white registrants.[5]

Within a year the Democrats were aided in overcoming the political obstacles to their much-desired ballot law by help from a most unexpected quarter; Republicans suddenly furnished the Democrats and the state a first-rate political scandal. Publication of the 1900 federal census for Maryland raised grave doubts, at least in Democratic circles, about the accuracy of the count. Reapportionment of the House of Delegates hinged on the census figures, and Democrats thought it odd that certain Republican counties showed a population growth just sufficient to increase their delegations while neighboring Democratic counties showed either an insufficient increase or a decrease in population.[6] According to preliminary estimates, six new delegates would be added to the lower house, and four of them would come from counties under Republican control. Five of the six counties that would receive additional delegates were in southern Maryland, a largely rural area not previously subject to startling population growth but an area long dominated by Republican Congressman Sydney Mudd.[7] Confident that scandal was brewing and that

3. *Ibid.*, January 27, 1900.
4. *Ibid.*, March 30, 1900.
5. *Ibid.*, March 3, 1900. There is no record of this survey in either the house or senate journals or documents for 1900.
6. *Baltimore Sun*, January 24, 1901.
7. Under the original 1900 federal census data for Maryland the counties of Anne Arundel, Charles, Kent, Montgomery, Prince George's, and St. Mary's would

it would benefit his party, Democratic Governor John Walter Smith, in February, 1901, called for a special session of the legislature to authorize a state census to correct "errors believed to exist in the enumeration in the recent United States Census of the population of this State" and for "reforming manifest and great abuses in the Election Law of this State."[8] The party leadership intended to use the special session for passage of the ballot bill it had hesitated to bring up in the regular session.

Party leaders converged on Annapolis in March to direct the work of the special session, and the ballot bill drew most of the attention and consumed most of the time of the legislature. Former United States Senator Gorman took up residence at the executive mansion to oversee the fight for the bill. John Prentiss Poe, dean of the University of Maryland Law School and reported author of the ballot bill, was on constant call for redrafting the bill or for offering assurances about its constitutionality.[9] With Democratic leaders bent on passage of the bill, Republican United States Senator Louis McComas left Washington and came to Annapolis to work against it. The Reform League, which had led the fight for the Republican election law of 1896, sent another Republican luminary, Charles Jerome Bonaparte, to oppose the change.[10]

The scandal, meanwhile, was breaking on schedule. On March 19, 1901, Stephen A. Abell, a census enumerator for St. Mary's County, was arrested in Washington, D.C., on a warrant sworn out by the chief clerk of the geographical division of the Census Bureau and charged with fraudulent enumeration. Abell, who confessed to the charge, implicated Congressman Sydney Mudd and Joseph Ching, a political aide of Mudd, in a conspiracy to return a padded count for southern Maryland. Although Mudd denied all knowledge of the plot and escaped legal action, further investigation turned up another census enumerator who also pleaded guilty to false enumeration and enough evidence to

have been entitled to one additional representative in the Maryland House of Delegates. All except Kent County are in southern Maryland and all except Montgomery and St. Mary's counties were under Republican rule in 1900 (*Sun Almanac*, 1903, p. 99).

8. "Proclamation of Governor John Walter Smith," *House Journal*, Extraordinary Session, 1901, p. 3.

9. *Baltimore Sun*, March 6, 9, 1901; John R. Lambert, *Arthur Pue Gorman* (Baton Rouge, 1953), pp. 285–87.

10. *Baltimore Sun*, March 12, 1901.

convict Ching of conspiracy in the plot.[11] Three Maryland counties were shown to have had their census counts padded, and the
United States Bureau of the Census made official recounts in
these three counties.[12] Revelation of the plot removed all controversy from the Democrats' proposal for a state census and
bolstered their arguments for a ballot law that would restrict
the franchise and cut into the power of those who had conceived
the fraud. In the house, both the election and the census bill
passed handily; in the narrowly controlled senate, the strict party-
division vote was fourteen Democrats for and eleven Republicans
against the bills.[13]

The new election law of 1901, as passed, eliminated easy
straight-ticket voting by prohibiting party groupings of candidates,
removed all party emblems from the ballot, and prohibited assistance for voters in marking their ballots except for those who were
physically disabled; it provided that candidates must be grouped
alphabetically, under the office they sought, with their party
affiliation spelled out after their names. It also provided that
voters who left the state even temporarily must file with their
local registration officials a legal declaration of their intention to
return—or lose their legal-residence qualification and their right
to vote. This last provision was aimed at the large Negro traffic
between southern Maryland and the District of Columbia.[14]

The first test of the new law came soon after its passage, in a
Baltimore city council election of May, 1901, and the results must
have caused great chagrin in Democratic circles. Republicans
had prepared for the election by opening schools in every precinct
to teach illiterate Negro voters how to recognize and pick out
the word " Republican " on the ballot. Democrats tried the same
tactic, but with little success; most of their illiterate constituents
were white and were unwilling to submit to instruction that the
Negroes accepted eagerly. When the votes were in, Republicans

11. *Ibid.*, March 20 and June 13, 1901. The National Civil Service Reform League
issued a summary pamphlet on the Maryland census frauds of 1900: " Frauds in
the Taking of the Federal Census in Maryland " (n. p., 1901).

12. The three counties were Anne Arundel, Charles, and St. Mary's. The
padding was not extensive in terms of numbers—just enough to have secured an
additional delegate for these counties had the plot succeeded. The original census
figures appeared in the *Baltimore Sun* (July 22, 1901); only the revised figures
appear in the published volumes of the federal census for 1900, and these are the
figures used in this study.

13. *Baltimore Sun*, March 21, 22, 1901; *Senate Journal*, 1901, pp. 114–17.

14. *Laws of Maryland*, Extraordinary Session, 1901, chap. 2, pp. 4–23.

discovered that they had carried the city by a plurality of more than 2,000, winning seventeen of the twenty-four seats in the first branch of the city council and all four of the second branch seats that were up for election. The only expectation that had been fulfilled by the new election law was the light turn-out, and the results must have left many Democrats wondering who had been disfranchised.[15]

The Democrats' doubts about the operation of the new law were confirmed in the fall of 1901 in a statewide election for delegates to the General Assembly: Republicans increased their representation in the House of Delegates from twenty-six to forty-three. In the 1902 congressional elections, Republicans took four of the state's six seats and ran up a statewide lead of some 8,000 votes over the Democrats.[16] Not only was the law having the opposite effect of what was intended, it was also proving extremely cumbersome to administer. The tally of the complex new ballots was so slow that it was several days before the results of elections were known. Dissatisfaction with the process of throwing out " incorrectly " marked ballots and the inevitable suspicion that attached to days-late returns forced general recognition that the law had failed. The *Baltimore Sun* caustically observed: " Tuesday's trial of the new Election law demonstrates conclusively that it will have to ' go way back and sit down,' in company with a good many distinguished statesmen." [17]

Ironically, their losses in recent elections made it difficult for the Democrats to make immediate or substantial changes in their backfiring election law; for the time being they had to content themselves with amendments that merely smoothed off some of the rougher edges. The Straus Election Law, passed in 1902, provided simply that the new ballot be printed in uniform type throughout the state, that it contain explicit direction for proper marking, and that additional election clerks be hired to speed the tally.[18]

15. *Baltimore Sun*, April 26, 27, and May 8, 1901. The total poll was about 67,000 from a registration total of 121,000. Two years earlier Baltimore's mayoralty election had polled 106,000 votes from a similar registration total. Although the two elections differed in the interest they generated, the election law undoubtedly contributed to the decline, as later elections confirm.

16. *Baltimore Sun*, November 7, 1901, and November 6, 1902.

17. Editorial of November 7, 1901.

18. *Laws of Maryland*, 1902, chap. 133, pp. 202 ff. Isaac Lobe Straus, an independent Democrat from Baltimore who sponsored the 1902 election law, became Democratic attorney general for Maryland in 1908.

The gubernatorial campaign of 1903 brought the election law issue to the forefront and proved that the present arrangement satisfied no one. Republicans, of course, wanted a return to the ballot law of 1896 and pledged to repeal all the changes made since that time by the Democrats.[19] Republican campaigners pointed to the sharp drop in voter turn-out, the numerous ballots thrown out for "irregularities," and the inconvenience of the new ballots even for literate voters. Democrats, too, were eager to change the new election law; in the three major elections held since its passage they had consistently lost ground to their Republican opponents and were genuinely suspicious of its operation. The Democrats did not specify how they would modify the law but their campaign left no doubt that the change would be toward further restriction and disfranchisement. "We believe that the political destinies of Maryland should be shaped and controlled by the white people of the State," the 1903 Democratic platform stated, "and we declare without reserve our resolute purpose to preserve in every conservative and constitutional way the political ascendancy of our race." [20]

Using the tactic that had worked so well for them in 1899, Democrats constructed their campaign around racist appeals and reached new excesses in public vilification of the Negro in Maryland. No longer did leading politicians hold back from public racism and leave the dirty work to underlings. The Democratic candidate for governor, Edwin Warfield, said:

I do not want to be Governor of this State unless I am elected to that high office by a majority of the white voters of Maryland. This election is a contest for the supremacy of the white race in Maryland. . . . The elevation of the negro is a well-nigh hopeless task, so long as they exercise like dumb, driven cattle, solidly and without intelligence or reason, their right of suffrage as a weapon of offense against the Democratic party, directed and guided by designing Republican politicians. What does he gain by such a course? The white man, the Democratic white man, is the real and true friend of the negro. . . . The white man is the highest type of the human family; the negro is the lowest. God has made no other race equal of the Caucasian, and neither

19. *Baltimore Sun*, September 18, 1903.
20. *Ibid.*, September 17, 1903.

amendments to the Constitution nor anything else can do what God has failed to do: that is, make the negro the equal of the white man.[21]

Arthur P. Gorman, recently elected to his fourth term in the United States Senate and back at the helm of the Maryland Democratic organization, expressed regret for the racism of the campaign. Nevertheless, Gorman added his share, observing:

So long as the negro is subordinated to the white man in every habitable part of the globe he is honest and faithful and may be elevated; but when you give to him political power and social equality, you transform him into a semifiend, treacherous and untrustworthy, altogether unfit for the responsibility of the management of the affairs of any community.[22]

As usual, the race issue put the Republicans on the defensive, but again they turned to instructing their illiterate constituents how to mark the complex ballot they would receive in November. Newspapers reported that Republicans conducted special night classes for this purpose in each Maryland county and that Negro attendance was high. Prospective voters who seemed unable to learn to mark the entire ballot correctly were taught to mark it for the Republican gubernatorial candidate only and to ignore the names of the other office-seekers.[23] But when the votes were in it was apparent that the Democrats had duplicated their 1899 victory. With a statewide plurality of 12,000 votes, Democrats retained control of the governor's office and achieved a two-to-one majority in both the house and the senate. Republicans carried only seven counties, all in their traditional bastions of strength in western and southern Maryland.[24]

The Democrats' electoral victory in 1903 was widely interpreted as a popular mandate for Negro disfranchisement—even Negroes seemed to agree that the question had been put and the verdict rendered. The *Baltimore Afro-American Ledger* observed sadly:

21. *Ibid.*, October 22, 1903.
22. *Ibid.*, October 25, 1903.
23. *Ibid.*, October 29, 1903.
24. *Sun Almanac*, 1904, p. 101. The gubernatorial election count was Democrats 108,548, Republicans 95,923. The legislature's division in 1904 would be nineteen Democrats and eight Republicans in the senate and seventy Democrats and thirty-one Republicans in the house.

There can be no mistake with respect to the significance of the Democratic victory last Tuesday in this city and state. The two respective tickets were headed by able and strong men, and the issue put to the forefront by the Democrats was bravely met by the opposing party, and the majority of the voters decided in favor of the plea put forward by the Democrats, to-wit: that disfranchisement and " Jim-Crowism " should obtain in the State of Maryland.

The Republican party which stood opposed to such outrageous treatment of colored citizens has been defeated, and Gormanism and disfranchisement indorsed. There is nothing for us to do but heroically take our medicine.[25]

When the heavily Democratic legislature met in 1904, Governor Warfield set its first obligation as revision of the election law and passage of a constitutional amendment " fixing a higher standard of qualification for the exercise of the elective franchise." [26] Senator Gorman and Dean Poe, now the semiofficial legal adviser of the Democratic party, again moved in to direct the party's strategy and to draw up the new election law and constitutional amendment.[27] The election law revision produced by the 1904 legislature was the Wilson ballot law, named for its sponsor, William R. Wilson of Queen Anne's County. Far from simplifying the ballot, the Wilson law prohibited the use of party emblems, party names, or party designations of any kind on the ballot; candidates could be identified only by their place of residence. An even more discriminatory feature was that the law applied to only eleven counties in the state, all of which had either large Negro populations or a history of Republican regularity: Anne Arundel, Calvert, Charles, Frederick, Garrett, Kent, Prince George's, St. Mary's, Somerset, Talbot, and Worcester counties. In these " Wilson-ballot counties " political parties were allowed to post lists of their candidates on the walls of polling places, which would let literate voters familiarize themselves with their party's candidates before entering the voting booth but would be of little use to illiterate voters.[28] The clear intent of the Wilson law was to make it impossible for the illiterate voter to cast an effective ballot in areas where the Republican party

25. Editorial of November 7, 1903.
26. Inaugural Address, *Senate Journal*, 1904, pp. 80–81.
27. Lambert, *Arthur Pue Gorman*, pp. 346–49.
28. *Laws of Maryland*, 1904, chap. 339, p. 601.

had shown electoral strength. According to the *Baltimore Sun*, "the new law is intended to prescribe indirectly an educational test for voters, which under the Constitution of the State cannot be done directly."[29]

The Republican politicians were resourceful in meeting this new threat to their constituency. Each election became a battle of wits between Republicans, determined to circumvent the effects of the Wilson law by mass instruction of their supporters, and Democrats, who were equally determined that the law should take its toll of Republican voters. In the 1904 congressional election Democrats in the Fifth District determined to use the new law to unseat the Republican incumbent Sydney E. Mudd, longtime boss of southern Maryland. They nominated their own candidate, Dr. Richard S. Hill, and to confuse the issue persuaded a man named John E. Mudd to run as an "Independent Republican." Undaunted by this trickery, Republicans instructed their followers to recognize "Sydney" as the name that contained "two pig yokes," or *y*'s.[30] The effectiveness of this instruction was demonstrated in the outcome: Congressman Sydney Mudd won handily over his Democratic opponent, and John E. Mudd received only 443 votes.[31] Congressman Mudd again displayed his mastery of the new ballot game in the 1905 state elections. Democrats in Mudd's home county of Charles entered a "Repudiation" slate of candidates whose names were similar to those of the Republican candidates. Mudd said nothing, but just before the deadline for ballot changes he withdrew the entire Republican ticket and filed a completely different slate—Lyon, Ryan, and Posey, all having the easily recognizable "pig yoke" in their names, and B. M. Wilmer and J. C. Wilmer, whose *W*'s became the subject of "double yoke" instruction.[32]

Not every county had a Sydney Mudd to do battle with the Democrats, however, and ballot trickery was rampant throughout the state. In 1905 Democrats in St. Mary's County persuaded a bogus "People's party" to enter a slate of candidates whose names resembled those on the Republican ticket. Republicans E. F. Greenwell, W. T. Wilkerson, and S. M. Jones had to compete against "People's party" candidates T. B. Greenwell, T. M.

29. Editorial of April 9, 1904.
30. *Baltimore Sun*, October 23, 1904.
31. *Sun Almanac*, 1905, p. 123.
32. *Baltimore Sun*, October 31, 1905.

Wilkerson, and J. M. Jones, as well as against their regular Democratic opponents. Also, because the Wilson ballot law did not require that candidates' names be listed alphabetically, as had the 1901 law, Democrats in Somerset, Worcester, and Kent counties made up their ballots with the Democratic candidates' names just above the thick black lines that separated the office groupings from one another; Democrats were instructed to mark the name just above the black line.[33] Even in non-Wilson-ballot counties where party names could appear on the ballot, fraud and trickery were common, as when Democrats sought to confuse Republican voters by entering " Repudiation " tickets on the ballots.[34]

Although the Wilson ballot law was in effect from 1904 until 1918, changes were made in its application to particular counties from time to time. In 1906 Frederick and Garrett counties were exempted from its operation and they returned to the ballot procedures of the 1901 ballot law, the basic law that governed all non-Wilson areas during this period. In 1908 Dorchester and Queen Anne's counties were added to the areas governed by the Wilson law. In 1914 all counties except the five southern Maryland counties of Anne Arundel, Calvert, Charles, Prince George's, and St. Mary's were exempted from the Wilson law.[35]

The ballot laws of 1901 and 1904 substantially reduced the number of voters, both white and Negro, who took part in Maryland elections. It is impossible, however, to say just what groups or how many voters were disfranchised by these two laws, and it would be erroneous to attribute all of the decrease in voter participation solely to their operation. Undoubtedly the economic discontent of the 1890s stimulated more intense voter interest than the relatively mild political issues of the early 1900s, and a comparison of voter turn-out in the two decades reflects some " normal " decrease in voter interest. Nevertheless, there was a marked drop in voter participation in all types of elections after the passage of the two ballot laws which is, in part, attributable to their restrictive provisions. Participation in presidential elections fell from a high of 88 percent of those eligible to vote in the 1890s to a high of 71 percent in the following decade. In gubernatorial elections the drop was from a high of 85 percent

33. *Ibid.*, October 24, 28, 1905.
34. *Ibid.*, October 24, 1905.
35. *Laws of Maryland*, 1906, chap. 498, p. 973; 1908, chap. 737, p. 103; and 1914, chap. 307, p. 458.

in the 1890s to a high of 65.5 percent in the early 1900s. And the drop in off-year congressional elections in the same period was from a high of 74 percent to a high of 63 percent (Figure 4).

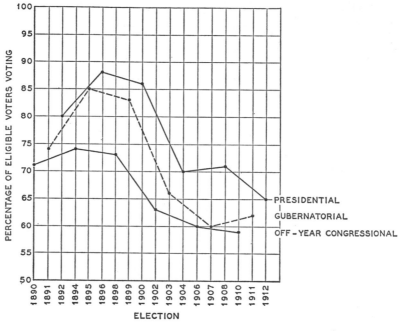

FIGURE 4

VOTER TURN-OUT IN MARYLAND BEFORE AND AFTER THE BALLOT-LAW
CHANGES OF 1901 AND 1904

There was a decline even in terms of the number of votes cast, despite a rapidly growing potential electorate. Marylanders cast 264,434 votes for president in 1900 but only 238,531 votes in 1908, and the 1908 vote represented the highest turn-out achieved after passage of the two ballot laws. The Maryland gubernatorial election attracted 251,189 voters in 1899 but only 215,967 voters in 1911. These decreases took place in a decade in which Maryland's potential electorate increased by 36,000.[36]

It is more difficult to separate the additional impact of the Wilson ballot law from the combined effect of both ballot laws,

36. U. S. Bureau of the Census, *Twelfth Census of the United States: 1900. Population*, 2: 188, and *Thirteenth Census of the United States: 1910. Population*, 2: 843–47.

but some pertinent observations can be made. The Wilson law applied to approximately one-half the area of the state but its impact was diminished in terms of the voting population: in 1900 only 16 percent of Maryland's eligible voters (male citizens twenty-one years and older) resided in this area.[37] Numerically, at least, the Wilson law affected a greater number of whites than Negroes; 31,674 eligible white voters resided in Wilson-law counties and only 19,654 eligible Negroes. Proportionately, however, the law caused greater hardship among the Negro voting group, as it was designed to do. Thirty-one percent of the state's eligible Negro voters resided in Wilson-law areas while only 13 percent of the state's white voters were so affected. This situation was compounded by the literacy rates of the two groups: of the eligible whites in the area, only 3,394 (11 percent) were listed as illiterate in the federal census of 1900 but 10,531 (54 percent) of the eligible Negroes were so listed.[38]

The Wilson law seems to have depressed voting participation somewhat more than the 1901 ballot law but its effect was less than might have been expected from the stringency of its provisions. Figure 5 compares the average voter turn-out in the areas that operated under the Wilson law of 1904 and in the areas that operated under the 1901 ballot law in presidential, gubernatorial, and off-year congressional elections from 1900 through 1912. The Wilson areas generally were several points below the non-Wilson areas in voter participation in presidential and gubernatorial elections, but the difference is not striking. It is significant, too, that in 1903, when both areas were still governed by the 1901 law, voter participation was already lower in counties where the Wilson ballot would go into effect. In off-year congressional elections, in 1906 and 1910, the turn-out in Wilson areas exceeded that in non-Wilson areas—a relationship that also existed in 1902, prior to enactment of the Wilson law.

37. From 1904 to 1912 nine counties operated continuously under the Wilson ballot law: Anne Arundel, Calvert, Charles, Kent, Prince George's, St. Mary's, Somerset, Talbot, and Worcester. From 1901 to 1912 Baltimore and ten counties operated continuously under the provisions of the 1901 ballot law: Allegany, Baltimore, Caroline, Carroll, Cecil, Harford, Howard, Montgomery, Washington, and Wicomico. Frederick, Garrett, Dorchester, and Queen Anne's were variable counties, operating part of the time under the 1901 law and part of the time under the Wilson law.

38. U.S. Bureau of the Census, *Twelfth Census of the United States: 1900. Population*, 1: 984.

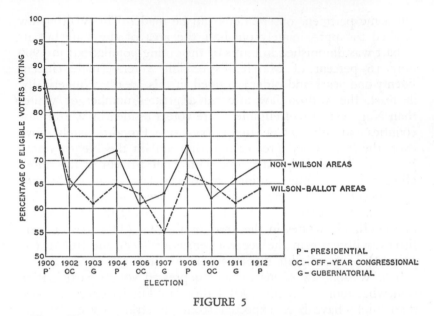

FIGURE 5

VOTER TURN-OUT IN AREAS UNDER THE BALLOT LAW OF 1901 AND IN AREAS
UNDER THE WILSON BALLOT LAW OF 1904 COMPARED

Apparently, then, the 1901 ballot law, which prohibited simple straight-ticket voting and party emblems on the ballot, had the greater effect on voter participation in Maryland. After its passage instruction by the political parties of illiterate and semiliterate voters became almost mandatory, and the added harassment of the Wilson ballot meant only that this instruction had to be more intensive. The Wilson law, however, led to greater ballot trickery and confusion in the areas where it was applied; and maintenance of voter participation in the face of these obstacles speaks highly of the political ingenuity of the minority party and the political performance of its constituents. Proponents of the Wilson law were among the first to acknowledge its relative ineffectiveness, and the continuing campaign for constitutional disfranchisement of the Negro, waged by the Democratic party after the law's enactment, is witness to this evaluation.

The Campaign for Constitutional Disfranchisement

The Democratic party made three separate attempts to remove the Negro from Maryland's political arena in the early 1900s, each in the form of a proposed amendment to the state constitution. They would, in essence, have established separate, unequal voting requirements for whites and Negroes. Each proposal was duly passed by a three-fifths majority of each house of the General Assembly and was submitted, as Maryland's constitution required, to the electorate for ratification. Each proposal, however, failed to win popular approval from Maryland voters.

The first and most serious threat to Negro suffrage in Maryland was the Poe amendment, passed by the General Assembly in 1904 and submitted to popular referendum in the autumn of 1905. Drafted by John Prentiss Poe of the University of Maryland Law School and passed by the same legislature that enacted the Wilson law, the Poe amendment was a frank imitation of deep-South voting restrictions. The amendment proposed to restrict voting privileges to male citizens who could qualify in one of four categories: as (1) a person able to read and to give a " reasonable explanation " of any section of the Maryland constitution submitted to him by the officers of registration; (2) a person unable to read but able " to understand and give a reasonable explanation " of a section of the constitution read to him by registration officials; (3) " a person who on the first day of January, 1869, or prior thereto, was entitled to vote under the laws of this State or of any other State of the United States wherein he then resided "; (4) a " male lineal descendent of such last-mentioned person who may be twenty-one (21) years of age or over in the year 1906." [39]

John Prentiss Poe explained, fully and frankly, the intent of the amendment he had drafted. He observed that the " understanding clause," embracing the first two categories under which potential voters might qualify, as well as the " grandfather clause," comprising the last two categories, had been borrowed from the constitutions of Southern states that had recently disfranchised the Negro. Mississippi had adopted the understanding clause in 1890 and Louisiana the grandfather clause in 1898. Most Maryland whites would qualify simply and easily under the grandfather clause, which exacted no test other than having been

39. The text of the Poe amendment does not appear in the *Laws of Maryland* nor in the house and senate journals and documents for 1904. Under constitutional procedure, however, the complete text of all constitutional amendments was published in at least one newspaper in each county prior to its submission to the electorate, and it is from this publication in the *Baltimore Sun* (August 29, 1905) that all pertinent quotations were taken.

entitled to vote prior to 1869—in one's own right or through one's forebears. Negroes, having had no legal right to vote in Maryland prior to 1870, would have to submit to and qualify under one of the two sections of the understanding clause.[40]

Still, Maryland encountered special problems in framing a disfranchising amendment, and these problems plagued the amendment's supporters from the outset. The foremost problem was the large body of naturalized citizens, politically active whites, who could not qualify under the grandfather clause. The federal census of 1900 lists 28,605 naturalized male citizens of voting age in Maryland, approximately 9 percent of the electorate.[41] Most of them probably had come of age and been naturalized after 1869 and therefore were unable to use the grandfather clause. Furthermore, even a native-born male of foreign parentage would be unable to qualify under the grandfather clause unless he or his father had qualified for suffrage prior to 1869. This raised the total of whites adversely affected by the pending amendment even higher. In 1900, 46,965 native-born white males of voting age and foreign parentage (either mother, father, or both) lived in Maryland and—if general population ratios hold for this group—only 10 percent of them had fathers who were native-born.[42] It is impossible to determine how many of the remaining 42,000 native-born males of voting age and foreign-born fathers had been eligible to vote prior to 1869 or had fathers naturalized and of age at that time, but if only half this group were adversely affected by the proposed amendment it would have amounted to 7 percent of the Maryland electorate. Thus the Poe amendment, in attempting to eliminate 20 percent of the state's electorate, which was Negro, was at the same time posing a serious threat to another 15 percent, which was white. Baltimore City was particularly sensitive to this threat because it was here that most of the state's foreign-born and first-generation citizens lived. In 1900 Baltimore's naturalized voting population and its Negro voting population were almost identical in size.[43]

40. *Baltimore Sun*, October 25, 1905.

41. U.S. Bureau of the Census, *Twelfth Census of the United States: 1900. Population*, 1: 984.

42. *Ibid.*, pp. 910–11, 808–9.

43. *Ibid.*, pp. 586, 984. In 1900, 73 percent of Maryland's naturalized male citizens of voting age lived in Baltimore, as did 70 percent of the state's native-born males of voting age and foreign parentage. The city had 20,840 naturalized males of voting age and 21,647 Negro males of voting age in 1900.

There is no indication that the framers of the Poe amendment intended to disfranchise or impair the registration of the large body of white voters of foreign parentage. Amendment supporters repeatedly asserted that no white voters would be disfranchised by the understanding clause, that literate and illiterate whites would be given easy clearance by the registrars, who possessed total discretion in administering the understanding test. Negroes who took the same test would fail to qualify.[44]

Maryland disfranchisement advocates faced another special problem: well over half of Maryland's adult Negro males were literate and could not be disfranchised by a simple reading test.[45] To meet this problem, the understanding clause of the Poe amendment was unusually harsh. By requiring a " reasonable explanation" of constitutional clauses, even from people who could read, the amendment exceeded the requirements in both South Carolina and Mississippi. Furthermore, after 1906 when the grandfather clause expired, every male who came of age— white or black—would be faced with the " reasonable explanation" test. The expiration of the grandfather clause, a standard device of Southern disfranchising schemes, was a measure for ensuring constitutionality, but after its expiration all potential voters had to submit themselves to the understanding test and the discretion of the registrars—a frightening prospect for many segments of the white population.

Still another problem plagued disfranchisement advocates in Maryland. Most Southern states set the effective date of their grandfather clause prior to 1867 in order to antedate the first Reconstruction Act and eliminate all Negroes from qualifying. If, however, Maryland did this, she would run afoul of her own restrictive Constitution of 1864, with its loyalty oaths and registry provisions, which had effectively disfranchised many whites and had been in effect until 1867. On the other hand, by making 1869 the effective date the Poe amendment actually conferred easy voting rights through its grandfather clause on a certain number of Negroes. Charles J. Bonaparte, a foremost opponent of the amendment, explained:

44. See Poe's address at the Lyric Theatre, Baltimore (*Baltimore Sun*, October 25, 1905).

45. U.S. Bureau of the Census, *Twelfth Census of the United States: 1900. Population*, 1: 984. There were 35,783 literate and 24,425 illiterate Negro males of voting age in Maryland at that time.

On January 1, 1869, the colored men of at least seven Southern states—North and South Carolina, Georgia, Florida, Alabama, Arkansas, and Louisiana—were entitled to vote, and voted in fact, although those in Maryland did not. The Poe Amendment, in truth, gives on its face Negroes not born in Maryland, or the great majority of them, a privileged position with respect not only to our own colored citizens, but to foreign-born white men as well.[46]

The number of Negroes who might have qualified under the grandfather clause was insignificant inasmuch as the bulk of Negro migration into Maryland was from Virginia, but the point raised by Bonaparte greatly embarrassed amendment supporters.[47]

For all its technicalities, its harshness, even its irony, the Poe amendment was a carefully drafted instrument; of the three disfranchising schemes presented in Maryland, it came closest to fulfilling contemporary requirements for ultimate constitutionality, and therein lay its greatest danger.

The Poe amendment generated intense controversy in Maryland from the time of its proposal. Republicans saw it as the gravest sort of threat to their institutional existence, and to a man they opposed its passage in the 1904 legislature. Republican legislative ranks were so diminished, however, that their opposition was not an effective obstacle to passage so long as the Democrats maintained party discipline. Astutely, the Democratic high command pressed for early legislative action and strove to deliver the necessary three-fifths majority before the normal, inevitable stress of a legislative session took its toll of party unity. The strategy worked and the amendment cleared both houses on a strict party-division vote by March 10, perhaps setting a record for quick passage of a major piece of legislation.[48]

Legislative approval came none too soon. Only one week later, discord within the Democratic party assumed major proportions and threatened to nullify all the careful planning of the party's old guard. Governor Edwin Warfield, backed by his attorney

46. Speech delivered at Salisbury, Md. (*Baltimore Sun*, October 26, 1905).
47. U.S. Bureau of the Census, *Twelfth Census of the United States: 1900. Population*, 1: 702–5.
48. The vote in the senate was seventeen Democrats for and seven Republicans against the amendment; in the house the vote was sixty-four Democrats for and twenty-seven Republicans opposed (*Senate Journal*, 1904, p. 499, and *House Journal*, 1904, pp. 821–30).

general, William S. Bryan, suddenly announced that he was not pleased with the amendment's understanding test and he indicated that he might not sign the measure.[49] This development thoroughly alarmed the old guard—if the governor vetoed the amendment it would have to be repassed later in the session by another three-fifths majority, when party discipline might be impossible to maintain. Constitutional amendments, along with ordinary bills, were routinely sent to the governor for his signature, but the constitution did not actually specify this procedure for amendments. Constitutionally, therefore, it was unclear whether a governor could veto a proposed amendment which already had three-fifths of the legislature behind it, or whether it was necessary even to send such an amendment to him. In this no-man's-land of constitutional ambiguity the legislature took one position and the governor another. On March 25 the Maryland senate resolved to bypass the governor and directed its secretary to deliver the amendment directly to the clerk of the Court of Appeals, who would have charge of putting it on the ballot in the next general election. Governor Warfield then sent a special message to the senate, advising it that its action was illegal—that the amendment could not lawfully be submitted to the people until after it had been approved by him or repassed over his veto—and that in its present form the amendment did not have his approval. He counseled the legislature to use the few remaining days of the session to pass an amendment more to his liking. The governor's message was referred, unread, to the senate's committee on constitutional amendments, which rejected it as constitutionally unsound, and the legality of the legislature's action was later upheld by the Maryland Court of Appeals.[50]

The key to this constitutional tug-of-war lay not in any real disagreement over Negro disfranchisement but in an eruption of the intraparty strife that had always beset the heterogeneous Democratic party of Maryland. The 1904 session of the legislature, while busily engaged in the " purification " of the white man's political and social order, also was faced with rescuing one of the state's largest industries.[51] Maryland's oyster industry was

49. *Baltimore Sun*, March 17, 1904.

50. *Senate Journal*, 1904, pp. 991–97, 1634–38, and Warfield *v.* Vandiver, 101 Md. Reports 78 (1905).

51. Besides the Poe amendment and the Wilson ballot law, the 1904 legislature passed two Jim Crow laws and four other bills that discriminated against Negro voters in local elections; see pp. 133–34 and 137 below.

in a state of deep depression: natural beds were depleted, there was little or no artificial culture, tongmen and dredgers barely showed a profit, and wholesalers and packers were unable to fill orders. Clearly, a system of artificial culture was essential for replenishing the beds and enabling the industry to maintain its competitive position with neighboring states. Baltimore packers were eager to plant oysters, but they needed legislation to ensure them the exclusive right to harvest their crops. Traditionally and legally, the waters and beds of Chesapeake Bay had always been regarded as the common property of all the people of the state, and a citizen could fish them anywhere upon payment of a small state license fee.[52] When the 1904 legislature attempted to lease parts of the bay to large corporations, thousands of independent oystermen and small farmers who supplemented their incomes with oyster fishing bitterly opposed this action. The lease system would require substantial investments of capital, which the small operators did not have, and they viewed the plan as an invitation to packers to set up their own source of supply, bypassing the independent fishermen and restricting them to the depleted natural beds. Packers and wholesalers were equally concerned that a system of artificial culture be devised to shore up the sagging industry. Vital economic interests were involved on both sides.[53]

The Haman oyster bill split the Democratic party down the middle, in a neat geographical fissure that divided western and middle Maryland counties, which favored the leasing plan, from the Eastern Shore and southern Maryland counties on Chesapeake Bay, which strongly opposed the plan.[54] Maryland Negroes then found that their political rights had been cast onto the weighing scales with the Maryland oyster. Business interests of the state threatened that if they could not have their way on the oyster legislation they would withhold their support from the plan to disfranchise the Negro. The *Baltimore Sun*, editorializing on " The Negro Versus the Oyster," conveyed the message plainly:

> The members of the Senate are beginning to realize that if they persist in their efforts to kill the Haman bill or render it absolutely ineffective by amendment, they will destroy any chance they may have of obtaining the sanction

52. William K. Brooks, *The Oyster* (Baltimore, 1905), pp. 140–75.
53. *Baltimore Sun*, March 21, 1904.
54. *Ibid.*, April 6, 1904.

of the people to the constitutional amendment which is designed to place the Democratic party securely in power.

The belief is universal among thinking men here that the people of Maryland will not agree to place practically unlimited power in the hands of a party which has shown itself so lost to the commercial interests and future prosperity of the State as to put petty political interests ahead of the material welfare of the whole people of the State. It is being said on all sides that the mass of the people would much prefer to continue to bear with the evil of the negro in politics than to place the welfare of the State in the hands of a party which shows absolutely no regard for the interests of the people.

The independent element of the Democratic party is already beginning to argue that the presence of the negroes in politics is at most a questionable evil, as they are said to keep the democratic leaders in check by making their hold insecure and conditional on the fulfillment of their duty to the people. . . .

In addition, it is being pointed out that the Eastern Shore and Southern Maryland, the sections of the State which feel most the effects of the negro votes, are the sections from which come most of the opposition to the Haman bill. . . . The western and middle counties are not at all overrun with the negroes, and they are content to let things go along as they are. If Southern and Eastern Maryland want to keep the negro in politics and on top in politics they have gone about it in exactly the right way.[55]

Material interests were again taking precedence over ideology in Maryland, but the very phrasing of the issue in such terms, although a monumental indignity to the Negro, was beneficial by displaying the skeleton of power politics for all to see. It was difficult for the Democratic party to maintain the purity of either a racist or reformist attitude toward disfranchisement after such a blatant political horse trade. The Haman oyster bill passed the legislature but it was so crippled by amendments that the governor, on the advice of its author, vetoed it as completely unworkable.[56] The loss of this leasing plan was a bitter pill

55. March 18, 1904.
56. *Baltimore Sun*, April 13, 1904.

for the commercial interests to swallow, and the bitterness engendered in the conflict cast a pall over the Democratic party's plans to disfranchise the Negro.

The referendum on the Poe amendment in 1905 created more excitement in Maryland than any other political issue since Reconstruction days. The issue dominated the conventions and the platforms of both parties, and even the election of state officials. " By common consent," the Democratic platform declared, " the only issue in this campaign is whether negro suffrage, put upon us against our will by force, shall be restricted and its power for evil destroyed." [57] Approval of the amendment meant so much to Democratic leader Arthur Gorman that, in a bid for support from independents who had long chafed at his tight control of the party, he promised to retire from politics if it won approval.[58] Each party set up special campaign committees to sponsor rallies in every part of the state, and both parties expressed willingness to sacrifice their entire ticket for a satisfactory outcome on the amendment. Democrats tried to compel all candidates and ward executives to declare for the amendment, threatening to deprive them of party funds and support if they did not.[59]

Anti-amendment activity was not confined to the Republican party—a host of special organizations entered the fray. Negroes organized the Maryland Suffrage League to fight the amendment. Concentrating on the Negro community, the Suffrage League worked through ministers, business and professional leaders, and lodge and secret-society leaders to instruct Negro voters to mark their ballots correctly.[60] In September, 1905, Harry Cummings reported to Booker T. Washington: " Our Suffrage League is down to good, hard, and earnest work and we shall endeavor to reach every one of the 53,000 colored voters of the State and not only explain to them the seriousness of the situation, but instruct them how to vote against the proposed Amendment." [61] Inde-

57. *Ibid.*, September 29, 1905.
58. Lambert, *Arthur Pue Gorman*, p. 351.
59. *Baltimore Sun*, October 5, 10, 1905.
60. *Baltimore Afro-American Ledger*, September 23, 1905.
61. Harry Cummings to Booker T. Washington, September 21, 1905, in The Booker T. Washington Papers, Library of Congress, Washington, D.C., box 2. Washington worked quietly and behind the scenes to encourage Maryland's Negro leaders in their fight against disfranchisement, arranging small monetary contributions from out of state to help them defeat the Poe and Straus amendments. Also see Washington to Cummings, November 3, 1905; Washington to Hugh M.

pendent Democrats formed their own organization, the Democratic Anti-Poe Amendment Committee, which concentrated on publicizing the defections of prominent Democrats.[62] The Maryland League of Foreign-Born Citizens was formed late in the campaign to coordinate the work of various nationality groups who were fighting the amendment. At its organizational meeting at least nine ethnic groups were represented: Germans, Poles, Bohemians, Croats, Lithuanians, Italians, Hungarians, Syrians, and Armenians.[63] The Baltimore Reform League, long a center for electoral and civil service reform, also played an active role in opposing the amendment.[64]

One of the most prominent Republican leaders in the amendment fight was Charles J. Bonaparte, who had just been appointed Secretary of the Navy by President Theodore Roosevelt. A man of aristocratic lineage and considerable wealth, Bonaparte had been a founder of the National Civil Service Reform League in the 1880s and its chairman from 1901 to 1905. Although a longtime foe of the Gorman-Rasin machine, Bonaparte was not considered a party regular by Maryland Republicans, and his elevation to cabinet rank, with the power and prestige it entailed, was widely resented.[65] Nevertheless, his position gave him control over the Republican party of Maryland, and his discharge of this responsibility in the amendment fight proved him a leader of great capacity; he mapped the strategy of the anti-amendment forces and carried the brunt of the speaking engagements. For three months before the referendum, scarcely a week passed without at least one major address by Bonaparte in some part of the state. His basic strategy was to keep Republican regulars and the Negro wing of the party in the background and to depend on Democratic disunity to defeat the amendment. Eager to give Democratic dissidents and independents as much free rein as possible, he strived to give the anti-amendment campaign a nonpartisan aura.[66]

Browne, secretary of The Committee of Twelve, July 13, 1909; Hugh M. Browne to Washington, September 20, 1909, in The Booker T. Washington Papers, boxes 2, 43.

62. *Baltimore Sun*, October 6, 13, 27, 1905.

63. *Ibid.*, October 15, 1905.

64. Eric Goldman, *Charles Jerome Bonaparte, Patrician Reformer: His Earlier Career* (Baltimore, 1943), p. 27.

65. *Ibid.*, pp. 9, 24, 81.

66. Jane L. Phelps, "Charles J. Bonaparte and Negro Suffrage in Maryland," *Maryland Historical Magazine*, 54 (December, 1959): 342–43.

The campaign reflected Bonaparte's strategy. Opponents attacked the amendment not so much for its disfranchisement of Negroes as for its possible effects on white voters. Very few foes of the amendment spoke out on the obvious injustice it would work on the Negro citizens; instead they focused on the registration perils for the foreign-born white citizens and on the danger the amendment presented to the two-party system. The two-party argument was directed especially to independent Democrats, along with forecasts that " Gormanism " and " ring rule " would fasten upon the state if the amendment were adopted. Republicans even considered a platform statement opposing Negro officeholding, but Bonaparte quashed the plan as too disruptive of Republican unity. But the platform deliberately kept the Negro at arm's length: " The Republican party of the State of Maryland favors no social equality among the races; favors no negro domination over the white people here or elsewhere, and can be depended upon to guard against the establishment of either. . . ." [67]

The odds against the Democrats increased as the weeks went by; they lacked a leader who could galvanize the pro-amendment forces as Bonaparte was doing for their opposition. Both the titular head of the Democratic party, Governor Warfield, and its ranking legal officer, Attorney General William S. Bryan, had joined the opposition. Logically, Senator Gorman, the prime mover behind the proposed amendment, should have assumed the role of public advocate, but the old charges of ring rule raised by the opposition forced the senior senator to remain in the background. The junior senator from Maryland, Isidor Rayner, had proved himself a master of racial invective in the Democrats' 1903 campaign, but, as the son of an immigrant German-Jew, he was under heavy pressure to oppose the amendment from both Jewish and ethnic groups. [68] Rayner, late in the campaign, announced his opposition to the amendment and flamboyantly challenged Gorman to a public debate on the proposal. Gorman ignored

67. *Baltimore Sun*, September 6, 7, 1905. Bonaparte also opposed this final statement but was overruled by other party leaders; see Charles J. Bonaparte to the Reverend George F. Bragg, Jr., September 26, 1905, and Bonaparte to John B. Hanna, September 14, 1905, in The Charles J. Bonaparte Papers, Library of Congress, Washington, D.C., box 162.

68. See esp. Rayner's addresses in Westminster and Baltimore in the 1903 campaign, in the *Baltimore Sun* (October 18, 22, 1903); also see Lambert, *Arthur Pue Gorman*, p. 354.

the challenge but the campaign ended as it had begun—with top Democratic leaders quarreling bitterly among themselves over their party's plan to disfranchise the Negro.[69]

The Poe amendment was defeated at the polls by a vote of 104,286 to 70,227.[70] Opponents of the amendment carried eighteen of the state's twenty-three counties, and carried Baltimore City almost two-to-one. It was a crushing defeat for the old guard, cutting down scores of Democratic candidates with the amendment. The newly elected House of Delegates faced a precarious party division: fifty-one Democrats, forty-seven Republicans, and three independents.

Bitterly, the Democrats analyzed their failure. Gorman was convinced he had been betrayed and sabotaged by Freeman Rasin in Baltimore—that the city machine had deliberately held back.[71] This assessment would have had more validity if Gorman had come close to carrying the rest of the state, but he had not. Rasin, who denied that he had not fought for the measure, gave a more realistic analysis of the defeat.

> The organization in the city supported the amendment as a party measure and did all that could be done for it, but the whole foreign vote was arrayed against it, the Republican party was solid, and the Democratic party was split. . . . We had practically no money at all in the city and it was an uphill fight all the time.[72]

In the years immediately following defeat of the Poe amendment the Democratic party underwent considerable change. The death of Senator Gorman in 1906, followed by that of Freeman Rasin in 1907, left the party without the clear lines of authority that had directed it for the past three decades.[73] As there was no one to step into the void left behind by the two organizational strongmen, the party experienced both the pleasures and the perils of internal democratization. With the bosses dead and many independents back in the fold, the party's program began to

69. *Baltimore Sun*, October 18, 20, 1905; Lambert, *Arthur Pue Gorman*, pp. 354–59.

70. *Maryland Manual*, 1905, p. 306.

71. Lambert, *Arthur Pue Gorman*, p. 360.

72. *Baltimore Sun*, November 8, 1905.

73. John R. Lambert, "Reconstruction to World War I," in *The Old Line State: A History of Maryland*, 3 vols., ed. Morris L. Radoff (Baltimore, 1956), 1: 122.

reflect new influences.[74] Reform became a key word in the Democratic vocabulary and party debate turned to the concerns of progressivism: direct primaries, a corrupt-practices act, a good roads policy, and direct election of United States senators.[75]

The Democrats' racism, however, remained constant amid all the change, and far from discouraged by the Poe amendment's decisive rejection, the new generation of Democrats determined to offer a new and improved disfranchising plan. Meeting in state convention in 1907, only two years after the Poe debacle, Democrats proclaimed their party " steadfast in its determination to eliminate the illiterate negro voter " and promised to submit another constitutional amendment for that purpose at the earliest possible time. They pledged that the new amendment would overcome the objections raised by the Poe plan and would fully protect the vote of all white citizens. After an encouraging victory in the gubernatorial race of 1907, Democrats unveiled their new plan, drafted by a committee of prominent lawyers that was headed by the newly elected attorney-general, Isaac Lobe Straus.[76] In keeping with the party's new mode of collective leadership, the entire drafting procedure was self-consciously democratic; there was careful consultation between all party leaders and reconciliation of all shades of opinion. The result was an almost incredible hodgepodge of provisions—surely the most lengthy and complex disfranchising plan ever seriously considered in the United States.

The Straus amendment—named for the attorney-general who supervised its drafting—designated six classes of persons who might vote in future elections in Maryland. The first four classes, which were conferred immediate voting rights, were designed to enfranchise all white males: (1) any person entitled to vote in or prior to January, 1869; (2) any male descendant of such person; (3) any foreign-born citizen naturalized between January 1, 1869, and the date of the amendment's adoption; and (4) any male descendant of such person. A person who qualified under any of these four categories and fulfilled residence and age requirements merely had to make a sworn personal affadavit to this effect, which registrars had to accept as *prima facie* evidence

74. *Baltimore Sun*, November 4, 1907.
75. See the Democratic platforms of 1907 and 1911, in the *Baltimore Sun*, August 9, 1907, and September 8, 1911.
76. *Baltimore Sun*, August 9, 1907, and January 30, 1908.

of qualification. The last two classes of the amendment were designed as categories under which Negroes would have to qualify in order to vote. According to the amendment, voting rights also would be extended to:

(5) a person who, in the presence of the officers of registration, shall in his own handwriting, with pen and ink, without any aid, suggestion or memorandum whatsoever and without any question or direction addressed to him by any of the officers of registration, make application to register correctly, stating in such application his name, age, date and place of birth, residence and occupation, at the time and for the two years next preceding, the name or names of his employer or employers, and whether he has previously voted, and if so, the State, county or city and district or precinct in which he voted last, and also the name in full of the President of the United States, of one of the Justices of the Supreme Court of the United States, of the Governor of Maryland, of one of the Judges of the Court of Appeals of Maryland and of the Mayor of Baltimore City, if the applicant resides in Baltimore City, or of one of the County Commissioners of the county in which the applicant resides; or

(6) a person, or the husband of a person, who owned and was assessed on the tax books for $500.00 of real or personal property, and had owned, paid taxes on, and had tax receipts for this property for the preceding two years.[77]

Aside from the all-but-impossible test it imposed on the majority of Negro applicants, the most notable feature of the Straus amendment was the absence of an expiration date for its "grandfather clause" and the companion naturalization clause. All previous disfranchising schemes that used a grandfather clause had specified expiration dates to ensure their constitutionality. The devious legal reasoning behind this technicality was that by the time the federal courts heard cases challenging the plan, the discriminatory grandfather clause would have expired, leaving the remaining provisions operative for whites and blacks alike. Straus defended the omission of a time limit, saying that the white people of Maryland would never approve a plan that subjected their children to either an educational or a property qualifi-

77. *Laws of Maryland*, 1908, chap. 26, pp. 300–304.

cation for voting. This omission cast considerable doubt on the constitutionality of the plan, according to Arthur P. Gorman, Jr., son of the late senator and himself a state senator from Howard County. Young Gorman, who made a valiant effort to persuade the party to include an expiration date, was outvoted in party caucus and acquiesed to the majority viewpoint.[78] Gorman's initial judgment was vindicated in 1915, however, when the United States Supreme Court struck down an Oklahoma grandfather clause that contained no time limit.[79] In their anxiety to secure its popular approval, the framers of the Straus amendment sacrificed the prime requisite of any such plan: compatibility with the United States Constitution and fundamental legality. All doubts, however, were buried in the massive campaign to sell the new plan to the voters. The Straus amendment cleared the heavily Democratic legislature easily in 1908, on a strict party-division vote, and went on the ballot for popular approval in the general election of 1909.[80]

In many ways the Straus amendment campaign was similar to the campaign for the Poe amendment four years before. Many of the same individuals and organizations took up their old positions for the new battle. The Democratic party again formed a special committee to campaign for amendment and assigned its passage high priority, overshadowing the contests for state comptroller and the legislature. Republicans were united in their opposition and gave defeat of the amendment their top priority. The League of Foreign-Born Voters again stepped forward to coordinate the opposition of the ethnic groups.[81] The Negro Suffrage League, after a slow start, again assumed major leadership in the Negro's fight.[82]

There were, however, important dissimilarities in the two campaigns, the most significant difference being the much stronger position of the latter-day Democratic party. This time no important Democrats defected, and such men as Senator Rayner, ex-Governor Warfield, and former Attorney General Bryan— who had opposed the Poe amendment—supported and campaigned

78. *Baltimore Sun*, February 3, 7, 1908.
79. Gwinn *v.* U. S., 238 U.S. 347.
80. The vote was 68 to 24 in the house and 18 to 9 in the senate (*House Journal*, 1908, p. 410, and *Senate Journal*, 1908, p. 361).
81. *Baltimore Sun*, September 12, 1909.
82. *Baltimore Afro-American Ledger*, October 26, 1909.

for the Straus plan.[83] Rayner took a very active role and, together with Isaac Lobe Straus, shouldered the major portion of the public campaign. Maryland Negroes were acutely conscious of the Jewish background of both Rayner and Straus; Straus had been dubbed " the Persecuting Attorney of the Colored Race " by the *Baltimore Afro-American Ledger*, which marveled at the race prejudice displayed by the Baltimore Jews and Irish.[84] Another important change was the Democrats' effort to wrap disfranchisement in the mantle of reform. In the Poe campaign there had been little attempt to justify disfranchisement of the Negro for it hardly occurred to anyone that justification was necessary; in the Straus campaign, however, there was a definite change of emphasis. Governor Austin Crothers, speaking for the amendment, made it a vital part of the Democratic program of reform— as desirable as primary election regulation, corrupt-practices legislation, and the road improvement program. Democrats spoke of Negro disfranchisement as " purification " and " elevation " of the electorate and the political process. The earlier idea was dismissed, that all Negroes would be disfranchised merely because they were Negroes—the Democratic party now contended that the Straus amendment would disfranchise only those Negroes who were " illiterate and thriftless." [85] Some, indeed, even argued that adoption of the amendment would be a positive blessing to the Negro community. In the words of Edwin Warfield, the former governor, passage of the amendment " would be the best thing that could happen " to Negroes. " It would help make them frugal and industrious and eager for an education so that they might exercise the highest privilege of an American citizen— that of participating in elections." [86]

Higher, more lofty grounds also were sought by some opponents of disfranchisement who based their case, at least in part, on the Negro's right to continued political participation. Although the major emphasis of the amendment's opponents continued to be its liabilities for whites, several significant attempts to defend the Negro's rights were made in the Straus campaign. James Cardinal Gibbons, the Catholic archbishop of Baltimore, con-

83. *Baltimore Sun*, September 15, 17, 28, 1909; *Baltimore American*, November 4, 1909.
84. Editorials of November 2 and December 7, 1907.
85. *Baltimore Sun*, September 15, 16, 23, 1909.
86. *Ibid.*, September 15, 1909.

demned the proposed disfranchisement as unjust.[87] President
William Howard Taft spoke out against the attempt " to impose
educational and other qualifications for the suffrage upon negroes
and to exempt everybody else from such qualifications "; he
called it a " gross injustice " and " a violation of the spirit of
the Fifteenth Amendment." [88] Charles R. Schirm, president of
the Maryland League of Republican Clubs, defended the Negro's
right to vote and boasted that the Republican party had always
favored " putting all men on an equal footing in regard to the
right of suffrage." [89]

Although the Democratic party came closer to selling disfranchisement to the people of Maryland in 1909 than it had
before or would again, the statewide vote was 89,808 for the
amendment and 106,069 against. Nine counties, all on the Eastern
Shore and in southern Maryland, supported the amendment, while
fourteen counties and Baltimore City opposed it.[90]

Defeat of the Straus amendment reflected, at least in part,
the distrust of disfranchisement by the large number of naturalized
and foreign-parentage citizens of Maryland. Naturalized citizens
of Baltimore and western Maryland could not forget the implica-
tions of the earlier Poe amendment and never quite understood
the difference between the two proposals. The Straus amendment
was not a threat to naturalized citizens, and the Democrats
worked diligently to convince them of this fact, but the very com-
plexity of the amendment bred suspicion. Republicans, of course,
took full advantage of the confusion and fears, and also garnered
support with the argument that the Straus plan would undermine
the two-party system. Voters in western Maryland and Baltimore
had no pressing interest in Negro disfranchisement and, in opposing the Straus amendment, indicated their unwillingness to
risk their own political rights and advantages for an end in
which they had little concern.

Although the Democrats had twice been rebuffed at the polls
and common sense would seem to dictate a decent burial of the
issue, the Democratic party had fallen victim to its own political
plot. Too many members of the party had come to believe its

87. *Ibid.*, January 25, 1908.
88. *Baltimore News*, Letter to the Editor, September 15, 1909.
89. *Baltimore American*, September 15, 1909.
90. *Sun Almanac*, 1910, pp. 131–56.

propaganda, and what had begun as a practical measure for enhancing the position and power of the party became an ideological trap. " A QUESTION IS NEVER SETTLED UNTIL IT IS SETTLED RIGHT! " the *Baltimore Sun* declared only a few days after the defeat of the Straus amendment.[91] The Democratic governor, Austin Crothers, immediately announced that he would ask the legislature to frame yet another disfranchising plan: " Those who favored the adoption of the amendment are only too anxious to re-enlist in the old war. They will never give up the fight until the proposition is adopted and made a part of the organic law of the State." [92]

Responsibility for drawing up the third and last disfranchisement plan of the diehards fell, suitably enough, to two Democrats from the heavily Negro and longtime Republican stronghold of Charles County. William J. Frere, the first Democratic state senator from Charles County since 1894, and Walter M. Digges, who owed his place in the House of Delegates to a narrow victory over the son of Congressman Sidney Mudd, were co-sponsors of what came to be known as the Digges amendment.[93] The Digges amendment conferred voting privileges on all the state's white male citizens of legal age and residence but required that all other male citizens—that is, Negroes—must have owned and paid taxes on at least $500 worth of real or personal property for at least two years prior to their application to register.[94] The amendment would be submitted to the people in the general election of 1911.

The legislature, which approved the amendment, also passed a series of bills that ordered an all-white statewide registration of voters and that excluded all others from participation in the general election of 1911. These bills would have excluded Negroes from voting even before the Digges amendment could be submitted and ratified.[95] This scheme, from a purely legal standpoint, was wild and incredible, and elicited nationwide rebuke. The *Nation* reported that Southern leaders were greatly alarmed at such a direct challenge to the Fifteenth Amendment, fearing its ultimate effect on their own carefully drawn evasions of the Constitution.[96] Governor Crothers at first defended the

91. Editorial of November 5, 1909.
92. *Baltimore Sun*, November 6, 1909.
93. *Ibid.*, April 3, 1910.
94. *Laws of Maryland*, 1910, chap. 253, pp. 446–48
95. *Baltimore Sun*, April 7, 1910.
96. April 7, 1910.

scheme as an "orderly and legal method of testing the Fifteenth Amendment," but rising resentment in Maryland forced him to veto the legislation for a new registration of voters before the 1911 election.[97] Thus the Digges amendment, which Crothers signed, was submitted to an unrestricted electorate in the fall of 1911.

The amendment fared badly from the start; its patent unconstitutionality gave Republicans an easy case against it and a good election issue. Democrats, at first enthusiastic, began to balk. As the gubernatorial campaign of 1911 introduced other problems, the state Democratic convention tacitly agreed that the amendment would not be pushed. The party's full effort was needed to elect the state ticket, headed by gubernatorial candidate Arthur P. Gorman, Jr., who had been nominated in a close and bitter primary battle, and now faced strong opposition from Republican Phillips Lee Goldsborough.[98] Democrats found they could not afford to subordinate the practical concerns of the ticket to their ideological predilections, as they had done before.

In the end, both the ticket and the amendment were lost; the Digges plan was overwhelmingly defeated in city and state. The final tally showed only 46,220 votes for the amendment and 83,920 against it.[99] Gorman was defeated by only some 3,000 votes, but it was fitting that the son of the man who had fathered Maryland's disfranchisement scheme should go down to defeat with the remnants of that plan.[100]

The election of 1911 gave Maryland its second Republican governor in four decades, and his ascent to power in 1912 marked the end of the disfranchisement era. The political liability of the issue had finally been recognized by the Democrats, and a Republican governor at the helm of state for the next four years made the futility of continued agitation clearly apparent.

Goldsborough, the newly elected Republican governor, said that the first concern of his administration was the right of the people "to express their will at the polls in the easiest manner possible," that "voting should be made easy, and not difficult" for all.[101] He pledged to do everything in his power to remove

97. *Baltimore Sun*, April 5, 9, 1910.
98. *Ibid.*, September 7, 1911.
99. *Sun Almanac*, 1912, p. 134.
100. *Maryland Manual*, 1912, p. 229.
101. *Baltimore Sun*, November 9, 1911.

the discriminatory Wilson ballot law from Maryland's statute books. Handicapped by a Democratic legislature throughout his term of office, Goldsborough was not wholly successful in redeeming his pledge, but in 1914 the number of counties that operated under the Wilson law was reduced from eleven to five. In 1918 the law was repealed and Marylanders again voted under uniform and nondiscriminatory election regulations.[102]

By-Products of the Disfranchisement Movement

Although disfranchisement failed in its major purpose in Maryland the movement took its toll in discriminatory legislation against the Negro. The most important by-product of the movement was the Jim Crow laws that segregated public transportation in the state. Less significant but nonetheless effective for a time, a series of local laws eliminated or curtailed Negro participation in the municipal elections of several Maryland towns.

Jim Crow legislation, first considered in Maryland in 1902, was initiated by Democratic delegates from southern Maryland and the Eastern Shore. Two bills, which required racial segregation on railroads and steamships, were introduced in the General Assembly and received a favorable report from the committee on corporations. Lobbying activity against the bills was intense, however, particularly by railroad and steamship companies, which feared the expense and responsibility of enforcing such regulations.[103] After four Democrats joined the Republican opponents, the house voted forty-five to forty-one to reject the report of its committee and killed the Jim Crow proposals. Later in the session segregationists attempted to pass a Jim Crow bill that applied only to railroads operating on the Eastern Shore, but this too was voted down, with still greater Democratic defection.[104]

The statewide election of 1903 and its substantial legislative majority for the Democratic party gave segregationists the opportunity they had been waiting for. Racist fervor had been at its peak during the campaign, and the following session of the General Assembly placed more discriminatory laws on the books of Maryland than any previous or subsequent legislature. Along

102. *Laws of Maryland*, 1914, chap. 307, p. 458, and 1918, chap. 51, p. 76.
103. *Baltimore Sun*, January 31, 1902.
104. *House Journal*, 1902, pp. 540–41, 1451–56. The vote was 58 against and 23 for the second proposal. There were 43 Republican members of the house at this time.

with the Wilson ballot law, the Poe amendment, and numerous local disfranchising laws, the General Assembly of 1904 enacted two Jim Crow laws imposing segregation of the races on all railroads and steamships in the state. The first law required all railroads to provide separate cars or compartments on all steam-operated passenger trains and to segregate the races within these facilities. It established fines for noncompliance by railroads and on the part of their conductors, and fines and prison terms for passengers who refused to comply. Parlor and sleeping cars and express trains that did not stop in Maryland were exempt. The steamship law required separate accommodations for white and colored in the sleeping and dining compartments and in the seating arrangements.[105] Except for one Republican in the house and one Democrat in the senate, the vote on both bills reflected party alignment: sixty-seven to twenty-five and sixteen to six. The laws were effective July 1, 1904.[106]

The first court test of the new legislation was a sharp setback for its framers. A Negro law professor at Howard University, W. H. Hart, traveling from Pennsylvania to the District of Columbia, refused to change to a segregated car in Maryland; he was promptly arrested and was fined by a Cecil County court.[107] Hart appealed, however, and the Maryland Court of Appeals ruled that the state statute was an unconstitutional infringement on interstate commerce and that only passengers whose journey began and ended in Maryland could be segregated under the state law.[108] Maryland was the first state to limit the operation of its Jim Crow legislation in this way.

For Maryland Negroes, Jim Crow laws were a new and startling development. Some scholars have suggested that racial segregation was taken for granted in the South after Reconstruction ended and that restrictive legislation merely formalized an existing pattern of race relations. Maryland's experience, however, seems to follow the more fluid pattern of race relations described by C. Vann Woodward in *The Strange Career of Jim Crow*.[109] Woodward pointed out the growth and intensification of segregation that followed the political upheavals of the 1890s, developments

---

105. *Laws of Maryland*, 1904, chap. 109, pp. 186–88, and chap. 110, pp. 188–89.
106. *House Journal*, 1904, pp. 577–79, and *Senate Journal*, 1904, pp. 690–91.
107. *Baltimore Afro-American Ledger*, March 25, 1905.
108. Hart *v.* State, 100 Md. Reports 595 (1905).
109. 2d rev. ed. (New York, 1966).

which ended a period of comparative permissiveness in race relations. Maryland Negroes in 1904 were frankly unfamiliar with segregated transportation, highly resentful of this change, and determined to fight back. John Murphy, editor of the *Baltimore Afro-American Ledger*, who returned from a tour of the South in 1903, felt called upon to explain to his readers what segregation in public transportation was like. With genuine amazement he described the " deplorable " conditions resulting from segregation. He spoke of the " humiliating " signs designating " Colored " and " White Only " facilities and the patent inequality in the accommodations furnished the two races. " Most of the cars in which I have ridden were scarcely fit for a dog to ride in. The stations are filthy. . . . Many of the cars are but boxes, and so crowded that it is impossible to get a seat." [110]

Maryland Negroes had lobbied actively against the Jim Crow legislation from the start. In 1902 a Negro delegation had appeared before the house committee on corporations with a petition signed by more than 1,000 white and Negro citizens who opposed the segregation proposals.[111] In 1904 the Negro Suffrage League, with chapters throughout the state, directed the opposition.[112] When their efforts failed and the bills were passed, Negro leaders called on their people to boycott the segregated facilities. Negro churches and social organizations, which often sponsored excursions on boats and trains during the summer months (an activity that combined fund-raising with pleasure), let it be known that excursions were out whenever Jim Crow facilities were required. Throughout the summer of 1904 the *Baltimore Afro-American Ledger*, backed by the Negro Suffrage League, crusaded against Negro rail and ship excursions.[113] The effectiveness of the boycott is impossible to assess, but many railroad and steamship companies took special advertisements in the *Ledger* to explain that they had opposed the laws from the start and complied with them only because they must.[114]

A Negro boycott which was quite effective was one which ended the personal services provided by Negroes for " Jim Crow "

110. *Baltimore Afro-American Ledger*, December 12, 1903, and January 16, 1904.
111. *Ibid.*, February 22, 1904.
112. *Ibid.*, January–March, 1904.
113. *Ibid.*, April–August, 1904. Scarcely an issue of this Negro weekly did not have either an editorial or a story on excursion boycott during this period.
114. *Baltimore Afro-American Ledger*, May 14, 1904.

Kerbin. A Democratic lawyer and a delegate from Worcester County, William G. Kerbin was sponsor of the segregation bills of 1904. Returning home from Annapolis after the 1904 session, Kerbin found that the Negroes of Worcester County had boycotted him altogether; "he could not get a negro woman to cook his meals . . . [nor] a negro to wash his clothes or iron his shirts or black his boots." Apparently the boycott lasted a long time and attracted attention throughout the state, humiliating and inconveniencing the once proud legislator.[115]

Additional Jim Crow legislation was passed in 1908. A new act, the passage of which indicated that the previous law had not been totally effective, required steamship companies to provide separate toilets and sleeping quarters for white and colored passengers under penalty of a fine of $50.00 a day for noncompliance. Another act required railroads operating in the heavily Negro counties of Prince George's, Charles, St. Mary's, Calvert, and Anne Arundel to provide separate cars rather than compartmented cars for the two races. Still another law instituted segregation on electric railways, but it was worded so as to exempt electric railways in Baltimore City, and in practice applied only to the Short Line between Baltimore and Annapolis and to the Washington, Baltimore and Annapolis Railway.[116]

The rise of racism associated with the disfranchisement movement led to a sharp increase in informal segregation of the races. Nowhere was this more apparent—or more resented by Negroes —than within the Republican party. Early in the century—at least until 1903—males of both races were free to take seats wherever they pleased at Republican rallies, although as a gesture to female spectators, there were galleries in the meeting halls of both parties that were "reserved for ladies." More and more often, however, Negroes tended to sit or to be seated together, and increasingly the whites monopolized the main floor and shunted the Negroes into the balconies. By 1907 the Republican party openly segregated its white and Negro members at public functions. "When the time comes that we have to be 'Jim Crowed' in a Republican meeting," the editor of the *Baltimore Afro-American Ledger* observed, "we are counted out entirely, and propose to stay out." In 1908, when Republicans held a rally in Baltimore

115. *Baltimore Sun*, October 25, 1907.
116. *Laws of Maryland*, 1908, chap. 617, p. 85, chap. 292, p. 86, and chap. 248, pp. 88-89; *Baltimore Sun*, March 31, 1908.

honoring Charles E. Hughes of New York, Negroes—including city councilman Harry S. Cummings—were directed to segregated galleries. Those who refused to comply were forced to leave by party functionaries.[117]

The *Afro-American* reported that a wave of segregation and segregationist sentiment was sweeping over other areas of city life. Whites began to complain about Negro attendance at the free concerts of the Peabody Institute. There was an attempt to segregate school teachers at lectures provided by the Baltimore school board. The absence of Negro hotels in Baltimore and the worsening exclusionist policies of the white hotels created a shortage of facilities for transient Negroes. The culmination of segregationist activity in Baltimore came in 1911 with the passage of a city ordinance decreeing residential separation of the races. Although areas that were already racially mixed were exempted, the ordinance prohibited the sale or occupancy of property in all-white or all-Negro city blocks to members of the other race.[118]

With the state's most liberal and cosmopolitan city caught up in the racist fever, other Maryland localities indulged in even more blatant discrimination. Impatient with the state's necessity to amend its constitution before barring Negroes from the polls and its failure to secure such amendment, several Maryland cities wrote disfranchising provisions into their city charters. Changes in a city's charter required only the approval of the General Assembly, which usually granted them without question when they had the backing of the local delegation. In 1904 the towns of Snow Hill, Crisfield, and Frederick secured charter amendments that restricted voting rights in their municipal elections, and in 1908 Annapolis, the capital city, followed this same route to Negro disfranchisement. Combining grandfather clauses with property qualifications, the charter amendments generally restricted the vote to males entitled to vote prior to 1868 and their male descendants or to persons who owned more than $500 worth of assessed property.[119] Enforcement of the disfranchising pro-

---

117. *Baltimore Sun*, October 15, 1903, November 2, 1905, October 11, 25, and November 2, 1907; *Baltimore Afro-American Ledger*, October 19, 1907, and October 3, 1908.

118. *Baltimore Afro-American Ledger*, March 7, 28, June 6, 1908, April 15, 1911.

119. *Laws of Maryland*, 1904, chap. 153, p. 263, chap. 335, pp. 585–95, chap. 564, p. 961, and 1908, chap. 525, pp. 347–48. The Annapolis provision also allowed all naturalized male citizens and their descendants to vote.

vision in Annapolis provoked the Maryland Republican party to action, after the *Afro-American* reported that only 100 of the 800 registered Negroes in the city could meet the new qualifications and that they stood to lose their only Negro representative in the city council.[120]

With former United States Attorney General Charles J. Bonaparte as counsel, a group of Annapolis Negroes who had been denied registration brought suit against the city registrars. The case was heard by the United States Circuit Court of Appeals in October, 1910, and Judge Thomas J. Morris delivered the first federal court decision invalidating a disfranchisement plan that was based on a grandfather clause. Morris ruled that the Annapolis plan, although not explicitly depriving persons of the right to vote because of race or color, disfranchised and discriminated against Negroes through its grandfather-clause exemption and therefore was unconstitutional as a violation of the Fifteenth Amendment.[121] Five years later this decision of the circuit court was upheld by the United States Supreme Court.[122] The Supreme Court handed down its Annapolis decision the same day that it invalidated Oklahoma's disfranchising scheme which also was based on a grandfather clause.[123] The Annapolis case was overshadowed by the Oklahoma decision, but the issue was the same in both cases, and in point of time the Annapolis case antedated the better-known Oklahoma case.

The Annapolis decision ended the only effective disfranchisement that Maryland Negroes experienced. The state's long and costly battle against Negro suffrage had excluded Negroes from local elections in only four towns and for approximately six years. In the courts of law, as earlier in the court of popular opinion, disfranchisement had failed in Maryland. The byproducts of the movement were bitter, and the total vote of Negroes and whites alike was down, but the effort to deny the Negro a significant part in the state's political life was not successful.

120. June 12, 1909.
121. Anderson *v.* Myers et al., 182 Federal Reporter 223 (1910).
122. Myers et al. *v.* Anderson, 238 U.S. 368 (1915).
123. Gwinn *v.* U.S., 238 U.S. 347 (1915).

CHAPTER 6

NEGRO POLITICAL PARTICIPATION

Assessment of the political participation of a minority group always is difficult, and the hazards are increased when this analysis attempts to study a period relatively remote from the present. Measures of reliability and the theoretical underpinnings of contemporary quantitative research are not available, and research involves a mass of data whose reliability can only be judged subjectively. Nevertheless, a large quantity of information relating to Negro political participation in Maryland is available and the opportunities for significant analysis seem to outweigh the hazards.

The basic political structure of Maryland and the rules that governed its electoral contests have been surveyed in the preceding chapters. Only against such a background can the credibility of the quantitative data that follows be assessed, and the findings are reassuring. The use of the Federal Enforcement Acts to protect Negro suffrage, the absence of a poll tax, the mixed effects of the ballot-law changes, and the failure of constitutional disfranchisement combined to produce a relatively open political environment in Maryland. Whites and Negroes alike could, if they desired, exercise their basic right to vote. Maryland's functioning two-party system and minority-party representation throughout the electoral process operated to check electoral corruption; therefore it is not unreasonable to assume that the votes cast received a generally honest count.[1] Such considerations are of prime importance for the period and the purpose of this study; the voting statistics of many states during this era are almost worthless

1. No case is made for the exact accuracy of the registration or election figures; given the nature of the registration and election processes of the day and the informal reporting of both, no such claim could reasonably be made. Nevertheless, the essential validity of the data in showing comparisons between groups, both racial and areal, and the trends within and between such groups appears sound. Tabular presentation of figures rounded off to the nearest decimal point convey a sense of accuracy that can be misleading, and the reader is forewarned that such is not the intent in this study nor is the data so interpreted.

because of legal and extralegal franchise restrictions and electoral manipulations.

The absence of such distortions in Maryland provides a unique opportunity for the observation of Negro political activity and the development of a Negro political tradition over a century of uninterrupted participation. Focusing on the formative years of this tradition—a period when exclusionist policies elsewhere usually have precluded any real inquiry into Negro political behavior—the present study reveals behavorial attributes that are both unexpected and instructive.

The most important finding of this inquiry is the high level of political involvement the society's lowest socioeconomic group exhibited. Despite the poverty, illiteracy, and social disorganization that characterized the Negro group at this time, despite psychological handicaps owing to their previous condition of servitude, and despite the open hostility of most of the white community, the initial response of Maryland Negroes to enfranchisement was enthusiastic and their participation in the electoral process was high.[2] This same initial response can be found in much of the South.[3] What is fully as important, however, is the durability of this enthusiasm which can be demonstrated only in states like Maryland which maintained equal racial access to the ballot box.[4] Negro registration and voting activity remained high,

2. See "The Negro Votes: The Election of 1870," in Chapter 1.

3. The highly positive response of Southern Negroes to enfranchisement has been described as "one of the most noteworthy accomplishments in the history of American politics" (Francis B. Simkins, *The South Old and New* [New York, 1949], p. 187). For specific references to the high initial level of Negro voter activity in various Southern states, see Vernon L. Wharton, *The Negro in Mississippi, 1865–1890* (Chapel Hill, 1947), p. 146; William A. Mabry, *The Negro in North Carolina Politics since Reconstruction* (Durham, N.C., 1940), p. 9; and Joel Williamson, *After Slavery: The Negro in South Carolina during Reconstruction, 1861–1877* (Chapel Hill, 1965), p. 343.

4. It should be noted that constitutional disfranchisement in the Southern states, a process that began in the 1890s, was preceded by an extensive period of "preliminary disfranchisement," originating in some states as early as the withdrawal of Union troops. Preliminary disfranchising techniques ranged from outright violence and intimidation to the more subtle devices of a poll tax and highly complex ballot procedures. Writing in 1894, prior to constitutional disfranchisement in all states except Mississippi, Stephen B. Weeks gave a useful survey of the restrictions on Negro suffrage during this preliminary period in "The History of Negro Suffrage in the South," *Political Science Quarterly*, 9 (December, 1894): 671–703. More recent discussions of some of these restrictive techniques can be found in George B. Tindall, *South Carolina Negroes, 1877–1900* (Columbia, S.C., 1952); Charles E. Wynes, *Race Relations in Virginia, 1870–1902* (Charlottesville, 1961); and Allen J. Going, *Bourbon Democracy in Alabama, 1874–1890* (Montgomery, 1951).

both in relation to that of whites and absolutely, for three decades after enfranchisement. Only after 1900 and the passage of two restrictive ballot laws were there important decreases in voter participation, and these decreases were almost as severe for whites as for Negroes.

Maryland's registration and election data also reveal a marked participation differential between the state's largely rural counties and its single urbanized area. Political participation in Baltimore City was consistently lower than in the counties, and, although this relationship held true for both whites and Negroes, registration data indicates that Negro participation was more adversely affected by urbanization than was white participation.

The low incidence of candidacy and officeholding by Maryland Negroes is in striking contrast to their high levels of voter participation. Independent Negro candidacies did not attract Negro support, and few Maryland Negroes offered themselves for elective office. Negro electoral success was confined to a handful of city council districts, usually predominantly Negro, and even in these districts success was highly dependent on party endorsement. The contrast is heightened by the fact that, while Maryland Negroes filled only a few low-level local offices, Negroes in Virginia were elected to every session of the state legislature from 1869 through 1890, Negroes in South Carolina were elected to every legislative session from 1868 through 1900, and Negroes in eight Southern states were elected to Congress at various times between 1870 and 1901.[5]

Voter Registration

Most Maryland counties kept unofficial counts of Negro registrants from the time of enfranchisement but not until 1882 did the General Assembly provide for a uniform registration that required the notation of "color."[6] Thereafter, until 1916, each county and Baltimore City gave a biennial report of the total Negro and white registered voters within their boundaries at the

5. Negroes held important state offices in other Southern states after Reconstruction, but the most complete state surveys of Negro office-holding are Luther P. Jackson, *Negro Office-Holders in Virginia, 1865–1895* (Norfolk, Va., 1945), and George B. Tindall, *South Carolina Negroes, 1877–1900*. Also see Samuel D. Smith, *The Negro in Congress, 1870–1901* (Chapel Hill, 1940).

6. *Laws of Maryland*, 1882, chap. 22, pp. 28 ff.

close of registration in even-number years.[7] Registration in Maryland, however, was for the most part not a periodic procedure but a cumulative process. From 1882 through 1912 there was no completely new registration of voters in Maryland counties, and from 1882 to 1892 there was none in Baltimore City. Registrars revised the lists annually and, assisted by party workers and interested citizens, attempted to strike the names of persons who had died or had moved from the various districts, but the nature

TABLE 11

PERCENTAGE OF ELIGIBLE WHITE AND NEGRO VOTERS REGISTERED IN BALTIMORE, THE COUNTIES, AND THE STATE, 1882–1912

Year	Baltimore City White	Negro			Maryland Counties White	Negro			State White	Negro		
1882...	79.7	69.9	(— 9.8)*		82.7	84.5	(+ 1.8)*		81.6	80.3	(— 1.3)*
1884...	89.1	78.5	(— 10.6)		97.8	97.2	(— 0.6)		94.3	91.6	(— 2.7)
1886...	90.7	62.1	(— 18.6)		100.6†	99.2	(— 1.4)		96.5	87.5	(— 9.0)
1888...	92.8	83.7	(— 9.1)		100.6†	102.9†	(+ 2.3)		97.3	96.7	(— 0.6)
1890...	83.4	68.5	(— 14.9)		98.4	98.8	(+ 0.4)		91.8	88.6	(— 3.2)
1892...	89.5	76.8	(— 12.7)		99.5	97.1	(— 2.4)		95.1	90.2	(— 4.9)
1894...	86.5	68.8	(— 17.7)		98.6	91.7	(— 6.9)		93.3	83.8	(— 9.5)
1896...	93.5	87.0	(— 6.5)		92.4	94.1	(+ 1.7)		92.9	91.6	(— 1.3)
1898...	85.7	85.8	(+ 0.1)		94.2	96.5	(+ 2.3)		90.4	92.7	(+ 2.3)
1900...	91.3	86.6	(— 4.7)		98.6	100.0	(+ 1.4)		95.4	95.1	(— 0.3)
1902...	75.1	70.0	(— 5.1)		92.0	94.0	(+ 2.0)		84.5	85.1	(+ 0.6)
1904...	88.8	76.2	(— 12.6)		91.4	91.9	(+ 0.5)		90.2	85.9	(— 4.3)
1906...	77.2	67.6	(— 9.6)		87.0	87.8	(+ 0.8)		82.7	79.9	(— 2.8)
1908...	83.7	67.8	(— 15.9)		89.2	87.5	(— 1.7)		86.8	79.6	(— 7.2)
1910...	75.2	61.5	(— 13.7)		87.9	86.3	(— 1.6)		82.5	76.1	(— 6.4)
1912...	74.0	55.4	(— 18.6)		91.6	86.8	(— 4.8)		83.7	73.2	(— 10.5)

* Point variation above or below white registration.
† The process of interpolating, or estimating, the eligible voting population between federal census years causes the percentage to rise above one hundred.

of the process made such attempts only partially successful. In Baltimore City this situation was changed in 1892, when biennial re-registration of all voters was required by law.[8] Table 11 compares Negro and white voter registration in Baltimore, the counties, and the state as a whole from 1882 through 1912.[9]

7. The *Sun Almanac* is the most convenient source for these registration figures; its volumes for 1883 through 1913 were utilized and were cross-checked with the *Maryland Manual*, an official publication of the office of the Maryland Secretary of State, for 1896 through 1913.
8. *Laws of Maryland*, 1892, chap. 368, pp. 513 ff.
9. The basic data from which these percentages were computed is presented in Appendix A.

Both white and Negro registration rates were remarkably high for the entire period. In part this resulted from the cumulative registration system that prevailed over most of the state and reflected the presence of a certain amount of " deadwood " in the lists; however, because neither the cumulative nor the periodic system seems to have operated with any racial bias, the somewhat inflationary tendency of the cumulative process was deemed unimportant for the comparative purposes of the present study.[10] The general decline after 1900 in registration rates for both races reflected a combination of factors. The increased mobility and urbanization of the population, a normal diminution of political involvement after an era of high political fervor, and the effects of the ballot laws of 1901 and 1904 contributed to the post-1900 drop. It should be noted, however, that the ballot laws did not change the registration procedure or requirements; their adverse effect on registration, by complicating the act of voting, was indirect and psychological.

For the state as a whole the rate of Negro registration lagged only slightly behind that of whites. The percentage of eligible Negroes who registered twice exceeded that of whites during the period, and in only five of sixteen years did Negro registration trail white registration by more than five percentage points.[11] Moreover, the lag in Negro registration was accounted for almost solely by the low Negro registration in Baltimore City, where the difference between Negro and white registration is striking: in nine out of sixteen years the difference exceeded ten percentage points and in only two years did it fall below five percentage points. In the counties, on the other hand, the rate of Negro registration usually exceeded that of whites; in nine out of sixteen years a larger percentage of eligible Negroes registered to vote than did whites.

10. In theory, a cumulative registration system is probably freer from racial bias than a periodic system, since the burden of periodic re-registration falls more heavily on lower socioeconomic groups, who have less time and fewer resources for political activity than do middle- and upper-income groups. The fact that most registration officials were white was an additional handicap to Negroes, an effect which increased with the number of times blacks had to confront these white officials. In practice, however, neither system appears to have imposed any racial disadvantage in Maryland. The lag in Negro registration in Baltimore, for example, was just as evident prior to 1892, under the cumulative system, as it was afterward, when periodic registration was required.

11. Negro registration rates exceeded those of whites in 1898 and 1902. In 1886, 1894, 1908, 1910, and 1912, however, Negro registration lagged appreciably behind white registration.

Lower registration rates are characteristic of a growing urban population; residence requirements diminish registration in a mobile population and political organization and manipulation of constituencies is more difficult. Thus the lower registration rates for both races in Baltimore City are easily explicable, but the striking differential between white and Negro registration within the city cannot be explained by such factors. Nor did the urbanization of the population, in this period in Maryland, operate with any particular racial bias. The eligible white and the eligible Negro voting populations of Baltimore City doubled in size from 1880 to 1910, but the city's whites consistently maintained a substantially higher voter registration rate.[12]

Low Negro registration in Baltimore probably reflected the weak condition of the local Republican organization. Both the quantitative and qualitative data point to such a conclusion. Throughout most of the period the city organization was considered the soft spot of the Republican party.[13] From 1896 through 1900, however—when the Republicans were in power on both the state and local levels and effective political organization became a practical necessity—Negro registration in Baltimore reached its highest level and came closest to achieving parity with that of whites. Further evidence that Negro registration was a function of local Republican organization and effort was the tendency of Baltimore's Negro registration to increase noticeably in presidential years. From 1882 through 1904 Negro registration rates rose in presidential election years and dropped back again in the off years.[14] This type of behavior fits the character of the city's Republican organization, which was dominated by federal patronage-holders and -seekers who were primarily interested in a good showing on the national level. This pattern is not found in Negro registration in the counties.

On the basis of registration activity, Maryland Negroes must be classified as active political participants. Encountering no legal obstacles to registration and supported by a two-party system of genuine strength, Negro Marylanders' average registration rate in the 1882–1912 period was 86.1 percent, and ranged from a

12. In 1880 Baltimore City had 62,801 eligible white and 13,455 eligible Negro voters; in 1910 the figures were 120,030 and 26,214 respectively.

13. See Chapter 3.

14. The only exception to this pattern occurred in 1898; this, however, was during the period when Republicans were in power in both the state and the city.

high of 96.7 percent to a low of 73.2 percent. Their performance compared quite favorably with that of Maryland's white population, whose registration averaged 89.9 percent during the same period and ranged from a high of 97.3 percent to a low of 81.6 percent. The consistently high registration of Negroes in Maryland's counties, many of which had substantial Negro populations, indicates that little covert or extralegal repression of Negro registration occurred in Maryland during this period. The relatively lower registration rate of Negroes in Baltimore, whose Negro population never exceeded 16.2 percent of the total population during the period, probably reflected the local weakness of the Republican party rather than an effort by local whites to deny them their rights.

Voter Turn-out

Analysis of Negro voting participation requires considerably more inference than determination of registration activity. Registration figures by race are available for most of the period, but there is no comparable data on the ballots cast by Negroes and by whites. And while Maryland Negroes generally kept pace with whites in registering to vote, this fact provides little assurance that their voting performance was similar. In most of the state, registration required only a single political act by each individual, while voter participation required continuous political affirmation.

In order to deal with the question of Negro voting participation, it was necessary first to establish general voter turn-out in each gubernatorial, presidential, and congressional election from 1870 through 1912 for each of the state's twenty three counties.[15] Our analysis then classified and grouped the counties according to the percentage of their Negro populations. Average turn-out in all elections for each decade was then computed and entered for each county. Finally, each population grouping's average turn-out by decade was figured and shown. The results of this comparative analysis appear in Table 12. Average turn-out by decade for the

15. Election figures for the period were secured from the *Baltimore Sun* for 1870 through 1880 and from the *Sun Almanac* for 1882 through 1913, supplemented by the *Maryland Manual* for 1896 through 1913. United States census data was utilized to establish the number of male citizens of voting age in each census year and interpolations were made for the intervening years. These figures are reproduced in Appendix B.

TABLE 12

AVERAGE VOTER TURN-OUT BY DECADE IN MARYLAND COUNTIES, GROUPED BY RACIAL COMPOSITION, 1870–1912 (Percentages)

Counties	1870–79 (10)*	1880–89 (10)*	1890–99 (10)*	1900–1912 (14)*
Group 1 (*less than 15% Negro*)				
Allegany	71.53	83.32	82.39	60.90
Baltimore	57.85	63.43	64.81	60.88
Carroll	76.01	86.90	85.90	73.54
Washington	88.16	90.34	87.92	69.36
Garrett †	....	85.68	79.94	61.43
Frederick	....	....	88.13	77.53
Cecil	....	....	....	69.29
Average	73.39	81.93	81.51	69.56
Group 2 (*15%–30% Negro*)				
Harford	73.27	78.51	81.82	70.85
Howard	77.39	78.61	85.40	71.35
Wicomico	75.14	78.77	81.40	73.91
Caroline	....	83.56	85.53	71.52
Cecil	74.40	79.70	78.41	....
Frederick	86.76	90.73	....	....
Montgomery	....	....	....	69.14
Average	77.39	81.65	82.51	71.35
Group 3 (*31%–45% Negro*)				
Dorchester	77.37	78.48	80.88	66.77
Kent	82.50	88.42	83.76	69.98
Queen Anne's	84.04	83.99	86.03	74.01
Somerset	71.59	70.22	73.30	48.94
Talbot	82.30	87.68	87.01	71.92
Worcester	74.20	78.36	76.96	62.97
Montgomery	82.64	90.89	87.05	....
Anne Arundel	....	....	70.42	58.08
Prince George's	....	....	80.28	58.57
Caroline	77.40	....	....	....
St. Mary's	....	....	....	72.28
Average	79.00	82.58	80.63	64.82
Group 4 (*more than 45% Negro*)				
Calvert	94.71	89.02	87.14	72.26
Charles	85.31	87.46	80.96	70.66
St. Mary's	86.01	91.28	89.40	....
Anne Arundel	80.62	72.23	....	....
Prince George's	81.72	89.26	....	....
Average	85.67	85.85	85.83	71.46
Baltimore City ‡	70.16	70.87	78.16	65.47
Maryland	75.00	77.51	79.47	66.09

* Total number of gubernatorial, presidential, and congressional elections held within the period.

† Omitted for the 1870–79 period because Garrett County did not exist prior to 1872.

‡ With a Negro population of slightly over 15 percent for most of the period, Baltimore was racially comparable to counties in Group 2; its averages are listed separately to avoid complicating an essentially racial analysis with urban-rural differentials in turn-out.

state as a whole and for Baltimore City are included for comparative purposes, but Baltimore is deliberately kept separate from the population groupings to avoid complicating what is essentially a racial analysis with an urban-rural factor.

Table 12 shows that in the early years of the period, during the 1870s and 1880s, average voter turn-out tended to rise as the percentage of Negro population rose. This relationship is particularly striking for the 1870s; during the 1880s the relationship persisted, but there was no difference in the average turn-out in areas whose population was less than 30 percent Negro. After 1890 Group 4 contains too few counties from which to generalize; for analytical purposes, therefore, it is necessary to regroup the counties of Groups 3 and 4 into a single class—areas of high Negro population (more than 30 percent)—and to follow the same procedure for Groups 1 and 2—areas of low Negro population (less than 30 percent). This process reveals that there was no significant difference in voter turn-out between areas of low and high Negro population for the 1890s. The average turn-out in low Negro population areas (counties shown in Table 12 under Groups 1 and 2) was 81.97 percent during the 1890s, while the turn-out in high Negro population areas (counties shown in Table 12 under Groups 3 and 4) averaged 81.93 percent. The same procedure for the 1900–1912 period reveals an inverse relationship between areas of high Negro population and turn-out performance, which reverses the earlier trend. From 1900 to 1912 the average turn-out rate for the high Negro population areas was 66.04 percent and the average for low Negro population areas was 70.82 percent.

The inference from these relationships is that Maryland Negroes followed through on their high registration rates with remarkably high levels of voter participation. Voter participation from 1870 to 1900 was high in Maryland, and counties with large Negro populations performed as well as or better than counties with small Negro populations. Qualitative data for the period indicates the absence of systematic or legal repression of Negro voters prior to 1900, and the quantitative data indicates the absence of informal repression. Negroes voted freely in Maryland, even in areas where their numbers constituted a major threat to white control.

After 1900 the situation was different, and two trends are apparent. First, there was a sharp drop in turn-out for each group and for every county in each group. Second, the drop in turn-out usually was greater in high Negro population counties than in low Negro population counties. Much of the general decrease in voter participation probably stemmed from the ballot law of 1901, which ended easy straight-ticket voting throughout the state. The discriminatory Wilson ballot law of 1904, which eliminated party identification of candidates on the ballots of eleven Maryland counties, appears to have further depressed participation in high Negro population areas. The original Wilson ballot law embraced nine of the eleven Maryland counties that had Negro populations of more than 30 percent in 1900 (Frederick and Garrett counties, both low Negro population areas, also were included, but were removed two years later). In 1908 Dorchester and Queen Anne's, the two remaining counties with Negro populations exceeding 30 percent, were added to the Wilson-ballot areas. Consequently, the difference in voter turn-out between Wilson-ballot and non-Wilson-ballot areas between 1900 and 1912 closely approximates the difference in turn-out between high and low Negro population areas of Maryland for that period. The average turn-out for the ten Maryland counties that were always exempt from the Wilson ballot was 69.07 percent; for the nine counties that continuously used the Wilson ballot the average turn-out for the same period was 65.07 percent.[16]

The turn-out differential ascribed to the Wilson ballot, however, is quite small compared to the general decline in turn-out that occurred between the early 1890s and 1900s. Turn-out in low Negro population counties dropped from an average 81.97 percent in the 1890s to an average 70.82 percent in the early 1900s—an eleven-point decline. High Negro population areas experienced a sixteen-point decline during the same period. These relatively sharp decreases suggest that the ballot law of 1901, eliminating straight-ticket voting and party emblem identification, had a more significant effect on voter participation in Maryland. Furthermore, although it is impossible to say how many whites and how many

16. This produced a 4-point differential between non-Wilson- and Wilson-ballot counties, compared with a 4.78-point differential between low and high Negro population areas for the 1900–1912 period. The ten non-Wilson-ballot counties were Allegany, Baltimore, Caroline, Carroll, Cecil, Harford, Howard, Montgomery, Washington, and Wicomico. The nine counties continuously under the Wilson ballot law from 1904 through 1912 were Anne Arundel, Calvert, Charles, Kent, Prince George's, St. Mary's, Somerset, Talbot, and Worcester.

Negroes were discouraged from voting by these two laws, it is clear that their adverse effects were not confined to the Negro population. It is even possible that more whites than Negroes were discouraged from voting by the ballot laws of 1901 and 1904. Table 13 shows the drop in average voter turn-out after the

TABLE 13

DECREASE IN VOTER TURN-OUT IN SELECTED COUNTIES AFTER ENACTMENT OF THE BALLOT LAWS OF 1901 AND 1904

| County | Negro Population in 1900 | Average Voter Turn-out | | Decrease |
		1890–99	1900–1912	
Garrett	1%	79.94%	61.43%	18.51
Allegany	3	82.39	60.90	21.49
Charles	55	80.96	70.66	10.30
Calvert	50	87.14	72.26	14.88

enactment of these laws in the two lowest and the two highest Negro population counties in Maryland. Generalization for the entire state from these selected extremes is unwarranted, but the data indicate that white political participation dropped substantially in the wake of the ballot laws.

No important racial difference appears in voter participation in the various types of elections we have investigated for the period. Table 14 divides Maryland counties into two roughly equal groups based on the percentage of their Negro populations (less or more than 30% Negro) and shows average voter turnout for each county and group in four types of elections during the 1870–1912 period. Areas of high and low Negro populations show remarkably similar turn-out averages in presidential, gubernatorial, and regular congressional elections. The only significant variance occurs in off-year congressional elections, when high Negro population areas tend to have a slightly higher participation average than the low Negro population areas. This, of course, may reflect a higher degree of party organization for both whites and Negroes in these high Negro population areas.

The data seem to rule out systematic discrimination against Negro voters in any particular type of election in Maryland— even in the suspect state elections, whose lack of federal surveillance gave ample opportunity for informal repression. Although

TABLE 14

AVERAGE VOTER TURN-OUT IN DIFFERENT TYPES OF ELECTIONS,
MARYLAND COUNTIES GROUPED BY RACIAL COMPOSITION,
1870–1912 (Percentages)

Counties	Presi-dential (11)*	Guber-natorial (11)*	Regular Con-gressional (11)*	Off-Year Con-gressional (11)*
Group A (less than 30% Negro)				
Allegany	79.09	71.36	76.66	66.06
Baltimore	68.25	64.15	63.17	51.08
Caroline †	81.19	83.25	77.30	73.36
Carroll	84.37	83.38	82.12	69.92
Cecil	80.67	76.11	76.92	65.86
Frederick	87.67	85.44	86.51	80.54
Garrett	79.41	72.59	77.97	64.87
Harford	81.32	76.07	78.42	66.63
Howard	80.80	81.67	78.10	69.69
Washington	85.34	82.79	84.06	78.28
Wicomico	80.43	78.00	77.53	72.00
Average	80.78	77.65	78.07	68.94
Group B (more than 30% Negro)				
Anne Arundel	71.98	70.71	69.82	64.37
Calvert	86.19	83.69	85.57	82.75
Charles	80.15	80.06	79.45	80.93
Dorchester	77.21	81.16	73.11	68.71
Kent	82.56	82.72	79.52	75.79
Montgomery †	85.22	78.75	83.68	77.23
Prince George's	78.49	75.33	76.85	72.29
Queen Anne's	84.86	81.47	81.83	76.99
St. Mary's	88.01	84.00	81.23	81.19
Somerset	64.16	70.28	64.05	59.35
Talbot	83.94	83.49	80.50	77.23
Worcester	75.74	72.02	73.66	67.38
Average	79.89	78.64	77.44	73.68
Baltimore City	76.66	70.10	73.02	62.79
Maryland	78.34	74.27	75.49	66.89

* Number of elections held during the period.
† In this racial category for most but not all of the period. Deviates from assigned category from 1870 to 1880.

individual instances of repression undoubtedly occurred, no pattern of consistent or substantial repression emerges from the data.

Similarly, the pattern of voter interest is roughly the same for each group of counties. Presidential elections attracted the greatest voter interest in both low and high Negro population areas. Participation in regular congressional elections was closely tied to presidential turn-out, and trailed the latter by only a few points. Interest in gubernatorial elections was slightly less than the interest in presidential elections; and off-year congressional elections attracted the least voter interest, although high Negro population areas tended to express slightly more interest than the "whiter" areas.

In summary, the quantitative data on voter turn-out for the 1870–1912 period indicates that Maryland Negroes were highly active participants in the voting process, both in relation to the performance of whites and in absolute terms. The effort to reduce the Negro vote by the stringent ballot laws of 1901 and 1904 was partially successful, but only at the expense of a substantial reduction in the white vote. In view of the Negro's lower socioeconomic and literacy levels and the hostility of the predominantly white community toward his political participation, his persistent exercise of his franchise throughout this period is remarkable. Political apathy, generally considered an all-but-irredeemable attribute of lower socioeconomic groups, and particularly of Negroes, was not the characteristic feature of Negro political behavior at this time. At the same time, the quantitative information indicates that covert repression of the Negro vote was at most sporadic and was not a widespread phenomenon in Maryland. Maryland whites did not rely on violence and intimidation to maintain their political sway. The disfranchisement movement in Maryland was largely an open political movement that relied on legal and semilegal means. Disfranchisement failed in Maryland both formally, when it was rejected as a policy by the state's electorate, and practically, as Negro voters continued to exercise their franchise rights despite legal harassment and a hostile climate of opinion.

Candidacy and Officeholding

The Negro's high level of participation in registration and voting in Maryland did not carry over into the loftier realm of officeholding. Negro candidates, a rarity in Maryland, were the subject of much comment but little serious attention, even by

Negroes. By 1912 not a single Negro had offered himself for a state office or for either house of the General Assembly. In the forty-two years between 1870 and 1912, three Negroes ran for Congress from Maryland and fifteen sought positions on town councils, and only seven councilmen were elected.

All three Negroes who ran for Congress were independents and none elicited a respectable showing for his efforts. In 1874 James H. Montgomery of Cumberland became Maryland's first Negro candidate for public office, standing for Congress from the state's Sixth District; he received only twenty-five votes.[17] In 1886 S. Q. Sanks of Baltimore received about the same degree of support in his race for the Fourth Congressional District seat. Charles T. Parker in 1898, running in the heavily Negro Fifth District, attracted only 274 voters from their traditional Republican allegiance.[18]

The major difficulty of the Negro congressional candidates was their lack of party endorsement and the aura of suspicion, propagated by the Republican party, that they were backed by the Democratic party in an effort to split the Republican vote. It is impossible to validate or to refute such charges, but it seems most probable that these candidacies began as genuine independent revolts against Republican leadership and received covert Democratic encouragement only after their inception. The negligible voter support these Negro candidates received suggests that their Democratic backing, which would have been financial in nature, was insignificant.

Somewhat greater Negro success was achieved in local government, but the first Negro candidacies for city council, which occurred in Baltimore in the 1880s, also met disinterest from the political parties and voters. Of the eight Negro independents who ran for the Baltimore city council between 1880 and 1890, none received more than a light scattering of votes.[19] A major breakthrough was made in 1890, however, when Harry Scythe Cummings secured the Republican nomination for councilman from Baltimore's eleventh ward, a ward with a predominantly Negro

17. *Cumberland Daily News*, October 29 and November 7, 1874.
18. *Baltimore Sun*, November 3, 1886, and November 10, 1898.
19. In 1880 there were three Negro candidates: James E. Fisher, G. E. Briscoe, and John H. Smith. In 1882 Professor John A. Draper and W. E. Wilkes ran for the council. In 1885 George P. T. Jones and Revel H. Fooks were the unsuccessful Negro candidates, followed by John W. Davis in 1886, the last Negro independent to run for the council (*Baltimore Sun*, October 26, 1880, October 29, 1882, October 26, 1885, and October 28, 1886).

population but a voter registration about equally split between whites and Negroes. Elected with a slim 105 vote majority, Cummings became the first Negro to hold elective office in Maryland.[20] Thereafter, with brief exceptions, Negroes maintained a representative in the lower branch of the Baltimore city council, always from a predominantly Negro ward.[21] Cummings served from 1890 to 1892, when he was defeated by a white Democrat.[22] In 1895 Dr. J. Marcus Cargill, a Negro physician, was elected for a one-year term, and he was reelected in 1896.[23] Cummings again filled the post from 1897 to 1899.[24] The position then fell to Cummings' real estate partner, a longtime worker for the Republican party, Hiram Watty, who served until 1905, when he was defeated by a white Democrat.[25] In 1907 Cummings was elected again and served until 1915.[26] For twenty-five years these three men, Cummings, Cargill, and Watty, shared the highest office accorded members of their race in Maryland.

Elsewhere in Maryland, four other Negroes achieved positions of comparable status in smaller municipalities. On the Eastern Shore two Negroes served successive terms on the Cambridge city council from the predominantly Negro second ward. H. Maynadier St. Clair, a successful businessman and undertaker, served from 1906 to 1910, and was followed by Nehemiah Henry, who served from 1910 to 1912.[27] In Annapolis, T. A. Thompson served as city councilman from 1905 to 1907, and was succeeded by J. Albert Adams, who served from 1907 until the local disfranchising ordinance of 1909 deprived Negroes of representation on the council.[28]

20. *Baltimore Sun*, November 5, 1890.
21. Ward boundaries and numbers changed frequently during the period.
22. *Baltimore Sun*, November 9, 1892.
23. *Ibid.*, November 6, 1895, and November 4, 1896.
24. *Ibid.*, November 3, 1897.
25. *Ibid.*, October 21, 1905. Watty held a succession of low-level federal patronage positions under the Republican party before his rise to elective office; these included inspector in the customs house, messenger to the collector of the port, and inspector in the Treasury Department's Baltimore office.
26. *Baltimore Sun*, August 5, 6, 1907; *Baltimore Afro-American Ledger*, May 6, 1911.
27. *Cambridge Daily Banner*, June 14, 1907, and April 27, 1911; *Baltimore Afro-American Ledger*, September 16, 1911. St. Clair went on to become the dominant political leader of his race in Cambridge for the next thirty years, serving on the city council for most of that time; little is known of Henry. See George R. Kent, "The Negro in Politics in Dorchester County, Maryland, 1920–1960" (M.A. thesis, University of Maryland, 1961), pp. 64–66.
28. *Annapolis Evening Capital*, July 8, 9, 1907; *Baltimore Afro-American Ledger*, September 16, 1911.

The low incidence of Negro candidacy in Maryland was not so much a matter of modest Negro aspiration as of tight party control. Negroes repeatedly sought racial representation on the Republican ticket but their requests were either ignored or rejected. The hopelessness of Negro independent candidacies had been abundantly demonstrated, and the Democratic party apparently never considered running a Negro, even in heavily Negro areas. For all practical purposes, Negro candidacy depended on the support of the white power structure of the Republican party, and the white response almost invariably was negative.

Negroes came closest to getting racial representation on the Republican ticket in 1897 when Baltimore Republicans, then in control of the city, held a spirited primary to determine which of its two party factions should have the honor of defeating the Democrats in the forthcoming city election. In this intraparty fight one of the factions promised that Negro representation on the Republican legislative ticket would be granted in return for Negro support. The support was freely given, and the faction was successful, but the promise proved to be a ruse. A white spokesman explained to the outraged Negroes:

> All were honest when you were given the promise that you should name one colored member of the legislative ticket in each of the three districts of Baltimore, but the question of race prejudice has since been aroused. I, myself, think that this could be fought down, but outside pressure has been brought to bear against the naming of colored men on the ticket, and the question of party success is involved. You should care more for party than for individuals. This has now become a question of reason and expediency rather than of pure equity and sentiment.[29]

Maryland Republicans, at the height of their power, could not be persuaded to endorse a few Negro legislative candidacies, and the events of the ensuing years brought even less hope for aspiring Negro politicians. The Democrats' return to power in 1900 and the beginning of the campaign to disfranchise the Negro made further talk of Negro candidacies pointless. The political energy of white and Negro Republicans was to be spent in the long fight to preserve the basic right to vote, and the extension of Negro rights and privileges became a dead issue.

29. *Baltimore Sun*, September 14, 1897; also see pp. 96–98 above.

CHAPTER 7

WHY DISFRANCHISEMENT FAILED

The successful maintenance of the Negro's voting rights against white attack and his active exercise of these rights during the disfranchisement era confer a unique quality upon the Maryland experience. In 1870, as again in 1910, Maryland ranked twelfth from the top in a classification of states by percentage of Negro population; all eleven states that had a greater proportion of Negroes found ways during this period to sharply curtail Negro political participation within their borders. Most of them —South Carolina, Mississippi, Louisiana, Alabama, Georgia, Virginia, and North Carolina—after enacting legislative measures to reduce Negro power, launched successful constitutional attacks on the Negro's basic right to vote. The other states—Florida, Texas, Tennessee, and Arkansas—contented themselves with legislative devices such as the poll tax, complicated ballot procedures, and prescribed white primaries to reduce the Negro to a condition of practical political impotence. Maryland whites tried most of these methods and failed.

In assessing the reasons for the failure of both practical and formal disfranchisement in Maryland, several important factors can be discerned, some of which were so interrelated that they can be separated only analytically. At least one of these factors was unique to Maryland; another was an accident of history, a freak of circumstance that was unrelated to racial politics but nevertheless helped preserve the franchise. Above all, it was the combination of factors that brought about a relatively sanguine resolution of the difficult racial-political problem in Maryland.

The size and the distribution of Maryland's Negro population were important for the Negro's absorption into the state's political structure. The Negro-white population ratio has been judged the single most important socioeconomic factor affecting Negro political participation in the South,[1] and Maryland's ratio—22.5 percent in 1870 and 17.9 percent in 1910—fell well within what might be deemed the limits of " tolerance " for the period under study. On the state level Maryland whites were unable to portray the Negro as a political threat, because of his obvious numerical minority status. Within the state, however, there were numerous local Negro-white population ratios that usually are associated with the restriction of Negro political activity. In 1870 the population in thirteen of Maryland's twenty-two counties was more than 30 percent Negro, and in 1910 eleven out of twenty-three counties still had Negro minorities of more than 30 percent. The failure of Negro political restriction in Maryland can be partially accounted for by the fact that the great majority of Maryland whites did not reside in these areas of high Negro concentration and could not be persuaded that the race issue was their paramount political concern. Even in 1870 only about one in six Maryland whites resided in areas of large Negro population; the number of whites in counties whose Negro population exceeded 30 percent was only 125,310, compared with a white population of 480,187 in Baltimore City and the counties whose Negro proportion was less than the crucial 30 percent. Only in the state legislature, where they were greatly overrepresented, were the whites of high Negro population areas able to promulgate some of their restrictive schemes; in matters requiring popular approval they failed.[2]

Population ratios, however, though very important, provide only a partial explanation of the Maryland experience. Both Tennessee and Texas, with Negro-white population ratios similar to those of Maryland for most of the period, sharply curtailed Negro

---

1. Donald R. Matthews and James W. Prothro, " Social and Economic Factors and Negro Voter Registration in the South," *American Political Science Review*, 57 (March, 1963): 28–32.

2. In 1870 a delegate in the Maryland house from the high Negro population areas of the state (thirteen counties whose populations were more than 30 percent Negro) represented approximately 7,170 constituents; a delegate from the low Negro population areas (Baltimore City and nine counties less than 30 percent Negro) represented approximately 11,541 constituents. By 1910 the disproportion had increased: a delegate from the high Negro population areas (eleven counties more than 30 percent Negro) represented 8,058 persons and a delegate from the low Negro population areas (Baltimore City and twelve counties less than 30 percent Negro) represented 14,931 persons. Inequitable representation was even more pronounced in the senate, where population played a lesser role in determining representation than in the house.

political activity within their borders, and Oklahoma, with a much smaller Negro population than Maryland's, virtually eliminated the Negro from its politics.[3]

To an important degree, Maryland's Negro population was itself responsible for its relatively successful absorption into Maryland's political structure—and for defeat of the repeated attempts to eject it from this structure. The high level of Negro voter participation and the tenacity with which it was maintained, even in adversity, has been shown. This intense political involvement of Maryland's Negro population can be partially accounted for on social and economic grounds. Although Negroes in Maryland, as elsewhere, generally occupied the lowest positions in the socio-economic hierarchy, several positive factors gave them an advantage over their brothers in the South. There had been a large, free Negro population in Maryland long before the Civil War and it had grown steadily and in an orderly manner over the years.[4] That its Negro population was almost half slave and half free by 1860 was a factor unique to Maryland, as was its corollary, that half of Maryland's Negro population brought substantial experience with social and economic independence, sometimes extending over two generations, into the political arena after the war.

The significance of this unique Negro inheritance should not be misinterpreted, however; manumission had brought little physical improvement in the condition of the freeman. The outstanding authority on the free Negro in Maryland observes:

3. The percentage of Negro population in each of these states was as follows (U. S. Bureau of the Census, *Negro Population in the United States, 1790–1915* [Washington, D.C., 1918], p. 51).

Year	Maryland	Tennessee	Texas	Oklahoma
1870	22.5%	25.6%	31.0%	..
1880	22.5	26.2	24.7	..
1890	20.7	24.4	21.8	8.4%
1900	19.8	23.8	20.4	7.0
1910	17.9	21.7	17.7	8.3

4. The slave and free Negro population of Maryland before the Civil War was as follows (James M. Wright, *The Free Negro in Maryland, 1634–1860* [New York, 1921], pp. 36–37):

Year	Slave	Free	Year	Slave	Free
1790	103,036	8,043	1830	102,994	52,938
1800	105,635	19,587	1840	89,737	62,078
1810	111,502	33,927	1850	90,368	74,723
1820	107,397	39,730	1860	87,189	83,942

As freemen they continued to live substantially like the slaves lived, to associate with slaves, and apart from formal rights to be indistinguishable from slaves. . . .

The rural free Negroes generally engaged themselves to the landholders, sometimes to their own manumittors, to work under agreements which, apart from small nominal wages, placed them in a position substantially like that of the slaves.[5]

Also, their mobility within the state was limited because of the likelihood that they would be mistaken for runaway slaves, although migration out of the state was encouraged.[6] Nevertheless, there were immeasurable psychological benefits from the change in legal status along with some quite tangible economic gains.

The free Negro enjoyed a wide liberty in getting a living. He had a right to engage in agriculture, in the mechanical trades, in business, or to hire himself to any employer whom he could serve and to collect and expend his earnings. The law barred him wholly from no legitimate calling saving politics and military service. . . .

Free Negroes enjoyed the right to hold property by all of the common methods of possession and ownership.[7]

The opportunity to manage his own affairs, maintain his family unit, quit an employer who abused him, and better himself if he could was the heritage of the free Negro. The large number of Negroes in Maryland who shared this valuable experience in social and economic independence must have given strong impetus to the group's later struggle for political survival.[8]

5. Wright, *Free Negro in Maryland*, pp. 43, 94.
6. *Ibid.*, pp. 113–18.
7. *Ibid.*, pp. 97, 106.
8. Compare Stanley M. Elkins' theory on the "infantilization" of personality the "closed" nature of the plantation system of slavery produced in the Southern United States, an effect that would have been greatly diminished in Maryland because of its large free Negro population (*Slavery: A Problem in American Institutional and Intellectual Life* [New York, 1963]). It is possible, however, to attach too much importance to this heritage of freedom. Kentucky, for instance, had a very small proportion of free Negroes relative to its slave population prior to the Civil War (10,684 free and 225,483 slave in 1860) but in the postwar period seems to have followed a permissive policy on Negro political participation —with results similar to those in Maryland, that is, a fairly high degree of Negro voter participation (see Jasper B. Shannon and Ruth McQuown, *Presidential Politics in Kentucky, 1824–1948* [Lexington, 1950]; Thomas D. Clark, *A History*

After the Civil War the economic and social position of Negroes in Maryland was distinguished by a very low incidence of tenant farming. Farther south, the overwhelming majority of Negroes engaged in agriculture were caught in the tenant system, but in Maryland and in Virginia this was not the case. From 1890 to 1910 only about 2,500 Maryland Negroes were tenant farmers, and between 3,000 and 4,000 Negroes owned their own farms. Most Negro males in rural Maryland were agricultural laborers, while their urban counterparts were general laborers or servants. Most Negro females were house servants, laundresses, or agricultural laborers.[9] Laborers and servants, whether rural or urban, had two important advantages over tenant farmers: access to cash wages and mobility. For most Negroes tenancy was simply another form of slavery; they were held on the land by a combination of heavy debt to their white landlords and a total lack of monetary reimbursement for their services. Negro laborers were in a much more independent position in relation to the white community, and in Maryland one manifestation of this independence was their migration from rural to urban areas. In 1870, 25.5 percent of all Maryland Negroes lived in urban areas; by 1910 the proportion had risen to 42.3 percent.[10] It seems only reasonable that another manifestation of this greater measure of independence was a higher degree of political involvement and self-expression.

Factors that bore primarily on the white population of Maryland also contributed to the state's relatively successful absorption of its Negro minority into its political life. Maryland was spared the bitterness of military defeat and, even more important, of the Reconstruction measures which salted the wounds of that defeat By the time the Negro was enfranchised in Maryland the government of the state was firmly in the hands of native whites, and the whites who had been politically proscribed during the war

of Kentucky [New York, 1937]; and E. Merton Coulter, The Civil War and Readjustment in Kentucky [Chapel Hill, 1926]). Unfortunately, the lack of a thorough review of Kentucky election laws and procedures in these sources precludes more than a tentative comparison between Maryland and Kentucky in the postwar period.

9. U.S. Bureau of the Census, Negro Population, 1790–1915 (Washington, D.C., 1918), pp. 518, 607. Few Negroes were employed by Maryland industries, even as laborers.

10. U.S. Bureau of the Census, Thirteenth Census of the United States: 1910. Abstract with Supplement for Maryland, pp. 568–71, 581.

were again active. The intensity of white feeling against Negro political activity was necessarily moderated by the fact that the Negro's entry into state politics cost the ruling whites very little— the loss of a few local governmental units to a rival party. This rival party, moreover, was firmly controlled by whites who showed no inclination toward sharing power with their Negro constituents, factors which further allayed white fears.

The importance of the Federal Enforcement Acts in protecting Negro suffrage during the long span of Democratic dominance in Maryland was considerable. Elsewhere these acts may have been ineffective or of little consequence, but this was not the case in Maryland. The administrative machinery created by the acts was used continuously in federal elections from 1870 through 1892 and served as a practical and psychological deterrent to discrimination in election procedures. Central to this deterrent ability was the political party system that federal authorities were called upon to oversee in Maryland. If there had not been a vigorous, broadly based minority party it is doubtful that the Enforcement Acts could have been widely or effectively used in Maryland. Maryland's Republican leaders were thoroughly familiar with the protections the acts afforded and the election-day patronage their implementation provided, and they did not hesitate to take full advantage of these benefits. Consequently, federal enforcement authorities did not have to police a massively hostile state, as in the South, but a state in which a sizable, well-organized minority desired their presence and actively supported their authority.

The heterogeneity of Maryland's white population was another major factor in maintaining voting rights. The mere presence of Maryland's naturalized and foreign-parentage citizens made it almost impossible to frame a plan that would effectively disfranchise the Negro without threatening a large segment of the white electorate. The active opposition of most of the state's ethnic groups contributed greatly to the failure of constitutional disfranchisement in Maryland. Even more basic, however, this diversity of origins in Maryland's population, reinforced by a diversity of economic interests in the state, supplied a firm foundation for a two-party system, which most Southern states lacked.

A quirk of constitutional phraseology also played a small but important part in preserving the Maryland Negro's right to vote. Article 15 of the Maryland Declaration of Rights flatly prohibited the state from levying a " poll tax." The prohibition had been designed to prevent the levy of a capitation, or head, tax and originally had nothing to do with the tax on voting that came to be known as a poll tax. The wording, nevertheless, was an effective constitutional barrier to Democratic legislatures in the post–Civil War era, when a franchise tax might well have been used to strike at Negro voting power. In 1891 Maryland Democrats sought to repeal this constitutional prohibition, ostensibly to enact a state income tax, but Maryland Republicans were quick to point out the implicit dangers to the franchise which repeal would entail, and the effort was defeated at the polls in a fairly close election. Thus, quite by chance, one of the most effective methods of reducing the Negro vote was not available to Maryland whites.

Finally, the existence and persistence of a genuine two-party system contributed substantially to the defeat of disfranchisement in Maryland. When the flames of racism burned brightest, Maryland had in its Republican party a kind of institutional firebreak which kept the conflagration under some control. Maryland's Republican party was not the shrunken and scorned nonentity found farther south but a party that had proved both its staying power and its capacity to govern. It was a party well aware of its dependence on its Negro constituency and a party that had achieved power, locally and statewide, with the Negro in its ranks. Thus, when the disfranchisement movement came to Maryland, it faced an organized center of opposition with a vital and recognized interest to protect. The attack on the Negro was immediately perceived as an attack on the party system, and the battle was fought on those grounds. Maryland Republicans fought disfranchisement not out of liberal sentiment nor for racial justice, nor did they so pretend; they fought to preserve their power and the means to that power, their party. They fought informal legislative disfranchisement, which sought to cut into their power through complicated and discriminatory ballot procedures, and they fought formal constitutional disfranchisement, which threatened their political existence. In both engagements they were largely successful, for the two-party system worked in an almost mechanistic manner to protect itself and the threatened Negro minority which had become one of its integral parts through a generation of political support.

Appendix A

VOTER REGISTRATION BY RACE IN MARYLAND, 1882–1912

Voter Registration by Race: Maryland

Year	Eligible Voters *		Registered Voters †		Percentage Registered	
	White	Negro	White	Negro	White	Negro
1882	175,072	49,246	142,765	39,521	81.55	80.25
1884	182,034	49,908	171,690	45,690	94.32	91.55
1886	188,996	50,570	182,375	44,265	96.50	87.53
1888	195,958	51,232	190,659	49,532	97.30	96.68
1890	202,922	51,895	186,327	45,960	91.82	88.56
1892	211,852	53,557	201,432	48,285	95.08	90.16
1894	220,782	55,219	205,932	46,262	93.27	83.78
1896	229,712	56,881	213,304	52,113	92.86	91.62
1898	238,642	58,543	215,785	54,280	90.42	92.72
1900	247,573	60,208	236,105	57,284	95.37	95.14
1902	254,027	60,959	214,736	51,873	84.53	85.10
1904	260,481	61,710	235,018	53,029	90.23	85.93
1906	266,935	62,461	220,830	49,922	82.73	79.93
1908	273,389	63,212	237,380	50,336	86.83	79.63
1910	279,844	63,963	230,719	48,693	82.45	76.13
1912	291,100	65,787	243,693	48,185	83.72	73.24

* Number of male citizens twenty-one years of age and over taken from United States census data for 1880, 1890, 1900, and 1920, with interpolations made from these figures for the intervening years.

† Information taken from the *Sun Almanac*, 1883–1913, and from the *Maryland Manual*, 1896–1913. Racial classification of registered voters was authorized by the state in 1882.

162

VOTER REGISTRATION BY RACE: BALTIMORE CITY

Year	Eligible Voters *		Registered Voters †		Percentage Registered	
	White	Negro	White	Negro	White	Negro
1882......	67,971	14,259	54,203	9,961	79.74	69.86
1884......	73,141	15,063	65,184	11,823	89.12	78.49
1886......	78,311	15,867	71,005	9,850	90.67	62.08
1888......	83,481	16,671	77,475	13,959	92.81	83.73
1890......	88,647	17,476	73,929	11,971	83.40	68.50
1892......	92,985	18,310	83,188	14,062	89.46	76.80
1894......	97,323	19,144	84,166	13,174	86.48	68.82
1896......	101,661	19,978	95,045	17,379	93.49	86.99
1898......	105,999	20,812	90,858	17,855	85.72	85.79
1900......	110,339	21,647	100,778	18,739	91.34	86.57
1902......	112,277	22,561	84,346	15,791	75.12	69.99
1904......	114,215	23,475	101,394	17,880	88.77	76.17
1906......	116,153	24,389	89,689	16,494	77.22	67.63
1908......	118,091	25,303	98,821	17,165	83.68	67.84
1910......	120,030	26,214	90,310	16,127	75.24	61.52
1912......	130,312	28,384	96,453	15,711	74.02	55.35

* Number of male citizens twenty-one years of age and over taken from United States census data for 1880, 1890, 1900, and 1920, with interpolations made from these figures for the intervening years.

† Information taken from the *Sun Almanac*, 1883–1913, and from the *Maryland Manual*, 1896–1913. Racial classification of registered voters was authorized by the state in 1882.

VOTER REGISTRATION BY RACE: MARYLAND COUNTIES

Year	Eligible Voters *		Registered Voters †		Percentage Registered	
	White	Negro	White	Negro	White	Negro
1882......	107,103	34,987	88,562	29,560	82.69	84.49
1884......	108,897	34,845	106,506	33,867	97.80	97.19
1886......	110,691	34,703	111,370	34,415	100.61	99.17
1888......	112,485	34,561	113,184	35,573	100.62	102.93
1890......	114,275	34,419	112,400	33,989	98.36	98.75
1892......	118,867	35,247	118,244	34,223	99.48	97.10
1894......	123,459	36,075	121,766	33,088	98.63	91.72
1896......	128,051	36,903	118,259	34,734	92.35	94.12
1898......	132,643	37,731	124,927	36,425	94.18	96.54
1900......	137,234	38,561	135,327	38,545	98.61	99.96
1902......	141,750	38,399	130,390	36,082	91.99	93.97
1904......	146,266	38,237	133,624	35,149	91.36	91.92
1906......	150,782	38,075	131,141	33,428	86.97	87.80
1908......	155,298	37,913	138,559	33,171	89.22	87.49
1910......	159,814	37,749	140,409	32,566	87.86	86.27
1912......	160,790	37,403	147,240	32,474	91.57	86.82

* Number of male citizens twenty-one years of age and over taken from United States census data for 1880, 1890, 1900, and 1920, with interpolations made from these figures for the intervening years.

† Information taken from the *Sun Almanac*, 1883–1913, and from the *Maryland Manual*, 1896–1913. Racial classification of registered voters was authorized by the state in 1882.

VOTER TURN-OUT IN MARYLAND, 1870–1912

VOTER TURN-OUT: MARYLAND

Election	Total Vote Cast *	Number of Eligible Voters †	Percentage Voting
Gubernatorial			
1871...........	132,728	174,530	76.05
1875...........	157,991	193,270	81.75
1879...........	159,472	212,010	75.22
1883...........	173,401	228,130	76.01
1887...........	190,076	243,378	78.10
1891...........	192,037	260,113	73.83
1895...........	240,105	281,297	85.36
1899...........	251,189	302,481	83.04
1903...........	208,686	318,590	65.50
1907...........	201,437	333,002	60.49
1911...........	215,967	350,348	61.64
Presidential			
1872...........	133,948	179,215	74.74
1876...........	163,846	197,955	82.77
1880...........	172,227	216,694	79.48
1884...........	186,019	231,942	80.20
1888...........	210,921	247,190	85.33
1892...........	213,275	265,409	80.36
1896...........	250,877	286,593	87.54
1900...........	264,434	307,781	85.92
1904...........	224,206	322,193	69.59
1908...........	238,531	336,605	70.86
1912...........	231,981	356,889	65.00

* Election figures were taken from the *Baltimore Sun* for 1870 through 1880 and from the *Sun Almanac* for 1882 through 1913, supplemented by the *Maryland Manual* for 1896 through 1913.

† United States census data were utilized to establish the number of male citizens of voting age for each census year, with interpolations made for intervening years.

Voter Turn-out: Maryland (Continued)

Election	Total Vote Cast *	Number of Eligible Voters †	Percentage Voting
Congressional			
1870...........	134,525	169,845	79.21
1872...........	134,349	179,215	74.97
1874...........	121,079	188,585	64.20
1876...........	162,520	197,955	82.10
1878...........	122,321	207,325	59.00
1880...........	171,027	216,694	78.93
1882...........	156,816	224,318	69.91
1884...........	183,738	231,942	79.22
1886...........	150,471	239,566	62.81
1888...........	210,284	247,190	85.07
1890...........	181,573	254,817	71.26
1892...........	211,444	265,409	79.67
1894...........	204,473	276,001	74.08
1896...........	248,494	286,593	86.71
1898...........	216,500	297,185	72.85
1900...........	263,611	307,781	85.65
1902...........	197,168	314,987	62.60
1904...........	208,060	322,193	64.58
1906...........	199,155	329,399	60.46
1908...........	212,319	336,605	63.08
1910...........	204,537	343,807	59.49
1912...........	179,927	356,889	50.42

Voter Turn-out: Baltimore City

Election	Total Vote Cast *	Number of Eligible Voters †	Percentage Voting
Gubernatorial			
1871...........	37,636	56,911	66.13
1875...........	58,821	65,507	89.79
1879...........	47,095	74,103	63.55
1883...........	56,609	85,217	66.43
1887...........	64,285	97,165	66.16
1891...........	70,677	108,709	65.01
1895...........	100,978	119,053	84.82
1899...........	104,835	129,397	81.02
1903...........	90,328	136,264	66.29
1907...........	89,259	141,968	62.87
1911...........	90,056	152,469	59.07

VOTER TURN-OUT: BALTIMORE CITY (Continued)

Election	Total Vote Cast *	Number of Eligible Voters †	Percentage Voting
Presidential			
1872...........	44,218	59,060	74.87
1876...........	54,257	67,656	80.20
1880...........	56,010	76,256	73.45
1884...........	61,874	88,204	70.15
1888...........	85,415	100,152	85.29
1892...........	89,430	111,295	80.35
1896...........	106,601	121,639	87.63
1900...........	113,008	131,986	85.62
1904...........	97,537	137,690	70.84
1908...........	103,423	143,394	72.13
1912...........	99,549	158,694	62.73
Congressional			
1870...........	39,245	54,762	71.66
1872...........	42,915	59,060	72.66
1874...........	32,959	63,358	52.02
1876...........	53,413	67,656	78.95
1878...........	37,238	71,954	51.75
1880...........	55,591	76,256	72.90
1882...........	56,482	82,230	68.69
1884...........	61,834	88,204	70.10
1886...........	47,373	94,178	50.30
1888...........	85,308	100,152	85.18
1890...........	74,258	106,123	69.97
1892...........	88,649	111,295	79.65
1894...........	84,904	116,467	72.90
1896...........	105,491	121,639	86.72
1898...........	93,186	126,811	73.48
1900...........	112,733	131,986	85.41
1902...........	80,780	134,838	59.91
1904...........	87,950	137,690	63.88
1906...........	87,132	140,542	62.00
1908...........	85,077	143,394	59.33
1910...........	84,967	146,244	58.10
1912...........	76,855	158,694	48.43

* Election figures were taken from the *Baltimore Sun* for 1870 through 1880 and from the *Sun Almanac* for 1882 through 1913, supplemented by the *Maryland Manual* for 1896 through 1913.

† United States census data were utilized to establish the number of male citizens of voting age for each census year, with interpolations made for intervening years.

VOTER TURN-OUT: ALLEGANY COUNTY

Election	Total Vote Cast *	Number of Eligible Voters †	Percentage Voting
Gubernatorial			
1871............	5,252	7,902	66.46
1875............	5,378	7,746	69.43
1879...........	5,745	7,590	75.69
1883...........	6,263	7,766	80.65
1887...........	6,847	8,046	85.10
1891...........	7,082	8,724	81.18
1895...........	9,029	10,608	85.12
1899...........	9,270	12,492	74.21
1903...........	7,966	13,719	58.07
1907...........	7,907	14,731	53.68
1911...........	8,771	15,824	55.43
Presidential			
1872...........	5,996	7,863	76.26
1876...........	6,518	7,707	84.57
1880...........	6,427	7,556	85.06
1884...........	6,208	7,836	79.22
1888...........	7,538	8,116	92.88
1892...........	8,312	9,195	90.40
1896...........	9,680	11,079	87.37
1900...........	10,880	12,960	83.95
1904...........	9,289	13,972	66.48
1908...........	10,591	14,984	70.68
1912...........	8,593	16,156	53.19
Congressional			
1870...........	4,833	7,941	60.86
1872...........	5,006	7,863	63.67
1874...........	5,136	7,785	65.97
1876...........	6,414	7,707	83.22
1878...........	5,276	7,629	69.16
1880...........	6,396	7,556	84.65
1882...........	5,154	7,696	66.97
1884............	6,625	7,836	84.55
1886...........	6,503	7,976	81.53
1888...........	7,317	8,116	92.62
1890...........	6,917	8,253	83.81
1892...........	8,217	9,195	89.36
1894...........	8,603	10,137	84.87
1896...........	9,591	11,079	86.57
1898...........	7,328	12,021	60.96
1900...........	10,790	12,960	83.26
1902...........	8,060	13,466	59.00
1904...........	8,273	13,972	59.21
1906...........	6,689	14,478	46.20
1908...........	9,721	14,984	64.88
1910...........	7,374	15,492	47.60
1912...........	8,292	16,156	51.33

* Election figures were taken from the *Baltimore Sun* for 1870 through 1880 and from the *Sun Almanac* for 1882 through 1913, supplemented by the *Maryland Manual* for 1896 through 1913.

† United States census data were utilized to establish the number of male citizens of voting age for each census year, with interpolations made for intervening years.

VOTER TURN-OUT: ANNE ARUNDEL COUNTY

Election	Total Vote Cast *	Number of Eligible Voters †	Percentage Voting
Gubernatorial			
1871............	5,106	5,969	85.54
1875............	4,973	6,409	77.59
1879............	6,117	6,849	89.31
1883............	5,767	7,454	77.37
1887............	5,953	8,110	73.40
1891............	5,904	8,754	67.44
1895............	6,749	9,358	72.12
1899............	7,283	9,962	73.11
1903............	5,376	10,090	53.28
1907............	5,282	10,058	52.52
1911............	5,781	10,301	56.12
Presidential			
1872............	4,795	6,079	78.88
1876............	5,375	6,519	82.45
1880............	5,204	6,962	74.75
1884............	5,865	7,618	76.99
1888............	6,085	8,274	73.54
1892............	6,319	8,905	70.96
1896............	7,342	9,509	77.21
1900............	7,546	10,114	74.61
1904............	5,980	10,082	59.31
1908............	6,435	10,050	64.03
1912............	6,245	10,568	59.09
Congressional			
1870............	5,024	5,859	85.75
1872............	4,831	6,079	79.47
1874............	5,009	6,299	79.52
1876............	5,358	6,519	82.19
1878............	4,414	6,739	65.50
1880............	5,157	6,962	74.07
1882............	4,468	7,290	61.30
1884............	5,889	7,618	77.30
1886............	4,930	7,946	62.04
1888............	5,915	8,274	71.49
1890............	5,570	8,603	64.75
1892............	6,273	8,905	70.44
1894............	6,079	9,207	66.03
1896............	7,251	9,509	76.25
1898............	6,463	9,811	65.88
1900............	7,445	10,114	73.61
1902............	5,596	10,098	55.42
1904............	5,733	10,082	56.86
1906............	5,459	10,066	54.23
1908............	6,042	10,050	60.12
1910............	4,778	10,034	47.62
1912............	4,890	10,568	46.27

* Election figures were taken from the *Baltimore Sun* for 1870 through 1880 and from the *Sun Almanac* for 1882 through 1913, supplemented by the *Maryland Manual* for 1896 through 1913.

† United States census data were utilized to establish the number of male citizens of voting age for each census year, with interpolations made for intervening years.

VOTER TURN-OUT: BALTIMORE COUNTY *

Election	Total Vote Cast †	Number of Eligible Voters ‡	Percentage Voting
Gubernatorial			
1871............	8,263	14,034	58.88
1875............	9,982	16,374	60.96
1879............	10,996	18,714	58.76
1883............	12,358	19,156	64.51
1887............	15,505	18,964	81.76
1891............	10,920	19,329	56.50
1895............	15,982	21,381	74.75
1899............	17,593	23,433	75.08
1903............	15,993	27,033	59.16
1907............	16,605	31,153	53.30
1911............	20,443	32,965	62.01
Presidential			
1872............	7,945	14,619	54.35
1876............	12,296	16,959	72.50
1880............	12,672	19,300	65.66
1884............	14,121	19,108	73.90
1888............	12,131	18,916	64.13
1892............	12,880	19,842	64.91
1896............	17,188	21,894	78.51
1900............	18,987	23,943	79.30
1904............	17,246	28,063	61.45
1908............	20,982	32,183	65.20
1912............	22,454	31,687	70.86
Congressional			
1870............	8,485	13,449	63.09
1872............	8,023	14,619	54.88
1874............	7,408	15,789	46.92
1876............	12,225	16,959	72.09
1878............	6,544	18,129	36.10
1880............	8,769	19,300	45.44
1882............	10,346	19,204	53.87
1884............	14,259	19,108	74.62
1886............	8,804	19,012	46.31
1888............	12,122	18,916	64.08
1890............	7,957	18,816	42.28
1892............	12,818	19,842	64.60
1894............	12,035	20,868	57.67
1896............	16,896	21,894	77.17
1898............	12,985	22,920	56.65
1900............	15,877	23,943	66.31
1902............	14,651	26,003	56.34
1904............	16,095	28,063	57.35
1906............	15,719	30,123	52.18
1908............	19,705	32,183	61.23
1910............	17,282	34,243	50.47
1912............	18,111	31,687	57.16

* Baltimore County's population growth was erratic because of annexations to Baltimore City between 1880 and 1890 and between 1910 and 1920.

† Election figures were taken from the *Baltimore Sun* for 1870 through 1880 and from the *Sun Almanac* for 1882 through 1913, supplemented by the *Maryland Manual* for 1896 through 1913.

‡ United States census data were utilized to establish the number of male citizens of voting age for each census year, with interpolations made for intervening years.

VOTER TURN-OUT: CALVERT COUNTY

Election	Total Vote Cast *	Number of Eligible Voters †	Percentage Voting
Gubernatorial			
1871............	1,981	1,875	105.65 ‡
1875............	2,060	2,023	101.83 ‡
1879............	1,807	2,171	83.23
1883............	2,052	2,239	91.65
1887............	2,145	2,283	93.96
1891............	1,654	2,343	70.59
1895............	2,174	2,451	88.70
1899............	2,362	2,559	92.30
1903............	1,433	2,561	55.96
1907............	1,730	2,533	68.30
1911............	1,904	2,508	75.92
Presidential			
1872............	1,762	1,912	92.16
1876............	2,008	2,060	97.48
1880............	2,012	2,206	91.21
1884............	2,019	2,250	89.73
1888............	2,149	2,294	93.68
1892............	2,163	2,370	91.27
1896............	2,233	2,478	90.11
1900............	2,319	2,582	89.81
1904............	1,792	2,554	70.16
1908............	1,813	2,526	71.77
1912............	1,773	2,505	70.78
Congressional			
1870............	1,942	1,838	105.66 ‡
1872............	1,787	1,912	93.46
1874............	1,910	1,986	96.17
1876............	2,004	2,060	97.28
1878............	1,864	2,134	87.35
1880............	2,009	2,206	91.07
1882............	1,692	2,228	75.94
1884............	2,012	2,250	89.42
1886............	1,864	2,272	82.04
1888............	2,098	2,294	91.46
1890............	2,128	2,316	91.88
1892............	2,153	2,370	90.84
1894............	2,088	2,424	86.14
1896............	2,204	2,478	88.94
1898............	2,041	2,532	80.61
1900............	2,307	2,582	89.35
1902............	1,713	2,568	66.71
1904............	1,831	2,554	71.69
1906............	1,661	2,540	65.39
1908............	1,701	2,526	67.34
1910............	1,959	2,511	78.02
1912............	1,765	2,505	70.46

* Election figures were taken from the *Baltimore Sun* for 1870 through 1880 and from the *Sun Almanac* for 1882 through 1913, supplemented by the *Maryland Manual* for 1896 through 1913.

† United States census data were utilized to establish the number of male citizens of voting age for each census year, with interpolations made for intervening years.

‡ Distortion produced by census underenumeration, interpolation, or overzealous voting. For all comparative purposes in the text, figure was reduced to 100 percent.

VOTER TURN-OUT: CAROLINE COUNTY

Election	Total Vote Cast *	Number of Eligible Voters †	Percentage Voting
Gubernatorial			
1871............	2,467	2,787	88.52
1875............	2,227	2,995	74.36
1879............	2,722	3,203	84.98
1883............	2,820	3,296	85.56
1887............	3,081	3,356	91.81
1891............	3,247	3,482	93.25
1895............	3,504	3,810	91.97
1899............	3,790	4,138	91.59
1903............	3,331	4,469	74.54
1907............	3,153	4,801	65.67
1911............	3,716	5,054	73.53
Presidential			
1872............	2,144	2,839	75.52
1876............	2,437	3,047	79.98
1880............	2,638	3,251	81.14
1884............	2,832	3,311	85.53
1888............	3,023	3,371	89.68
1892............	2,946	3,564	82.66
1896............	3,480	3,892	89.41
1900............	3,721	4,220	88.18
1904............	3,370	4,552	74.03
1908............	3,659	4,884	74.92
1912............	3,645	5,056	72.09
Congressional			
1870............	2,333	2,735	85.30
1872............	2,179	2,839	76.75
1874............	2,046	2,943	69.52
1876....	2,323	3,047	76.24
1878............	1,980	3,151	62.84
1880............	2,636	3,251	81.08
1882............	2,235	3,281	68.12
1884	2,845	3,311	85.93
1886............	2,592	3,341	77.58
1888............	3,006	3,371	89.17
1890............	2,756	3,400	81.06
1892............	2,917	3,564	81.85
1894............	2,783	3,728	74.65
1896............	3,442	3,892	88.43
1898............	3,260	4,056	80.38
1900............	3,711	4,220	87.94
1902............	2,841	4,386	64.77
1904............	3,193	4,552	70.15
1906............	3,563	4,718	75.52
1908............	3,484	4,884	71.33
1910............	3,395	5,052	67.20
1912............	2,093	5,056	41.40

* Election figures were taken from the *Baltimore Sun* for 1870 through 1880 and from the *Sun Almanac* for 1882 through 1913, supplemented by the *Maryland Manual* for 1896 through 1913.

† United States census data were utilized to establish the number of male citizens of voting age for each census year, with interpolations made for intervening years.

VOTER TURN-OUT: CARROLL COUNTY

Election	Total Vote Cast *	Number of Eligible Voters †	Percentage Voting
Gubernatorial			
1871	5,446	6,832	79.71
1875	5,667	7,156	79.19
1879	6,516	7,480	87.11
1883	6,973	7,749	89.99
1887	7,206	8,005	90.02
1891	7,529	8,287	90.85
1895	7,903	8,618	91.70
1899	8,224	8,958	91.81
1903	6,862	9,201	74.58
1907	6,456	9,413	68.59
1911	7,083	9,624	73.60
Presidential			
1872	5,095	6,913	73.70
1876	6,207	7,237	85.77
1880	6,630	7,557	87.73
1884	6,797	7,813	87.00
1888	7,616	8,069	94.39
1892	7,274	8,363	86.98
1896	8,140	8,703	93.53
1900	8,340	9,042	92.24
1904	7,027	9,254	75.93
1908	7,217	9,466	76.24
1912	7,216	9,676	74.58
Congressional			
1870	5,524	6,751	81.82
1872	5,146	6,913	74.44
1874	4,819	7,075	68.11
1876	6,182	7,237	85.42
1878	3,314	7,399	44.79
1880	6,600	7,557	87.34
1882	6,131	7,685	79.78
1884	6,826	7,813	87.37
1886	5,658	7,941	71.25
1888	7,595	8,069	94.13
1890	5,958	8,193	72.72
1892	7,267	8,363	86.89
1894	6,414	8,533	75.17
1896	8,076	8,703	92.80
1898	6,791	8,873	76.54
1900	8,325	9,042	92.07
1902	6,356	9,148	69.48
1904	6,411	9,254	69.28
1906	6,122	9,360	65.41
1908	6,772	9,466	71.54
1910	6,130	9,572	64.04
1912	6,003	9,676	62.04

* Election figures were taken from the *Baltimore Sun* for 1870 through 1880 and from the *Sun Almanac* for 1882 through 1913, supplemented by the *Maryland Manual* for 1896 through 1913.

† United States census data were utilized to establish the number of male citizens of voting age for each census year, with interpolations made for intervening years.

Voter Turn-out: Cecil County

Election	Total Vote Cast *	Number of Eligible Voters †	Percentage Voting
Gubernatorial			
1871............	5,212	6,337	82.25
1875............	5,180	6,533	79.29
1879............	5,496	6,729	81.68
1883...........	5,260	6,793	77.43
1887...........	5,438	6,817	79.77
1891...........	5,246	6,836	76.74
1895...........	5,147	6,856	75.07
1899...........	5,845	6,876	85.01
1903...........	4,832	6,860	70.44
1907...........	4,297	6,832	62.90
1911...........	4,545	6,824	66.60
Presidential			
1872...........	4,650	6,386	72.82
1876...........	5,478	6,582	83.23
1880...........	5,657	6,775	83.50
1884...........	5,570	6,799	81.92
1888...........	5,939	6,823	87.04
1892...........	5,459	6,841	79.80
1896...........	6,230	6,861	90.80
1900...........	6,066	6,881	88.16
1904...........	5,037	6,853	73.50
1908...........	5,280	6,825	77.36
1912...........	4,736	6,836	69.28
Congressional			
1870...........	4,912	6,288	78.12
1872...........	4,767	6,386	74.65
1874...........	4,066	6,484	62.71
1876...........	5,472	6,582	83.14
1878...........	3,079	6,680	46.09
1880...........	5,652	6,775	83.42
1882...........	4,532	6,787	66.77
1884.........	5,599	6,799	82.35
1886...........	4,616	6,811	67.77
1888...........	5,939	6,823	87.04
1890...........	4,311	6,831	63.11
1892...........	5,282	6,841	77.21
1894...........	5,063	6,851	73.90
1896...........	6,163	6,861	89.83
1898...........	4,990	6,871	72.62
1900...........	6,063	6,881	88.11
1902...........	4,449	6,867	64.79
1904...........	4,529	6,853	66.09
1906...........	4,492	6,839	65.68
1908...........	5,000	6,825	73.26
1910...........	4,285	6,812	62.90
1912...........	2,804	6,836	41.02

* Election figures were taken from the *Baltimore Sun* for 1870 through 1880 and from the *Sun Almanac* for 1882 through 1913, supplemented by the *Maryland Manual* for 1896 through 1913.

† United States census data were utilized to establish the number of male citizens of voting age for each census year, with interpolations made for intervening years.

VOTER TURN-OUT: CHARLES COUNTY

Election	Total Vote Cast *	Number of Eligible Voters †	Percentage Voting
Gubernatorial			
1871............	2,975	3,427	86.81
1875............	3,129	3,671	85.24
1879............	3,484	3,915	88.99
1883............	3,304	3,818	86.54
1887............	3,475	3,602	96.47
1891............	2,877	3,519	81.76
1895............	3,330	3,831	86.92
1899............	3,540	4,143	85.45
1903............	2,329	4,121	56.52
1907............	2,277	3,993	57.02
1911............	2,731	3,956	69.03
Presidential			
1872............	2,791	3,488	80.02
1876............	3,303	3,732	88.50
1880............	3,575	3,980	89.82
1884............	3,391	3,764	90.09
1888............	2,873	3,548	80.98
1892............	2,391	3,597	66.47
1896............	3,529	3,909	90.28
1900............	3,662	4,217	86.84
1904............	2,870	4,089	70.19
1908............	2,871	3,961	72.48
1912............	2,646	4,012	65.95
Congressional			
1870............	3,138	3,366	93.23
1872............	2,823	3,488	80.93
1874............	2,914	3,610	80.72
1876............	3,288	3,732	88.10
1878............	3,105	3,854	80.57
1880............	3,545	3,980	89.07
1882............	3,195	3,872	82.52
1884............	3,401	3,764	90.36
1886............	3,215	3,656	87.94
1888............	2,867	3,548	80.81
1890............	3,002	3,441	87.24
1892............	2,234	3,597	62.11
1894............	2,933	3,753	78.15
1896............	3,509	3,909	89.77
1898............	3,312	4,065	81.48
1900............	3,661	4,217	86.82
1902............	3,003	4,153	72.31
1904............	2,921	4,089	71.44
1906............	2,930	4,025	72.80
1908............	2,898	3,961	73.16
1910............	2,859	3,900	73.31
1912............	2,462	4,012	61.37

* Election figures were taken from the *Baltimore Sun* for 1870 through 1880 and from the *Sun Almanac* for 1882 through 1913, supplemented by the *Maryland Manual* for 1896 through 1913.

† United States census data were utilized to establish the number of male citizens of voting age for each census year, with interpolations made for intervening years.

Voter Turn-out: Dorchester County

Election	Total Vote Cast *	Number of Eligible Voters †	Percentage Voting
Gubernatorial			
1871............	3,805	4,516	84.26
1875............	3,739	4,944	75.63
1879............	4,844	5,372	90.17
1883............	4,887	5,687	85.93
1887............	5,259	5,971	88.08
1891............	5,704	6,283	90.78
1895............	5,947	6,671	89.15
1899............	6,532	7,059	92.53
1903............	5,105	7,307	69.86
1907............	4,531	7,507	60.36
1911............	5,061	7,669	65.99
Presidential			
1872............	3,608	4,623	78.04
1876............	3,901	5,051	77.23
1880............	4,374	5,474	79.91
1884............	4,624	5,758	80.31
1888............	4,851	6,042	80.29
1892............	4,597	6,380	72.05
1896............	5,835	6,768	86.21
1900............	6,242	7,157	87.22
1904............	4,869	7,357	66.18
1908............	5,485	7,557	72.58
1912............	5,329	7,686	69.33
Congressional			
1870............	3,778	4,409	85.69
1872............	3,655	4,623	79.06
1874............	3,056	4,837	63.18
1876............	3,879	5,051	76.80
1878............	3,353	5,265	63.68
1880............	4,361	5,474	79.67
1882............	3,698	5,616	65.85
1884............	4,637	5,738	80.33
1886............	3,781	5,900	64.08
1888............	4,845	6,042	80.19
1890............	4,433	6,186	71.66
1892............	4,548	6,380	71.29
1894............	4,649	6,574	70.72
1896............	5,821	6,768	86.01
1898............	5,459	6,962	78.41
1900............	6,231	7,157	87.06
1902............	4,787	7,257	65.96
1904............	4,622	7,357	62.82
1906............	4,864	7,457	65.23
1908............	5,293	7,557	70.04
1910............	4,696	7,652	61.37
1912............	2,364	7,686	30.76

* Election figures were taken from the *Baltimore Sun* for 1870 through 1880 and from the *Sun Almanac* for 1882 through 1913, supplemented by the *Maryland Manual* for 1896 through 1913.

† United States census data were utilized to establish the number of male citizens of voting age for each census year, with interpolations made for intervening years.

VOTER TURN-OUT: FREDERICK COUNTY

Election	Total Vote Cast *	Number of Eligible Voters †	Percentage Voting
Gubernatorial			
1871............	9,739	10,586	92.00
1875............	9,418	11,114	84.74
1879............	10,656	11,642	91.53
1883............	10,405	11,937	87.17
1887............	11,244	12,157	92.49
1891............	11,042	12,448	88.71
1895............	11,821	12,968	91.16
1899............	11,916	13,488	88.35
1903............	10,507	13,755	76.39
1907............	9,999	13,943	71.71
1911............	10,693	14,135	75.65
Presidential			
1872............	8,864	10,718	82.70
1876............	10,235	11,246	91.01
1880............	11,042	11,772	93.80
1884............	10,702	11,992	89.24
1888............	11,440	12,212	93.68
1892............	11,434	12,578	90.91
1896............	11,940	13,098	91.16
1900............	12,457	13,614	91.50
1904............	10,956	13,802	79.38
1908............	11,316	13,990	80.89
1912............	11,360	14,190	80.06
Congressional			
1870............	9,403	10,454	89.95
1872............	8,991	10,718	83.89
1874............	8,599	10,982	78.30
1876............	10,226	11,246	90.93
1878............	9,504	11,510	82.57
1880............	11,002	11,772	93.46
1882............	9,955	11,882	83.78
1884............	10,832	11,992	90.33
1886............	10,869	12,102	89.81
1888............	11,428	12,212	93.58
1890............	10,608	12,318	86.12
1892............	11,405	12,578	90.67
1894............	11,240	12,838	87.55
1896............	11,863	13,098	90.57
1898............	10,167	13,358	76.11
1900............	12,446	13,614	91.42
1902............	9,961	13,708	72.67
1904............	10,428	13,802	75.55
1906............	8,829	13,896	63.54
1908............	10,565	13,990	75.52
1910............	10,636	14,080	75.54
1912............	10,735	14,190	75.65

* Election figures were taken from the *Baltimore Sun* for 1870 through 1880 and from the *Sun Almanac* for 1882 through 1913, supplemented by the *Maryland Manual* for 1896 through 1913.

† United States census data were utilized to establish the number of male citizens of voting age for each census year, with interpolations made for intervening years.

VOTER TURN-OUT: GARRETT COUNTY *

Election	Total Vote Cast †	Number of Eligible Voters ‡	Percentage Voting
Gubernatorial			
1871............	....	....	....
1875............	1,510	....	....
1879............	2,125	....	....
1883............	2,364	2,827	83.62
1887............	2,648	3,071	86.23
1891............	2,752	3,363	81.83
1895............	3,214	3,811	84.33
1899............	3,246	4,259	76.22
1903............	2,666	4,532	58.83
1907............	2,611	4,740	55.08
1911............	2,668	4,887	54.59
Presidential			
1872............	....	....	....
1876............	1,973	....	....
1880............	2,334	2,644	88.28
1884............	2,541	2,888	87.98
1888............	2,792	3,132	89.14
1892............	2,960	3,475	85.18
1896............	3,392	3,923	86.46
1900............	3,580	4,376	81.81
1904............	3,063	4,584	66.82
1908............	3,316	4,792	69.20
1912............	2,920	4,879	59.85
Congressional			
1870............	....	....	....
1872............	....	....	....
1874............	1,212	....	....
1876............	1,970	....	....
1878............	1,815	....	....
1880............	2,330	2,644	88.12
1882............	2,025	2,766	73.21
1884............	2,589	2,888	89.65
1886............	2,443	3,010	81.16
1888............	2,799	3,132	89.37
1890............	2,597	3,251	79.88
1892............	2,949	3,475	84.86
1894............	2,797	3,699	75.62
1896............	3,370	3,923	85.90
1898............	2,450	4,147	59.08
1900............	3,582	4,376	81.86
1902............	2,601	4,480	58.06
1904............	2,814	4,584	61.39
1906............	2,104	4,688	44.88
1908............	3,149	4,792	65.71
1910............	2,304	4,895	47.07
1912............	2,679	4,879	54.91

* Garrett County was formed from a portion of Allegany County in 1872. Because there are no data on the county's number of eligible voters before the federal census of 1880, turn-out cannot be computed for the years prior to that date.

† Election figures were taken from the *Baltimore Sun* for 1870 through 1880 and from the *Sun Almanac* for 1882 through 1913, supplemented by the *Maryland Manual* for 1896 through 1913.

‡ United States census data were utilized to establish the number of male citizens of voting age for each census year, with interpolations made for intervening years.

VOTER TURN-OUT: HARFORD COUNTY

Election	Total Vote Cast *	Number of Eligible Voters †	Percentage Voting
Gubernatorial			
1871............	4,444	5,322	83.50
1875............	4,372	5,990	72.99
1879............	4,100	6,658	61.58
1883............	5,394	7,002	77.04
1887............	5,662	7,242	78.18
1891............	5,918	7,435	79.60
1895............	6,738	7,495	89.90
1899............	6,660	7,555	88.27
1903............	5,825	7,702	75.63
1907............	5,024	7,878	63.77
1911............	5,392	8,133	66.30
Presidential			
1872............	4,077	5,489	74.28
1876............	5,078	6,157	82.48
1880............	5,492	6,822	80.50
1884............	5,833	7,062	82.60
1888............	6,413	7,302	87.83
1892............	6,022	7,450	80.83
1896............	7,105	7,510	94.61
1900............	6,924	7,570	91.47
1904............	5,833	7,746	75.30
1908............	5,972	7,922	75.39
1912............	5,713	8,255	69.21
Congressional			
1870............	4,674	5,155	90.67
1872............	4,198	5,489	76.48
1874............	3,799	5,823	65.24
1876............	5,056	6,157	82.12
1878............	2,814	6,491	43.35
1880............	5,449	6,822	79.87
1882............	5,037	6,942	72.56
1884............	5,868	7,062	83.09
1886............	4,028	7,182	56.08
1888............	6,380	7,302	87.37
1890............	4,504	7,420	60.70
1892............	6,007	7,450	80.63
1894............	5,620	7,480	75.13
1896............	7,051	7,510	93.89
1898............	5,626	7,540	74.62
1900............	6,893	7,570	91.06
1902............	5,063	7,658	66.11
1904............	5,319	7,746	68.67
1906............	4,974	7,834	63.49
1908............	5,434	7,922	68.59
1910............	5,203	8,011	64.95
1912............	4,284	8,255	51.90

* Election figures were taken from the *Baltimore Sun* for 1870 through 1880 and from the *Sun Almanac* for 1882 through 1913, supplemented by the *Maryland Manual* for 1896 through 1913.
† United States census data were utilized to establish the number of male citizens of voting age for each census year, with interpolations made for intervening years.

VOTER TURN-OUT: HOWARD COUNTY

Election	Total Vote Cast *	Number of Eligible Voters †	Percentage Voting
Gubernatorial			
1871............	2,650	3,213	82.48
1875............	2,891	3,485	82.96
1879............	3,406	3,757	90.66
1883............	3,126	3,856	81.07
1887............	2,954	3,896	75.82
1891............	3,200	3,958	80.85
1895............	3,794	4,102	92.49
1899............	3,733	4,246	87.92
1903............	3,325	4,283	77.63
1907............	3,039	4,289	70.86
1911............	3,250	4,296	75.65
Presidential			
1872............	2,501	3,281	76.23
1876............	2,830	3,553	79.65
1880............	3,152	3,826	82.38
1884............	3,125	3,866	80.83
1888............	3,360	3,906	86.02
1892............	3,410	3,994	85.38
1896............	3,870	4,138	93.52
1900............	3,783	4,278	88.43
1904............	3,226	4,284	75.30
1908............	3,097	4,290	72.19
1912............	2,960	4,298	68.87
Congressional			
1870............	2,639	3,145	83.91
1872............	2,515	3,281	76.65
1874............	2,318	3,417	67.84
1876............	2,822	3,553	79.43
1878............	1,995	3,689	54.08
1880............	3,144	3,826	82.17
1882............	2,848	3,846	74.05
1884............	3,136	3,866	81.12
1886............	2,199	3,886	56.59
1888............	3,360	3,906	86.02
1890............	3,166	3,922	80.72
1892............	3,398	3,994	85.08
1894............	3,384	4,066	83.23
1896............	3,836	4,138	92.70
1898............	3,036	4,210	72.11
1900............	3,763	4,278	87.96
1902............	2,644	4,281	61.76
1904............	3,050	4,284	71.20
1906............	2,682	4,287	62.56
1908............	2,735	4,290	63.75
1910............	2,994	4,294	69.73
1912............	2,281	4,298	53.07

* Election figures were taken from the *Baltimore Sun* for 1870 through 1880 and from the *Sun Almanac* for 1882 through 1913, supplemented by the *Maryland Manual* for 1896 through 1913.
† United States census data were utilized to establish the number of male citizens of voting age for each census year, with interpolations made for intervening years.

VOTER TURN-OUT: KENT COUNTY

Election	Total Vote Cast *	Number of Eligible Voters †	Percentage Voting
Gubernatorial			
1871............	3,607	4,167	86.56
1875............	3,358	4,263	78.77
1879............	4,207	4,359	96.51
1883............	4,084	4,451	91.75
1887............	4,246	4,547	93.38
1891............	4,139	4,704	87.99
1895............	4,413	5,024	87.84
1899............	4,706	5,344	88.06
1903............	3,616	5,270	68.61
1907............	3,080	5,070	60.75
1911............	3,394	4,871	69.68
Presidential			
1872............	3,281	4,191	78.29
1876............	3,622	4,287	84.49
1880............	3,822	4,379	87.28
1884............	4,200	4,475	93.85
1888............	4,188	4,571	91.62
1892............	3,990	4,784	83.40
1896............	4,465	5,104	86.87
1900............	4,573	5,420	84.37
1904............	3,843	5,220	73.62
1908............	3,731	5,020	74.32
1912............	3,380	4,824	70.07
Congressional			
1870............	3,563	4,143	86.00
1872............	3,333	4,191	79.53
1874............	3,161	4,239	74.57
1876............	3,616	4,287	84.35
1878............	3,293	4,335	75.96
1880............	3,832	4,379	87.51
1882............	3,362	4,427	75.94
1884............	4,216	4,475	94.21
1886............	3,492	4,523	77.21
1888............	4,178	4,571	91.40
1890............	3,690	4,624	79.80
1892............	3,983	4,784	83.26
1894............	3,592	4,944	72.65
1896............	4,461	5,104	87.40
1898............	4,228	5,264	80.32
1900............	4,575	5,420	84.41
1902............	3,559	5,320	66.90
1904............	3,793	5,220	72.66
1906............	3,581	5,120	69.94
1908............	3,526	5,020	70.24
1910............	3,661	4,918	74.44
1912............	1,918	4,824·	39.76

* Election figures were taken from the *Baltimore Sun* for 1870 through 1880 and from the *Sun Almanac* for 1882 through 1913, supplemented by the *Maryland Manual* for 1896 through 1913.

† United States census data were utilized to establish the number of male citizens of voting age for each census year, with interpolations made for intervening years.

VOTER TURN-OUT: MONTGOMERY COUNTY

Election	Total Vote Cast *	Number of Eligible Voters †	Percentage Voting
Gubernatorial			
1871............	4,097	4,977	82.32
1875............	4,059	5,433	74.71
1879............	4,772	5,661	84.30
1883............	5,361	6,158	87.06
1887............	5,611	6,370	88.08
1891............	5,623	6,665	84.37
1895............	6,370	7,221	88.21
1899............	6,561	7,777	84.36
1903............	5,725	8,161	70.15
1907............	5,263	8,489	62.00
1911............	5,356	8,831	60.65
Presidential			
1872............	4,070	5,091	79.95
1876............	4,949	5,547	89.22
1880............	5,623	5,999	93.73
1884............	5,640	6,211	90.81
1888............	6,126	6,423	95.38
1892............	6,155	6,804	90.46
1896............	6,846	7,360	93.02
1900............	7,151	7,915	90.35
1904............	5,882	8,243	71.36
1908............	6,275	8,571	73.21
1912............	6,241	8,926	69.92
Congressional			
1870............	4,227	4,863	86.92
1872............	4,133	5,091	81.18
1874............	3,985	5,319	74.92
1876............	4,951	5,547	89.26
1878............	4,828	5,775	83.60
1880............	5,630	5,999	93.85
1882............	5,265	6,105	86.24
1884............	5,719	6,211	92.08
1886............	5,463	6,317	86.48
1888............	6,111	6,423	95.14
1890............	5,841	6,526	89.50
1892............	6,153	6,804	90.43
1894............	5,947	7,082	83.97
1896............	6,799	7,360	92.38
1898............	5,633	7,638	73.75
1900............	7,131	7,915	90.09
1902............	4,999	8,079	61.88
1904............	5,536	8,243	67.16
1906............	4,652	8,407	55.33
1908............	5,682	8,571	66.29
1910............	5,851	8,736	66.97
1912............	5,593	8,926	62.66

* Election figures were taken from the *Baltimore Sun* for 1870 through 1880 and from the *Sun Almanac* for 1882 through 1913, supplemented by the *Maryland Manual* for 1896 through 1913.

† United States census data were utilized to establish the number of male citizens of voting age for each census year, with interpolations made for intervening years.

VOTER TURN-OUT: PRINCE GEORGE'S COUNTY

Election	Total Vote Cast *	Number of Eligible Voters †	Percentage Voting
Gubernatorial			
1871............	4,476	5,135	87.17
1875............	4,714	5,603	84.13
1879............	5,237	6,071	86.26
1883............	5,511	6,181	89.16
1887............	5,200	6,165	84.35
1891............	5,001	6,286	79.56
1895............	5,923	6,826	86.77
1899............	6,107	7,366	82.91
1903............	4,219	8,141	51.82
1907............	4,028	8,997	44.77
1911............	5,077	9,813	51.74
Presidential			
1872............	3,895	5,252	74.16
1876............	5,041	5,720	88.13
1880............	5,385	6,193	86.95
1884............	5,820	6,177	94.22
1888............	6,121	6,161	99.35
1892............	5,121	6,421	79.75
1896............	5,811	6,961	83.48
1900............	6,279	7,499	83.73
1904............	5,139	8,355	61.51
1908............	5,397	9,211	58.59
1912............	5,341	9,987	53.48
Congressional			
1870............	4,441	5,018	88.50
1872............	3,957	5,252	75.34
1874............	4,356	5,486	79.40
1876............	5,033	5,720	87.99
1878............	3,937	5,954	66.12
1880............	5,379	6,193	86.86
1882............	4,840	6,185	78.25
1884............	5,843	6,177	94.59
1886............	4,935	6,169	79.99
1888............	6,093	6,161	98.90
1890............	4,877	6,151	79.29
1892............	5,098	6,421	79.40
1894............	5,033	6,691	75.22
1896............	5,746	6,961	82.55
1898............	5,340	7,231	73.85
1900............	6,251	7,499	83.36
1902............	4,880	7,927	61.56
1904............	4,930	8,355	59.01
1906............	4,739	8,783	53.96
1908............	5,122	9,211	55.61
1910............	5,692	9,639	59.05
1912............	4,175	9,987	41.80

* Election figures were taken from the *Baltimore Sun* for 1870 through 1880 and from the *Sun Almanac* for 1882 through 1913, supplemented by the *Maryland Manual* for 1896 through 1913.

† United States census data were utilized to establish the number of male citizens of voting age for each census year, with interpolations made for intervening years.

Voter Turn-out: Queen Anne's County

Election	Total Vote Cast *	Number of Eligible Voters †	Percentage Voting
Gubernatorial			
1871.............	3,736	3,826	97.65
1875.............	3,439	4,238	81.15
1879.............	3,779	4,650	81.27
1883.............	3,936	4,725	83.30
1887.............	4,145	4,689	88.40
1891.............	3,740	4,682	79.88
1895.............	4,304	4,762	90.38
1899.............	4,380	4,842	90.46
1903.............	3,429	4,792	71.56
1907.............	2,910	4,696	61.97
1911.............	3,237	4,613	70.17
Presidential			
1872.............	3,462	3,929	88.11
1876.............	3,625	4,341	83.51
1880.............	3,973	4,752	83.61
1884.............	4,052	4,716	85.92
1888.............	4,197	4,680	89.68
1892.............	4,023	4,702	85.56
1896.............	4,616	4,782	96.53
1900.............	4,538	4,864	93.30
1904.............	3,885	4,768	81.48
1908.............	3,334	4,672	71.36
1912.............	3,426	4,605	74.40
Congressional			
1870.............	3,653	3,723	98.12
1872.............	3,505	3,929	89.21
1874.............	3,061	4,135	74.03
1876.............	3,625	4,341	83.51
1878.............	2,902	4,547	63.82
1880.............	3,975	4,752	83.65
1882.............	3,745	4,734	79.11
1884.............	4,075	4,716	86.41
1886.............	3,311	4,689	70.48
1888.............	4,183	4,680	89.38
1890.............	3,577	4,662	76.72
1892.............	4,011	4,702	85.30
1894.............	3,636	4,742	76.68
1896.............	4,574	4,782	95.65
1898.............	4,007	4,822	83.10
1900.............	4,552	4,864	93.59
1902.............	3,601	4,816	74.77
1904.............	3,759	4,768	78.84
1906.............	3,628	4,720	76.86
1908.............	3,382	4,672	72.39
1910.............	3,384	4,621	73.23
1912.............	1,941	4,605	42.15

* Election figures were taken from the *Baltimore Sun* for 1870 through 1880 and from the *Sun Almanac* for 1882 through 1913, supplemented by the *Maryland Manual* for 1896 through 1913.

† United States census data were utilized to establish the number of male citizens of voting age for each census year, with interpolations made for intervening years.

VOTER TURN-OUT: ST. MARY'S COUNTY

Election	Total Vote Cast *	Number of Eligible Voters †	Percentage Voting
Gubernatorial			
1871............	2,916	3,279	88.93
1875............	2,907	3,431	84.73
1879............	3,363	3,583	93.86
1883............	3,119	3,578	87.17
1887............	3,349	3,518	95.20
1891............	3,256	3,533	92.16
1895............	3,384	3,773	89.69
1899............	3,608	4,013	89.91
1903............	3,698	4,016	92.08
1907............	2,131	3,940	54.09
1911............	2,184	3,885	56.22
Presidential			
1872............	2,676	3,317	80.68
1876............	3,042	3,469	87.69
1880............	3,302	3,623	91.14
1884............	3,313	3,563	92.98
1888............	3,357	3,503	95.83
1892............	3,220	3,593	89.62
1896............	3,551	3,833	92.64
1900............	3,696	4,073	90.74
1904............	2,446	3,997	61.20
1908............	3,642	3,921	92.88
1912............	3,602	3,884	92.74
Congressional			
1870............	3,090	3,241	95.34
1872............	2,706	3,317	81.58
1874............	2,777	3,393	81.84
1876............	3,036	3,469	87.52
1878............	2,764	3,545	77.97
1880............	3,300	3,623	91.08
1882............	3,130	3,593	87.11
1884............	3,330	3,563	93.46
1886............	2,951	3,533	83.53
1888............	3,339	3,503	95.32
1890............	3,150	3,473	90.70
1892............	3,223	3,593	89.70
1894............	3,076	3,713	82.84
1896............	3,530	3,833	92.09
1898............	3,345	3,953	84.62
1900............	3,692	4,073	90.65
1902............	3,092	4,035	76.63
1904............	2,738	3,997	68.50
1906............	2,528	3,959	63.85
1908............	2,095	3,921	53.43
1910............	2,669	3,886	68.68
1912............	1,949	3,884	50.18

* Election figures were taken from the *Baltimore Sun* for 1870 through 1880 and from the *Sun Almanac* for 1882 through 1913, supplemented by the *Maryland Manual* for 1896 through 1913.

† United States census data were utilized to establish the number of male citizens of voting age for each census year, with interpolations made for intervening years.

VOTER TURN-OUT: SOMERSET COUNTY

Election	Total Vote Cast *	Number of Eligible Voters †	Percentage Voting
Gubernatorial			
1871............	3,392	4,214	80.49
1875............	3,371	4,574	73.70
1879............	3,936	4,934	79.77
1883............	4,431	5,285	83.84
1887............	4,797	5,633	85.16
1891............	4,113	5,978	69.14
1895............	5,401	6,302	85.70
1899............	5,905	6,626	89.12
1903............	2,214	6,825	32.44
1907............	3,386	6,989	48.45
1911............	3,204	7,084	45.23
Presidential			
1872............	2,745	4,304	63.78
1876............	3,700	4,664	79.33
1880............	3,793	5,024	75.50
1884............	3,756	5,372	69.92
1888............	4,071	5,720	71.17
1892............	3,991	6,059	65.87
1896............	5,209	6,383	81.61
1900............	5,221	6,702	77.90
1904............	3,637	6,866	52.97
1908............	2,484	7,030	35.33
1912............	2,287	7,058	32.40
Congressional			
1870............	3,363	4,124	81.54
1872............	2,809	4,304	65.26
1874............	2,861	4,484	63.80
1876............	3,699	4,664	79.31
1878............	2,370	4,844	48.93
1880............	3,594	5,024	71.54
1882............	2,534	5,198	48.75
1884............	3,776	5,372	70.29
1886............	3,071	5,546	55.37
1888............	4,044	5,720	70.70
1890............	3,091	5,897	52.42
1892............	3,949	6,059	65.18
1894............	4,496	6,221	72.27
1896............	5,196	6,383	81.40
1898............	4,597	6,545	70.24
1900............	5,186	6,702	77.38
1902............	3,773	6,784	55.62
1904............	3,470	6,866	50.54
1906............	3,656	6,948	52.62
1908............	3,433	7,030	48.83
1910............	3,648	7,110	51.31
1912............	1,700	7,058	24.09

* Election figures were taken from the *Baltimore Sun* for 1870 through 1880 and from the *Sun Almanac* for 1882 through 1913, supplemented by the *Maryland Manual* for 1896 through 1913.

† United States census data were utilized to establish the number of male citizens of voting age for each census year, with interpolations made for intervening years.

VOTER TURN-OUT: TALBOT COUNTY

Election	Total Vote Cast *	Number of Eligible Voters †	Percentage Voting
Gubernatorial			
1871............	3,272	3,862	84.72
1875............	3,387	4,230	80.07
1879............	4,293	4,598	93.37
1883............	4,373	4,809	90.93
1887............	4,588	4,965	92.41
1891............	4,742	5,114	92.73
1895............	4,841	5,254	92.14
1899............	4,966	5,394	92.07
1903............	3,668	5,433	67.51
1907............	3,298	5,435	60.68
1911............	3,893	5,420	71.83
Presidential			
1872...........	3,184	3,954	80.53
1876...........	3,620	4,322	83.76
1880...........	4,136	4,692	88.15
1884...........	4,421	4,848	91.19
1888...........	4,510	5,004	90.13
1892...........	4,295	5,149	83.41
1896...........	4,936	5,289	93.33
1900...........	4,977	5,431	91.64
1904...........	3,956	5,433	72.81
1908...........	4,034	5,435	74.22
1912...........	4,006	5,403	74.14
Congressional			
1870...........	3,260	3,770	86.47
1872...........	3,210	3,954	81.18
1874...........	3,314	4,138	80.09
1876...........	3,605	4,322	83.41
1878...........	3,127	4,506	69.40
1880...........	4,137	4,692	88.17
1882...........	3,735	4,770	78.30
1884...........	4,425	4,848	91.27
1886...........	3,782	4,926	76.78
1888...........	4,479	5,004	89.51
1890...........	4,253	5,079	83.74
1892...........	4,276	5,149	83.05
1894...........	3,865	5,219	74.06
1896...........	4,905	5,289	92.74
1898...........	4,439	5,359	82.83
1900...........	4,960	5,431	91.33
1902...........	4,045	5,432	74.47
1904...........	3,878	5,433	71.38
1906...........	3,778	5,434	69.53
1908...........	3,996	5,435	73.52
1910...........	4,017	5,437	73.88
1912...........	2,157	5,403	39.92

* Election figures were taken from the *Baltimore Sun* for 1870 through 1880 and from the *Sun Almanac* for 1882 through 1913, supplemented by the *Maryland Manual* for 1896 through 1913.

† United States census data were utilized to establish the number of male citizens of voting age for each census year, with interpolations made for intervening years.

VOTER TURN-OUT: WASHINGTON COUNTY

Election	Total Vote Cast *	Number of Eligible Voters †	Percentage Voting
Gubernatorial			
1871............	7,392	7,920	93.33
1875............	7,399	8,416	87.92
1879............	8,214	8,912	92.17
1883............	7,941	9,274	85.63
1887............	8,704	9,586	90.80
1891............	8,678	10,023	86.58
1895............	9,737	10,827	89.93
1899............	10,261	11,631	88.22
1903............	8,554	12,343	69.30
1907............	7,874	13,023	60.46
1911............	9,203	13,852	66.44
Presidential			
1872............	6,742	8,044	83.81
1876............	7,905	8,540	92.56
1880............	8,110	9,040	89.71
1884............	8,589	9,352	91.84
1888............	9,107	9,664	94.24
1892............	9,273	10,224	90.70
1896............	10,133	11,028	91.88
1900............	10,519	11,833	88.90
1904............	8,833	12,513	76.72
1908............	9,377	13,193	71.08
1912............	9,540	14,174	67.31
Congressional			
1870............	7,040	7,796	90.31
1872............	7,010	8,044	87.15
1874............	6,939	8,292	83.68
1876............	7,879	8,540	92.26
1878............	6,893	8,788	78.44
1880............	8,118	9,040	89.80
1882............	7,761	9,196	84.40
1884............	8,609	9,352	92.06
1886............	8,651	9,508	90.99
1888............	9,075	9,664	93.91
1890............	8,432	9,822	85.85
1892............	9,257	10,224	90.54
1894............	9,268	10,626	87.22
1896............	10,031	11,028	90.96
1898............	8,839	11,430	77.33
1900............	10,500	11,833	88.73
1902............	8,231	12,173	67.62
1904............	8,442	12,513	67.47
1906............	6,906	12,853	53.73
1908............	8,825	13,193	66.89
1910............	8,322	13,530	61.51
1912............	9,199	14,174	64.90

* Election figures were taken from the *Baltimore Sun* for 1870 through 1880 and from the *Sun Almanac* for 1882 through 1913, supplemented by the *Maryland Manual* for 1896 through 1913.

† United States census data were utilized to establish the number of male citizens of voting age for each census year, with interpolations made for intervening years.

VOTER TURN-OUT: WICOMICO COUNTY

Election	Total Vote Cast *	Number of Eligible Voters †	Percentage Voting
Gubernatorial			
1871............	2,686	3,544	75.79
1875............	2,890	3,828	75.50
1879............	3,336	4,112	81.13
1883............	3,417	4,354	78.48
1887............	3,831	4,582	83.61
1891............	4,047	4,866	83.17
1895............	4,370	5,310	82.30
1899............	5,357	5,754	93.10
1903............	4,364	6,289	69.39
1907............	4,420	6,849	64.53
1911............	5,211	7,334	71.05
Presidential			
1872............	2,549	3,615	70.51
1876............	3,154	3,899	80.89
1880............	3,406	4,183	81.42
1884............	3,616	4,411	81.98
1888............	3,887	4,639	83.79
1892............	4,026	4,977	80.89
1896............	4,622	5,421	85.26
1900............	5,374	5,869	91.57
1904............	4,900	6,429	76.22
1908............	5,182	6,989	74.15
1912............	5,772	7,395	78.05
Congressional			
1870............	2,877	3,473	82.84
1872............	2,650	3,615	73.31
1874............	2,569	3,757	68.40
1876............	3,154	3,899	80.89
1878............	2,511	4,041	62.14
1880............	3,408	4,183	81.47
1882............	2,718	4,297	63.25
1884............	3,630	4,411	82.29
1886............	3,071	4,525	67.87
1888............	3,873	4,639	83.49
1890............	3,318	4,755	69.78
1892............	3,963	4,977	79.63
1894............	3,680	5,199	70.78
1896............	4,596	5,421	84.78
1898............	4,757	5,643	84.30
1900............	5,335	5,869	90.90
1902............	4,867	6,149	79.15
1904............	4,800	6,429	74.66
1906............	4,823	6,709	71.89
1908............	5,086	6,989	72.77
1910............	5,211	7,273	71.65
1912............	3,601	7,395	48.70

* Election figures were taken from the *Baltimore Sun* for 1870 through 1880 and from the *Sun Almanac* for 1882 through 1913, supplemented by the *Maryland Manual* for 1896 through 1913.

† United States census data were utilized to establish the number of male citizens of voting age for each census year, with interpolations made for intervening years.

Voter Turn-out: Worcester County

Election	Total Vote Cast *	Number of Eligible Voters †	Percentage Voting
Gubernatorial			
1871............	2,232	3,631	61.47
1875............	3,125	3,987	78.38
1879............	3,216	4,343	74.05
1883............	3,646	4,506	80.91
1887............	3,903	4,610	84.66
1891............	3,350	4,745	70.60
1895............	4,242	4,969	85.37
1899............	4,500	5,193	86.66
1903............	3,621	5,435	66.62
1907............	2,879	5,683	50.66
1911............	3,114	5,888	52.89
Presidential			
1872............	2,899	3,720	77.93
1876............	3,292	4,076	80.77
1880............	3,658	4,428	82.61
1884............	3,705	4,532	81.75
1888............	3,732	4,636	80.50
1892............	3,584	4,801	74.65
1896............	4,123	5,025	82.05
1900............	4,690	5,249	89.35
1904............	3,608	5,497	65.64
1908............	3,618	5,745	62.98
1912............	3,247	5,911	54.93
Congressional			
1870............	3,091	3,542	87.27
1872............	2,949	3,720	79.27
1874............	2,742	3,898	70.34
1876............	3,290	4,076	80.72
1878............	2,204	4,254	51.81
1880............	3,626	4,428	81.89
1882............	2,931	4,480	65.42
1884............	3,763	4,532	83.03
1886............	2,860	4,584	62.39
1888............	3,730	4,636	80.46
1890............	3,179	4,689	67.80
1892............	3,453	4,801	71.92
1894............	3,288	4,913	66.92
1896............	4,092	5,025	81.43
1898............	4,221	5,137	82.17
1900............	4,688	5,249	89.31
1902............	3,616	5,373	67.30
1904............	3,545	5,497	64.49
1906............	3,644	5,621	64.83
1908............	3,596	5,745	62.59
1910............	3,220	5,865	54.90
1912............	2,076	5,911	35.12

* Election figures were taken from the *Baltimore Sun* for 1870 through 1880 and from the *Sun Almanac* for 1882 through 1913, supplemented by the *Maryland Manual* for 1896 through 1913.

† United States census data were utilized to establish the number of male citizens of voting age for each census year, with interpolations made for intervening years.

BIBLIOGRAPHICAL NOTE

The basic framework of Maryland politics from 1870 to 1912 must be reconstructed from primary sources because of the lack of secondary works that deal with this period of the state's history. Newspapers and public documents provide the major sources of information.

The state was fortunate in having an outstanding newspaper, the *Baltimore Sun*, which supplied both detailed and continuous coverage of political events. Maintaining regular correspondents in all areas of the state, the *Baltimore Sun* provided a statewide coverage unique in Maryland and rarely equaled in other states. Legislative sessions, political conventions, and campaign and election activity were regularly and fully reported. A normally Democratic paper with independent proclivities, the *Baltimore Sun* was not only a reporter of events but a major influence in the political arena. Its Republican counterpart, the *Baltimore American*, was generally too partisan, even factional, to serve as a general guide to events and issues, but it furnishes useful editorial content. Other newspapers that are helpful in reconstructing regional reaction to the volatile issues of Negro rights are the *Port Tobacco Times and Charles County Advertiser* in southern Maryland, the *Chestertown Transcript* and the *Cambridge Daily Banner* on the Eastern Shore, and the *Frederick Examiner* in western Maryland.

Negro opinion began to find journalistic expression in Maryland in the *Baltimore Afro-American*, a weekly newspaper founded in 1893 as "the only organ of the Race published in Maryland." Edited by William M. Alexander, a Baltimore minister and an activist in the Brotherhood of Liberty and other Negro-rights organizations, the newspaper is available for parts of 1893 and from 1895 to 1898. In 1898 a second Negro weekly, the *Baltimore Ledger,* appeared under the editorial direction of George F. Bragg, also a Baltimore minister. For almost two years the papers were published concurrently, more in a spirit of cooperation than competition. In 1900 John H. Murphy, a former laborer and job-printer, merged the two newspapers under his own editorial and financial control as the *Baltimore Afro-American Ledger*. Continuous issues are available to 1913.

An invaluable source of political information is the *Sun Almanac*, published annually by the *Baltimore Sun* from 1876 through 1913, which offers a convenient and remarkably complete set of voter registration and election statistics, lists of state and local officials (usually with their party affiliations), and lists of political party officials. It supplies all state and federal election returns for Maryland as well as the results of many purely local elections. Registration and election returns are broken down by county, ward, and sometimes by precinct level. After 1896 the state

190

assumed responsibility for publication of a similar guide, the *Maryland Manual*, which offers complete registration and election data but omits the party data available in the *Sun Almanac*.

The *Documents*, *Journals*, and *Laws* of the Maryland General Assembly are essential for tracing the course of public policy toward the Negro. Particularly valuable are the formal addresses of Maryland governors to the General Assembly that detail administration priorities, and the reports of the State Board of Education, which are found in the *Documents*. Only cursory accounts of legislative proceedings are given in the *Journals* but roll-call votes are recorded; by cross-checking these votes with the party affiliations provided in the *Sun Almanac*, party alignments on issues may be reconstructed. The *Laws* must be laboriously checked, session by session, to keep up with the changing regulations that governed elections, public education, and civil rights. Indexes to session laws are fairly adequate for statewide legislation but are quite inadequate for the mounting volume of local legislation, some of which pertained to racial matters.

Federal census publications are particularly important in determining the number of eligible voters in an area, a process central to judging registration and election participation. Use of these publications for this purpose, however, involves some rather special problems. For example, not until 1890 were males of voting age designated by race at the county level, although this information is available for the state as a whole and for the major cities in the preceding two decades. Furthermore, the censuses of 1880 and 1890 did not adequately distinguish between naturalized citizens and aliens in its county-level category of foreign-born males of voting age. I have adjusted the county figures by computing general rates of naturalization among the foreign-born for the state and for Baltimore City (for which adequate data are available) and have deduced from these two rates a general rate of naturalization for the counties. Inasmuch as the overwhelming majority of Maryland's foreign-born lived in Baltimore City, the adjustments required in the county figures were minor.

Manuscript sources were generally disappointing. The collections of leading state political figures—such as Lloyd Lowndes, William Pinckney Whyte, and Henry Stockbridge, all in the possession of the Maryland Historical Society in Baltimore—consist mainly of scrapbooks of newspaper clippings. The Arthur Pue Gorman Papers at the Maryland Historical Society contain correspondence and drafts of speeches as well as scrapbooks, but there is little that is not more readily available in John R. Lambert's biography of the senator. The Gorman Papers and the Isidor Rayner Papers in the Southern Historical Collection, Chapel Hill, N.C., contain only scrapbooks of news clippings. The most useful collection is that of Charles Jerome Bonaparte's papers, in the Library of Congress. Bonaparte carried on a large correspondence about Maryland

Republican party matters, some of it with Negro Marylanders. The main topic was patronage, but there is much good material on the inner workings of the party. The Booker T. Washington Papers, also in the Library of Congress, contain scattered bits of correspondence that reflect Washington's concern with the Maryland disfranchisement campaigns of 1905 and 1909 and his aid to Maryland Negroes during these crucial years.

General histories of Maryland are weak in their treatment of the post–Civil War period, reflecting the serious lack of monographic work on this era. Matthew Page Andrews, *History of Maryland: Province and State* (New York, 1929), provides a rather limited amount of general information. Somewhat better is Morris L. Radoff, ed., *The Old Line State: A History of Maryland*, 3 vols. (Baltimore, 1956), which contains a good chapter on the 1870–1914 period, written by John R. Lambert. James B. Crooks' valuable contribution to the period, *Politics and Progress: The Rise of Urban Progressivism in Baltimore, 1895–1911* (Baton Rouge, 1968), unfortunately appeared too late to be of material aid in the preparation of this study.

Several good books furnish essential background material on the Negro in Maryland and on Maryland politics prior to 1870. Charles L. Wagandt, *The Mighty Revolution: Negro Emancipation in Maryland, 1862–1864* (Baltimore, 1964), is an outstanding study. The Negro's pre–Civil War condition is ably described in Jeffrey R. Brackett, *The Negro in Maryland: A Study of the Institution of Slavery* (Baltimore, 1889), and in James M. Wright, *The Free Negro in Maryland, 1634–1860* (New York, 1921). Other useful works are Charles Branch Clark, *Politics in Maryland during the Civil War* (Chestertown, Md., 1952), and two books by William Starr Myers, *The Maryland Constitution of 1864* (Baltimore, 1901) and *The Self-Reconstruction of Maryland, 1864–1867* (Baltimore, 1909). A recent study of the complex political party realignments in Maryland after the war is Richard P. Fuke, " The Break-up of the Maryland Union Party, 1866 " (M.A. thesis, University of Maryland, 1965).

Several biographies are helpful in studying the 1870–1912 period. Foremost is John R. Lambert's *Arthur Pue Gorman* (Baton Rouge, 1953), a fine account of the state and national activities of Maryland's leading Democratic politician during this period. Eric Goldman, *Charles Jerome Bonaparte; Patrician Reformer; His Earlier Career* (Baltimore, 1943), is helpful but does not cover the period when Bonaparte was most influential in state and national Republican politics. Benjamin Quarles, *Frederick Douglass* (Washington, D.C., 1948), and Philip S. Foner, ed., *The Life and Writings of Frederick Douglass*, 4 vols. (New York, 1950–55), provide insight into the political thought of a Negro leader who was a source of guidance for many Marylanders. Biographical information on Maryland Negro leaders is extremely difficult to locate. There are numerous state biographical guides, such as B. F. Johnson, ed., *Men of Mark in Maryland*, 4 vols. (Baltimore, 1910), but Negroes always were excluded from these general compilations. George F. Bragg, Jr., *Men of Maryland* (Baltimore, 1925), a small volume devoted exclusively to Negro Marylanders, provides some assistance but omits many Negro politicians.

Miscellaneous essays and memoirs deal with special aspects of the period. Jeffrey R. Brackett, *Notes on the Progress of the Colored People of Maryland Since the War* (Baltimore, 1890), is an undocumented essay. Frank R. Kent, *The Story of Maryland Politics* (Baltimore, 1911), lacks documentation but is an interesting firsthand account by the *Baltimore Sun*'s leading political reporter. Gerald W. Johnson, Frank R. Kent, and H. L. Mencken, *The Sunpapers of Baltimore* (New York, 1937), is a useful history of the state's most powerful newspaper. Eugene W. Goll, "The Poe Amendment's Defeat: Maryland Voters Reject the Negro Disfranchisement Movement, 1903–1905" (M.A. thesis, University of Maryland, 1966), is a detailed account of one of the three attempts to disfranchise Maryland Negroes.

The most relevant general works on the Negro in the post–Reconstruction era are C. Vann Woodward, *Origins of the New South, 1877–1913* (Baton Rouge, 1951), and *The Strange Career of Jim Crow*, 2d rev. ed. (New York, 1966); Rayford Logan, *The Negro in American Life and Thought: The Nadir, 1877–1901* (New York, 1954); August Meier, *Negro Thought in America, 1880–1915* (Ann Arbor, 1963); and Gilbert T. Stephenson, *Race Distinctions in American Law* (New York, 1910). Numerous studies of other states' experience during the period provide valuable comparative insights and information. The most useful are George B. Tindall, *South Carolina Negroes, 1877–1900* (Columbia, S.C., 1952); Vernon L. Wharton, *The Negro in Mississippi, 1865–1890* (Chapel Hill, 1947); Frenise Logan, *The Negro in North Carolina, 1876–1894* (Chapel Hill, 1964); Helen G. Edmonds, *The Negro and Fusion Politics in North Carolina* (Chapel Hill, 1951); William A. Mabry, *The Negro in North Carolina Politics Since Reconstruction* (Durham, N.C., 1940); Charles E. Wynes, *Race Relations in Virginia, 1870–1902* (Charlottesville, 1961); Luther P. Jackson, *Negro Office-Holders in Virginia, 1865–1895* (Norfolk, Va., 1945); Allen J. Going, *Bourbon Democracy in Alabama, 1874–1890* (Montgomery, 1951); A. A. Taylor, *The Negro in Tennessee, 1864–1880* (Washington, D.C., 1941); Clarence Bacote, "The Negro in Georgia Politics, 1880–1908" (Ph.D. dissertation, University of Chicago, 1955); and Olive Hall Shadgett, *The Republican Party in Georgia from Reconstruction through 1900* (Athens, Ga., 1964). Leslie H. Fishel, Jr., "The North and the Negro, 1865–1900" (Ph.D. dissertation, Harvard University, 1954), provides a needed standard of comparison with the status of Northern Negroes during the period.

INDEX

Abell, Edwin F., 41
Abell, Stephen A., 104
Adams, J. Albert, 153
Alabama, 155
Alexander, William M., 190
Allegany County, 19, 40, 53, 67
American Colonization Society, 57
Andrews, Henry F., 87, 90
Annapolis, 137–38, 153
Anne Arundel County, 27, 30, 53, 65n, 105n, 109, 111, 136
Archer, Stevenson, 26, 27, 51–52
Arkansas, 155
Australian ballot, 52, 92

Ballot law of 1901, 104, 105–6, 111, 113–14, 143, 148–49, 151
Ballot law of 1904. *See* Wilson ballot law
Baltimore: and Democratic party, 35–38, 39, 56–57; and independent Democrats, 41–42, 43, 45, 47, 72–73; and industrialism, 19; nationality groups in, 7–8, 36n, 116, 130; Negro Democratic ward clubs in, 57; and Negro education, 64n, 93–94; Negro employes, 94–95; Negro population of, 4–5, 116, 144; Negro protest groups in, 77n, 80; representation in General Assembly, 68; and Republican party, 71–73, 96–98; secession sentiment in, 6–7; segregation in, 23, 135, 137; voter participation in, 141, 146, 165–66; voter registration in, 52–53, 142, 143–44, 145, 163
Baltimore Afro-American Ledger, 135, 190
Baltimore and Ohio Railroad, 41, 43n, 49
Baltimore County, 19, 52n
Baltimore Sun, 84, 90, 190
Baughman, L. Victor, 55
Bell, John, 6
Bonaparte, Charles Jerome, 74, 104, 117–18, 123–24, 138
Bond, Hugh Lennox, 10, 18, 19, 21n
Bowie, Oden, 16, 18, 24, 63
Bradford, Augustus W., 8, 11
Bragg, George F., 190

Breckinridge, John C., 6
Briscoe, G. E., 152n
Brooks, Walter B., 49, 80
Brown, Frank, 51, 85
Brown, H. J., 76–77
Bryan, William Jennings, 90
Bryan, William S., 119, 124, 128–29
Bryant, George Wellington, 95, 99

Calvert County, 30, 40, 65n, 66, 67, 109, 111, 136
Cambridge, 153
Cargill, J. Marcus, 94, 153
Caroline County, 65n
Carroll County, 19
Cecil County, 19, 52n
Census fraud of 1900, 103–5
Charles County, 25–26, 27, 30, 40, 53, 65n, 66, 67, 105n, 109, 111, 131, 136
Cheltenham Reformatory for Colored Boys, 96
Child labor, 47, 53
Ching, Joseph, 104–5
Citizens' Reform party, 33n, 34n, 41, 43, 44
Civil rights, 13, 17–18, 61, 63, 80
Civil Rights Act of 1875, 58, 85
Civil Service Reform League, 123
Cleveland, Grover, 36, 37, 40, 83, 85
Colored Advisory Committee, 79
Colored Citizens' League, 99
Colored Democratic Association, 27, 56
Colored Equal Rights League, 76, 77n, 79–80
Colored People's Conference, 99
Congressional elections, participation in, 149–51
Conservative Unionists, 11, 16
Constitution: of 1776, 3n; of 1851, 12; of 1864, 12, 16, 17, 117; of 1867, 17–18, 19, 51, 61, 119
Constitutional convention: of 1864, 12; of 1867, 17
Cowen, John K., 41, 49, 90
Cox, Christopher, 13n
Creswell, John A. J., 10, 15n, 20, 21n, 73, 74
Crisfield, 137

195